The Story of a Great Medieval Book

 rethinking the middle ages • volume two
SERIES EDITORS: PAUL EDWARD DUTTON AND JOHN SHINNERS

Ist ein grosser man gewesen.
("He was a great man.")

—LUTHER ON PETER LOMBARD,
FROM HIS "TABLE TALKS" (D. MARTIN LUTHERS WERKE,
TR 2: 2544B; DATED 1532)

The Story of a Great Medieval Book
Peter Lombard's *Sentences*

Philipp W. Rosemann

broadview press

©2007 Philipp W. Rosemann

Library and Archives Canada Cataloguing in Publication

Rosemann, Philipp W.
    The story of a great medieval book : Peter Lombard's Sentences / Philipp W. Rosemann.

(Rethinking the Middle Ages ; v. 2)
Includes bibliographical references and index.

ISBN-13: 978-1-55111-718-8
ISBN-10: 1-55111-718-5

    1. Peter Lombard, Bishop of Paris, ca. 1100-1160. Sententiarum libri IV.
2. Catholic Church—Doctrines—Early works to 1800—Textbooks. 3. Theology—Early works to 1800—Textbooks. I. Title. II. Series.

BX1749.P4R68 2007   230'.2   C2006-906053-3

Broadview Press is an independent, international publishing house, incorporated in 1985. Broadview believes in shared ownership, both with its employees and with the general public; since the year 2000 Broadview shares have traded publicly on the Toronto Venture Exchange under the symbol BDP.

We welcome comments and suggestions regarding any aspect of our publications—please feel free to contact us at the addresses below or at broadview@broadviewpress.com.

North America:
PO Box 1243, Peterborough,
Ontario, Canada K9J 7H5
PO Box 1015, 3576 California Road,
Orchard Park, NY, USA 14127
Tel: (705) 743-8990;
Fax: (705) 743-8353

E-mail: customerservice@
broadviewpress.com

UK, Ireland, and continental Europe:
NBN Plymbridge
Estover Road
Plymouth PL6 7PY UK

Tel: 44 (0) 1752 202300
Fax: 44 (0) 1752 202330

E-mail: enquiries@nbnplymbridge.com

Australia and New Zealand:
UNIREPS,
University of New South Wales
Sydney, NSW, 2052 Australia

Tel: 61 2 9664 0999
Fax: 61 2 9664 5420

E-mail: info.press@unsw.edu.au

www.broadviewpress.com

Book design and composition by George Kirkpatrick
PRINTED IN CANADA

Contents

Illustrations

Acknowledgements

THE INSPIRATION for this book came from a remark Marcia Colish made in her magisterial two-volume study of Peter Lombard and his intellectual environment: "I was struck by the fact that medievalists would be able to survey and map the *terra incognita* that remains in our knowledge of much of the history of speculative thought from the middle of the twelfth century to the end of the period if the *Sentence* commentaries of all the scholastics known to have made them could be studied in chronological order and in a comparative way."[1] Professor Colish's idea fascinated me, despite the impossibility involved in realizing her dream: it would require, as she added, "a large international équipe of medievalists with unlimited funding."[2] But what about a less ambitious project—not a comprehensive survey of all extant commentaries on the *Book of Sentences* but a brief history of some of the most influential ones? This is what I hope to have accomplished in this book.

The opportunity to embark on this project in seriousness presented itself when Paul Dutton and John Shinners expressed an interest in it for their new series, "Rethinking the Middle Ages." John Shinners subsequently invited me to deliver a series of three lectures at Notre Dame, co-sponsored by his own college, Saint Mary's, the Medieval Institute of the University of Notre Dame, and Broadview Press. This book has profited much from the discussions that occurred at Notre Dame in

connection with these lectures: apart from John Shinners, I would like to thank, in particular, Stephen Dumont, Kent Emery, Jr., and Marina Smyth for their suggestions and criticisms. I also met a wonderful group of graduate students at Notre Dame whose interest in my work did much to encourage me. My thanks go especially to Julia Schneider.

John Shinners, who read the manuscript with meticulous care before it went to press, suggested countless improvements that helped me keep the book free from unnecessary technicalities. While I hope to have advanced scholarship on the history of the *Sentences* literature, the book is intended to be accessible to students who are beginning to study medieval intellectual history.

Marcia Colish also read a draft of the work and kindly provided a long list of important suggestions. My colleague Francis Swietek, of the University of Dallas, gave welcome advice of a paleographical and philological nature on some of the unedited sources. He also read the entire manuscript and offered observations on a number of points. Christopher Schabel, of the University of Cyprus, helped me to nuance some of my claims concerning the fourteenth century. I alone am responsible for any remaining shortcomings.

By granting me sabbatical leave for the fall of 2004, the University of Dallas made it possible for me to start researching and writing the book. The University also awarded me a Haggar Scholarship toward some of the expenses that I incurred in obtaining manuscript copies and illustrations. I gratefully acknowledge the University's consistent support of my research.

As always, I am grateful to the William A. Blakley Library and its staff. The library's first-rate collections in medieval intellectual history are continuing to grow, and an efficient interlibrary loan service enabled me to obtain materials that are not available in Irving.

Finally, a word of thanks to the libraries that assisted me in procuring reproductions of manuscripts: the British Library in London, the John Rylands University Library of Manchester, the *Biblioteca nazionale* in Naples, and the *Ratsschulbibliothek* at Zwickau. Dottoressa Beatrice De Magistris, of the University of Dallas Rome Campus, kindly communicated with the *Biblioteca nazionale* on my behalf. At Manchester, Mr. John Hodgson, Keeper of Manuscripts, was generous with his time in helping me identify the call number of the codex containing *Filia Magistri*.

Abbreviations

Mediaeval Commentaries	*Mediaeval Commentaries on the* Sentences *of Peter Lombard: Current Research*, vol. 1, ed. G.R. Evans (Leiden/Boston/Cologne: Brill, 2002).
Peter Lombard, *Sentences*	Magistri Petri Lombardi *Sententiae in IV libris distinctae*, ed. Ignatius Brady, O.F.M., 2 vols., Spicilegium Bonaventurianum 4–5 (Grottaferrata: Editiones Collegii S. Bonaventurae Ad Claras Aquas, 1971–81). Vol. 1 contains Books I and II; vol. 2 contains Books III and IV. All translations from the *Sentences* are my own.
PL	*Patrologia latina, cursus completus*, 221 vols., ed. J.-P. Migne (Paris: J.-P. Migne, 1844–65).
Rosemann, *Peter Lombard*	Philipp W. Rosemann, *Peter Lombard*, Great Medieval Thinkers (New York: Oxford University Press, 2004).

RTAM   *Recherches de théologie ancienne et médiévale*
        (Louvain: Abbaye du Mont César). Vol. 1
        (1929)–63 (1996). Continued as *RTPM*.

RTPM   *Recherches de théologie et philosophie médiévales*
        (Louvain: Peeters). Started with vol. 64 (1997).

Stegmüller, *Repertorium*   Friedrich Stegmüller, *Repertorium commentariorum in Sententias Petri Lombardi*, 2 vols.
        (Würzburg: Schöningh, 1947).

All English translations from Scripture follow the Douay-Rheims version, which has been chosen for its closeness to the Vulgate: *The Holy Bible, translated from the Latin Vulgate ... the whole revised and diligently compared with the Latin Vulgate by Bishop Richard Challoner* (Baltimore: John Murphy, 1889; reprinted, Rockford, IL: TAN Books and Publishers, 2000).

Introduction: The *Book of Sentences* and the Structure of Traditions

Habent sua fata libelli, the Roman grammarian Terentianus Maurus said: "Books have their fates." The fate of a great book, however, is inextricably tied up with the fate of the culture to which it belongs; indeed, in civilizations that developed systems of writing, the history of a culture is to a large extent the history of the great books that have shaped it and, in turn, have reflected (upon) its development.

What, then, is a great book? Perhaps the safest way of determining greatness in this area is through influence. The German language has coined an apposite term in this regard, *Wirkungsgeschichte*, which literally translates as "history of effect." A great book, on this account, would be one that has exerted great effect: a book, in other words, which successive generations of people have read and reread because it helped them think about and mold their lives. Great books tell powerful stories, such as those of Ulysses, Jesus, King Arthur, or Doctor Faust. Because the stories are so powerful, they are told not once but over and over again, and each time they undergo modifications. Material from previous versions is updated, altered, or dropped, while additions occur where the old narrative has proven inadequate.

On the account just offered, the book whose *Wirkungsgeschichte* forms the subject matter of the present volume is a most unlikely candidate for

greatness. To begin with, it was a university textbook, serving as the standard manual of scholastic theology in the Christian West between the early thirteenth century and, roughly, the Council of Trent in the sixteenth. Now one may think what one will about textbooks—that they are an extremely useful literary genre, indispensable to the handing down, assimilation, and digestion of knowledge; nevertheless, it is doubtless not in this category that books are written which are apt to survive the test of the ages. For textbooks typically lack originality. Instead of adding to existing knowledge, telling a new story, or at least developing an old story in significant ways, they normally content themselves with reliable recapitulation. The case of our famous theology textbook exemplifies this tendency: in large measure, it consists of mere quotation from the works of other authors, especially Augustine.

Against this background, how can we explain the unparalleled success of Peter Lombard's *Book of Sentences*, which is, among all the works of Christian literature, the one to have elicited the largest number of commentaries—only Scripture itself excepted? The *Sentences* must have related the story of Jesus effectively enough for generations of theologians and their students to find the book a valuable tool for reflection. In truth, however, it is not quite accurate to say that the *Sentences* offered an account of the "story" of Jesus. A story, at least in the most basic sense of the word, narrates events according to a chronological structure. The Gospel according to St. Luke is a good example: "Forasmuch as many have taken in hand to set forth in order a narration of the things that have been accomplished among us ... [i]t seemed good to me also, having diligently attained to all things from the beginning, to write to thee in order, most excellent Theophilus ..." (Luke 1:1 and 3). In its literalness, the old Douay-Rheims version manages to convey very faithfully Luke's emphasis upon the good "order" (*taxis* in Greek) of the story that is about to be told here. Luke clearly means the chronological order of events.

Now the *Book of Sentences* certainly possesses an order, but it is no longer the chronological one of the original story of Jesus. When the *Sentences* were composed, in the middle of the twelfth century, Christianity had reached a stage in its development where it was ready to move decisively from the historico-biblical to a much more "logical," reasoned account of its faith.[1] To be sure, already in the centuries preceding Peter Lombard's, Christian thinkers had accomplished more than a

simple telling and retelling of Scripture. They had asked, and answered, many "theo-logical" questions that the Bible raised upon closer inspection—questions that sought the *logos*, the coherent rationale, behind the actions of God (*theos*), his prophets, and his people. For example, what is the precise relationship between the Old and the New Testaments, that is to say, how does the Christian faith continue the Jewish tradition yet also break with it in radical and decisive ways? How are we to understand the words of the Last Supper, "This is my body" (Mt. 26:27)? In different places of the Gospels, Jesus speaks of God as his "Father" and mentions a divine "Spirit": is Christianity not a tritheism, then? Through investigation of these and many other theological matters, a tradition gradually built around Scripture—a multi-layered tradition, for later generations of thinkers continued to refer to earlier strands of inquiry, adopting and adapting ideas that had come before them in order to arrive at an increasingly sophisticated explication of the Christian faith. Thus, one can imagine the Christian tradition as a kind of "onion," composed of concentric circles around a scriptural core (see Figure 1).

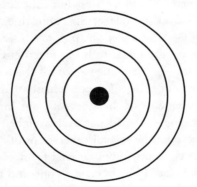

Figure 1: The "onion" of the Christian tradition

The "onion" quite aptly represents certain characteristics of the Christian intellectual tradition—and, indeed, of any tradition, Christian, intellectual, or otherwise. One of these characteristics has to do with the fact that, as the tradition develops, it steadily moves away from its center;

in other words, access to the center comes to be increasingly mediated. A ninth-century author reads Scripture with different eyes than a fourth-century author: his eyes have been sharpened by the insights of his predecessor—but maybe the emphases, oversights, and omissions of the same predecessor have also blinded them to certain aspects of the original text. Thus, a tradition will periodically feel the need for a robust return to its center: a "renaissance" of some sort will occur in order to balance the interplay between centrifugal and centripetal forces in our "onion."[2]

The image of the onion also throws into relief the fact that, as a tradition develops, it grows—first of all, simply in terms of material being accumulated. Therefore, the ninth-century author will find it more demanding to assimilate the wealth of the tradition than did his colleague writing in the fourth. It is for this reason that, from fairly early times, the Christian tradition devised tools to facilitate the collection, ordering, and transmission of authoritative texts, that is to say, of texts that, having been judged orthodox, made it into the onion. (The relationship between the onion and its outside is a matter that we cannot consider here.) One of the literary genres for such a gathering of authoritative material was the sentence collection. Already in the fifth century, Prosper of Aquitaine, who was a disciple of St. Augustine, composed a work entitled *The Book of the Sentences of St. Augustine* (*Liber sententiarum Sancti Augustini*), in which he attempted to bring together the most important theological statements—or "sentences"—of his teacher.[3]

By the twelfth century, the Western Christian tradition had translated all the major elements of the story of Jesus into theology. There was no scriptural passage that had not been weighed in light of similar passages, commented upon by several generations of exegetes, elucidated by means of abstract concepts (often derived from non-Christian philosophical sources), and placed in a doctrinal context. One of the principal differences between the biblical narrative and doctrine is that the latter is articulated according to the order of reason. A treatise on, say, the Eucharist or grace and free will addresses these topics not following a chronology of scriptural events, but rather in a chain of logically connected arguments. A major step, however, had yet to be accomplished at the time of Peter Lombard: the methodical arrangement of all the elements of Christian doctrine into a coherent whole, into a theological *system*.

It has been said that "systematic theology was the invention of the early twelfth century."[4] There are a number of reasons why time was ripe for this step. The professionalization of theology is one of them, that is, the fact that theology was increasingly taught by independent masters who neither were monks nor were charged with pastoral responsibilities in a parish or diocese. These masters reinvented theology as a self-contained discipline, not primarily aimed at contemplation, spiritual edification, or moral education, but rather functioning according to its own pedagogical and curricular needs. This new kind of theology was thus "scholastic," that is, designed for formal instruction in professional schools. Yet even monks contributed to the emerging field of systematic theology, though ultimately with less success than the new scholastic masters.

In order to understand the need for systematic theology, it is helpful to return to our "onion" for a moment. We have spoken of an interplay between centrifugal and centripetal forces in the Christian intellectual tradition. This interplay can be viewed in terms of a dialectical relationship between the *one* center of the tradition, Scripture,[5] and the *many* authoritative texts in which this center is spelled out and unfolded in all its implications. The unfolding ultimately calls for a folding-back, lest the unity of the tradition be lost. A renaissance is such a folding-back— but so is systematic theology, which can be conceived of as an effort to hold the multiple parts of Christian theology in one unified, methodically constituted whole.

The greatness of Peter Lombard's *Book of Sentences*—its unequalled *Wirkungsgeschichte* that we are still trying to explain—can be attributed to the fact that it folded the tradition back into the unity that it needed by the twelfth century: a highly differentiated unity, in which the voices of the Bible itself, of its earliest interpreters—the Fathers of the Church—and of the medieval theologians retained their distinctness while being woven into a harmonious composition of systematic theology. This is, indeed, what the *Book of Sentences* accomplished: it placed thousands of quotations in a coherent overall scheme, attempting to represent the positions of different interpreters faithfully while synthesizing divergent opinions, frequently adjudicating among competing views, and occasionally pronouncing particularly profound problems to be insoluble (see Figure 2).

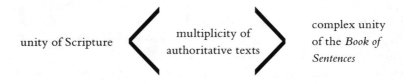

Figure 2: Unity and multiplicity in the Christian tradition

Subsequently, due to the need to which it responded and thanks to its clearly perceived superiority by comparison with other contemporary sentence collections, the *Book of Sentences* became itself the center of a textual tradition, of an "onion." Father Joseph de Ghellinck, who can be regarded as the founder of modern Peter Lombard studies, wrote of the *Sentences* that "it is legitimate to see in [this work] the point of arrival of all the preceding endeavors; at the same time, it is from this work that all the later efforts took their point of departure."[6] Just as initially the Christian tradition expanded, explicating the contents of its scriptural center, and then contracted in the twelfth century when the moment came for comprehensive theological synthesis, so from the latter half of the twelfth century the *Book of Sentences* itself functioned as the starting point of a complex textual tradition.

How did this tradition develop? According to what rhythm did it unfold? Did it have discernible layers and stages? Where did it lead? This is the first set of questions that the following four chapters will attempt to address.

The interest of this investigation is not limited to the *Book of Sentences* and its history. It can, in fact, be expected to shed light on the structure of textual traditions as such—in the Christian Middle Ages, the West, and maybe even beyond them. For one may ask, is there a typical pattern to the way in which the Western tradition received the great texts that are at its core? The preceding pages suggest a hypothesis: the Western tradition reads its great texts in a dialectical movement of expansion and contraction. This movement is constituted by a constant tension between

a textual center and its periphery: as the area surrounding the center expands in successive layers of explication and elaboration, this expansion will reach a point where a return to the center becomes necessary in order to avoid a dispersal of the tradition into unrelated fragments (see, once again, Figure 2). Let us find out whether it is in this manner that the *Book of Sentences* was received by its readers.

There is a second cluster of questions to which a study of the *Wirkungsgeschichte* of the *Book of Sentences* is in a privileged position to respond. The history of the reception of the *Sentences* spans the centuries from the later Middle Ages right to the dawn of the modern age. During this period, every theologian was expected to comment upon the *Sentences* as part of his university lectures. Indeed, even monastic thinkers who kept a distance from the scholastic milieu, such as Denys the Carthusian in the fifteenth century, were drawn into the orbit of Peter Lombard's great work and composed commentaries. As a consequence, the literary genre of the *Sentences* commentary is able to serve as a window upon a long and crucial segment of the Western Christian tradition. It witnesses—and of course contributed to—the major transformations in the structures of thought that occurred during more than three centuries: Peter Lombard completed the second redaction of the *Book of Sentences* in 1158; Martin Luther was one of the last great theologians to comment upon the work, in glosses that date from 1509–11. It is particularly intriguing to ask whether, and in what ways, the transition from medieval to modern thought makes itself felt in the *Sentences* literature: Is it in the methodology of theological reflection? Or perhaps even in certain formal features of the genre, that is to say, in the literary structures in which theological reflection was couched?

The two sets of questions that we have just formulated are, obviously, quite closely related. The development of the textual tradition of the *Sentences* commentary is connected with the evolution of the literary form of the genre; and this evolution, in turn, reflects and influenced changing approaches to theological reflection. The methodological parameters of our study are set, then. The following chapters will study the reception of the *Book of Sentences* by examining the literary form of some of the most influential commentaries that the work received between the latter half of the twelfth century and the beginning of the sixteenth.[7] At the same time, we will ask how the authors of these commentaries

conceived of the theological project: did they view theology primarily as contemplative or as scientific? Which authorities did they draw on? How did they view the relationship between theology and other branches of knowledge? Each of the four chapters is devoted to one of the centuries during which the *Sentences* exercised their greatest influence: the twelfth, thirteenth, fourteenth, and fifteenth. The final chapter concludes with the glosses upon the *Book of Sentences* that Martin Luther composed at the end of the first decade of the sixteenth century.

Chapter One: The Twelfth Century
From the *Sentences* to Abbreviations and Glosses

THE CHRISTIAN tradition evolved in several distinctive phases, which one can imagine as successive layers in our "onion." In the apostolic age, the Gospels recorded four interpretations of the life of Jesus Christ in narrative form; to this narrative, the Pauline epistles already added a dimension of theoretical reflection on the meaning and implications of the Christian faith. The Letter to the Galatians, for example, explores the relationship between the old (Jewish) law and the new faith. The Church Fathers pushed this reflection further, and in dialogue with the heritage of Greco-Roman philosophy developed well-defined doctrines; the term "Trinity," for instance, was coined at this stage in order to articulate the relationship among God the Father, the Son, and the Holy Spirit. Councils of bishops frequently stepped in to adjudicate among competing theories. In the Latin West, the patristic age culminated in the works of St. Augustine (354–430).

After the "dark ages" that followed the disintegration of the Western half of the Roman Empire, the Carolingian period was characterized by educational reforms that lent new vigor to Christian intellectual life. The Emperor Charlemagne (768–814) encouraged the cathedral schools and monasteries in his realm to improve their standards of instruction,

seeing to it that they were equipped with sound Bibles, free from textual corruption. Charlemagne's initiatives provided the foundation for several centuries of theological reflection on topics such as the Eucharist, predestination and free will, and numerous others. With the exception of John Scottus Eriugena (ca. 800–ca. 877), however, no thinker attempted a large-scale theoretical account of the Christian faith as a whole. Eriugena was something of an eccentric figure, as his main work, the *Periphyseon*, drew much more heavily upon Greek sources than was customary at the time.

The crucial step from treatises on individual theological topics to theological *systems* defines the original contribution of the twelfth century to the development of the Western Christian tradition. The need for a comprehensive and coherent account of all elements of the faith was first felt in the practical domain. For the salvation of souls, it is more important to know what constitutes a valid ordination, marriage, or Mass than to grasp all the fine points of Trinitarian theology! This is why it is in the field of canon law—the regulations governing the daily life of the Church—that the first comprehensive manuals were created. But the methods used in the compilation of these canon-law books also proved to be fruitful for more theoretically oriented theologians. From the canonists, they learned two things in particular: how to arrange large amounts of material in a systematic order, and how to reconcile seemingly opposed statements from authoritative sources, such as councils or Church Fathers. Now, as we already know from the Introduction, collections of "sentences" had existed since the fifth century; yet the movement toward systematic theology did not take center stage until after the creation of such comprehensive canon law collections such as the *Decretum* and *Panormia* by Ivo of Chartres (ca. 1040–1115).[1]

There are other reasons as well behind the quest for theological systems that occurred in the twelfth century. In the Introduction, we saw the rise of professional schools of theology run by independent masters; this development had everything to do with the prosperity of urban centers, the relative ease of travel, and hence the desire and ability of city-dwellers to pursue higher education.[2] Many schools competed for students, but in the first half of the twelfth century, Paris evolved into what the late English medievalist Sir Richard Southern called "the scholastic metropolis of northern Europe."[3] Masters and students from all

over the continent flocked to the vibrant city, which was rapidly eclipsing older centers of learning such as Laon, Rheims, and Chartres.

Peter Lombard (1095/1100–1160) and the *Book of Sentences*

In the 1130s, Peter Lombard left his native Italy in order to complete his theological education at Rheims, which had established its reputation in the eleventh century. Rheims was, moreover, not too far from Laon, where the school of Master Anselm created the *Glossa ordinaria*, or "standard Gloss"—a compilation of excerpts from the Fathers and medieval authorities that were placed in the margins and between the lines of the text of Scripture to serve as commentary. The *Glossa ordinaria* was the most advanced tool of biblical studies at the time, and in fact continued to be used until the eighteenth century.[4]

In 1136, however, Peter Lombard decided to move on, no doubt attracted by the rising fame of the Parisian masters. By 1140, a dozen schools of theology were operating within the city or in its immediate vicinity. They included the famous abbey of St. Victor and the school of the brilliant, controversial, scandal-ridden Peter Abelard (1079–1142) on the Mount Sainte-Geneviève. The Lombard—the name often used to refer to Peter Lombard—became closely associated with the Victorines, attending the lectures of Hugh of St. Victor (1097/1101–1141), who was the author of an influential manual of theology entitled *De sacramentis christianae fidei* (*On the Sacraments of the Christian Faith*). In the *De sacramentis*, Hugh endeavored to render a complete account of the faith by arranging the authoritative "sentences" of the tradition according to the order of salvation history: creation, the Fall, the history of Israel, the Incarnation.... However, Peter Lombard also immersed himself in the works of Abelard, who in the various versions of his *Theologia* experimented with a more "logical" schema, dividing the theological material into faith, charity, and sacraments. In another work of Abelard's, *Sic et non* (*Yes and No*), the Lombard found the codification of a set of rules for the reconciliation of conflicting "sentences." What if, on a given theological issue, Augustine seemed to contradict Jerome or, indeed, if quotations from Augustine's own works did not always appear consistent? Abelard's rules stipulated, among other things, that careful attention should be paid to the authenticity of quoted sources, that one

needed to reckon with the possibility of textual corruptions, and that one could resolve seeming contradictions by noticing instances where authors use identical words with different meanings.

In the 1140s, Peter Lombard became affiliated with the cathedral school of Notre Dame (which by 1200 would, together with other Parisian colleges, form the University of Paris). He was to teach at Notre Dame for some twenty years, until his election as bishop of Paris in 1159. The *Book of Sentences* was the fruit of this teaching career—and, of course, the education preceding it—at the heart of the scholastic metropolis of northern Europe. There, he lived in constant dialogue—and friendly competition, no doubt!—with the leading theologians of the day. In the *Book of Sentences*, the twelfth century's quest for a comprehensive theological system came to a (provisional) conclusion.

The full title of the *Book of Sentences* is *Sententiae in quatuor libris distinctae*, "Sentences divided into four books." The four books deal, respectively, with God and the Trinity; creation (including the creation of angels and of man, and questions surrounding the Fall); Christology; and, finally, the sacraments and eschatology. In order to arrive at this division of the theological material, Peter Lombard learned from his contemporaries. His schema still has an unmistakable historico-biblical element to it: God, the creator, makes heaven and earth, angels and man; creation leads to the Fall and to sin, which Christ's saving work overcomes; this work of salvation is mediated to us through the sacraments; and whether the human being embraces or rejects this divine grace determines the shape of life in the hereafter for each of us. The *Sentences*, however, overlay this historical schema with a more "rational" one, which Peter Lombard derived from St. Augustine (rather than having recourse to the Abelardian one). He explains it in the opening chapters of the work. In his treatise *De doctrina christiana* (*On Christian Teaching*), Augustine made a twofold distinction between things and signs, enjoyment and use, developing a kind of theological semiotics. Everything that exists, suggested Augustine, is ultimately nothing but a sign of its Creator, the only "thing" in the strictest sense of the term. Therefore, all these created signs ought to be merely "used" in the human quest for the vision of God in the hereafter. Enjoyment, on the other hand, is something that should be reserved for God himself, for to enjoy anything less—to rest in it—would imply a failure to recognize its

proper function as a pointer to the Ultimate. Although Peter Lombard himself never articulates the matter quite so clearly, the four books of the *Sentences* reflect the dialectical relationship between thing and sign, enjoyment and use. Beginning with *the* Thing, God (Book I), the work moves on to a consideration of all the created things that are only to be used (Book II). Human beings occupy an intermediary position in this hierarchy, since they cannot be reduced to mere means on the way to God; they possess a dignity that makes them worth being enjoyed, albeit only "in God" (still Book II).[5] Christ, as God-man, is in a sense both the Way and the Goal: thus, he is the Sign-Thing *par excellence* (Book III). The sacraments, finally, are signs of grace (Book IV).

Each of the four books falls into chapters: 210 chapters in the first, 269 in the second, 164 in the third, and 290 in the fourth book. The subject matter of each chapter is summarized in a short heading, which is repeated—although not always verbatim—in the general table of contents that appears at the beginning of the *Sentences*. Tables of contents had been in use since around the year 500;[6] nevertheless, the practice seems to have remained controversial and not universally accepted. Indeed, Robert of Melun, author of a sentences collection contemporaneous with that of Peter Lombard, declares in his preface, "It is custom rather than reason that compels me to precede this work with titles and to divide it by means of titles placed within it."[7] Peter Lombard, for his part, appears rather proud of his table of contents. He concludes his prologue with an explanation of its advantages: "Again, so that what is sought might appear more easily, we have begun by providing the titles by which the chapters of the individual books are distinguished."[8] A table of contents makes it possible to consult a book selectively, the choice of topics to be read being determined by the reader's own interests. This kind of approach was new in the twelfth century, for prior to the rise of scholasticism, the paradigmatic medieval style of reading had been contemplative and ruminative. In the monasteries, books served a religious goal: that of assimilating the reader, through words, to the Word; to lead him or her through Scripture, and the great commentators upon Scripture, to the Author himself. Entire books were therefore read slowly and repeatedly, in community, and aloud. In Peter Lombard and his fellow Parisians, we see a more professorial attitude to the text.[9]

In keeping with the exigencies of a scholarly reference work, the *Book*

of Sentences possesses a variety of other features to facilitate consultation. Not only the individual chapters, but paragraphs within chapters, too, are frequently introduced by short headings, written in red characters. These so-called "rubrics" (from the Latin *ruber*, "red") let the headings stand out from the text, making it possible to scan the outline of its argument at a glance. Furthermore, Peter Lombard makes sure to document the sources of his authoritative quotations—of his "sentences"—with the greatest accuracy that was possible in his day, that is to say, through references by author, title, and book or chapter. Here we have the precursor to the (distinctly modern) footnote, which acknowledges the individual ownership of certain texts, distinguishing borrowed ideas and phrases from "original" contributions.[10]

The preface to the *Sentences* is in striking contrast to the tone of scholarly professionalism that pervades much of the body of the work. It hearkens back to an older style of writing, one that confounds the voice of the author with that of the texts he quotes. Metaphors from Scripture, rather than the precise conceptual language of the scholastic master, are employed to characterize the project upon which Peter Lombard is about to embark. This is how the preface opens:

> Longing to cast something of our want and poverty along with the little poor woman into the treasury of the Lord [see Mark 12:41–44], to scale the heights, we have presumed to undertake a work beyond our powers, placing the trust for completion and the wages of the work upon the Samaritan, who, having taken out two pence for the care of the half-dead man, promised to repay all to the one spending over and above that [see Luke 10:35]. The truth of the one making the promise delights us, but the immensity of the work frightens us; the desire to advance urges us on, but the weakness of failing dissuades us, [a weakness] which the zeal for the house of the Lord conquers.[11]

The *Book of Sentences*, then, is itself a transitional work, standing at the threshold between older approaches to theological writing and the developing movement of scholastic theology.

It is now time for us to turn to an examination of the ways in which the work was received among its earliest readers. In the twelfth century,

two very distinct strands are discernible in the history of the *Sentences*: in one, they were contracted; in the other, expanded upon.

Abbreviations of the Sentences

The *Book of Sentences* is of course itself a contraction or condensation of the tradition preceding it. In the prologue, Peter Lombard explains, "[This work] gathers together, in a brief volume, the sentences of the Fathers, side by side with their testimonies, so that it might not be necessary for someone searching to go through a large number of books—[someone] to whom the anthology offers without labor what he seeks."[12] Nevertheless, the text of the *Sentences* is not exactly short: in the modern critical edition, it fills about 1,100 pages. Perhaps medieval masters had a different sense of brevity than we do: a century after the Lombard, Thomas Aquinas would, in the prologue to the *Summa theologiae*, speak of his intention to offer the young reader a "brief" treatment of sacred doctrine—and proceed to write a work even longer than Peter Lombard's. Be that as it may, as the *Sentences* began to be disseminated beyond the boundaries of the cathedral school of Notre Dame, masters who used the text in their teaching felt a need to abbreviate the abbreviation further, and in this manner to render it more manageable. Almost a century ago a Belgian medievalist, Raymond Martin, made the first—and to date only—attempt to categorize the different kinds of abridgments that arose in the reception of the *Book of Sentences*. He distinguished several kinds of *Sentences* abbreviations:[13]

1. Versified abbreviations, which fulfilled the pedagogical purpose of facilitating memorization, condensed the entire *Book of Sentences* into a few manuscript folios. Evidently, the purpose here was not to summarize any detailed theological discussions, but only the outline of the work. Numerous surviving manuscripts testify to the popularity of this genre.[14]

2. Among the abbreviations in prose, some concentrated on only one or several books of the *Sentences*, omitting others. There are also manuscripts that offer just a few excerpts, chosen in light of specific interests.[15]

3. Most of the abbreviations, however, provided summaries of the *Book of Sentences* as a whole. We shall examine two of the most famous and widespread of these in a moment, namely, the abbreviation by Master Bandinus and the one known under the title *Filia Magistri*, "Daughter of the Master."

4. Occasionally, as the *Sentences* were transmitted to successive generations of masters and students, earlier abridgments were subjected to further abbreviation. In this manner, the study aids became increasingly concise, but obviously also more superficial.[16]

Martin regarded two other kinds of study aids as abbreviations, though it may be better to consider them separately. They are, on the one hand, dictionaries of theological terms occurring in the *Sentences*; some manuscripts use the expression *verborum significationes*, "meanings of words," to identify the contents of such lexica.[17] On the other hand, some masters prepared analytical, alphabetical, or even synoptic tables to render the *Sentences* more accessible. It appears, however, that these latter research tools were the product of the thirteenth century rather than the twelfth. We will return to them at greater length in the next chapter.

The Abbreviation by Master Bandinus

One of the first abridgments of the *Sentences*, which was also to become one of the most widespread, was authored by a certain Master Bandinus.[18] Unfortunately, we know very little about him, except that he taught in Paris during the second half of the twelfth century. His abbreviation of the *Sentences*, however, enjoyed an influence that extended even into the modern age. In 1516, John Eck, Luther's celebrated adversary, rediscovered Bandinus's abbreviation in a manuscript at the abbey of Melk. The learned Eck immediately noticed the close similarity between Bandinus's work and the *Book of Sentences*, wondering which of the two was original and which guilty of "plagiarism"! Amazingly from a contemporary point of view, the first printed edition of the abbreviation, which appeared at Vienna in 1519, adjudicated this question in Bandinus's favor—an opinion that was reproduced in the second modern printing, which appeared at Louvain in 1555. As late as 1834, the German Protestant theologian

Friedrich Wilhelm Rettberg devoted a short treatise to the question of the priority between the *Sentences* and its abbreviated version, finally laying the debate to rest through a careful comparison of the two texts.[19]

The popularity of this abbreviation is easy to understand remaining, for the most part, scrupulously faithful to Peter Lombard's teachings, it boils the text down to its essential arguments. This no-nonsense manual reduces the entire prologue of the *Book of Sentences* to a half-sentence, after which it immediately proceeds to chapter 1:

> **The general subject matter of all Scripture: things and signs. What a thing is and what a sign.** Wishing to furnish students, by heavenly favor, with some compendium about the divine matters, we are immediately reminded that there are two things with which the teaching about God is primarily concerned, namely, things and signs. For, as Augustine says, "all teaching is about either things or signs. But we call 'things' those entities that are not employed to signify something; 'signs,' on the other hand, we call entities the use of which consists in signifying"—such as the sacraments of both Laws.[20]

"Wishing" (*cupientes*) picks up the very first word of Peter Lombard's prologue, in which the author of the *Sentences* explains, rather poetically and extensively, the purpose of his work. In Bandinus, the statement of intent is much more succinct. Apart from this one word, there is no other quotation from the original prologue. Rather, Bandinus states his aim in words that are either directly borrowed from or paraphrase the beginning of chapter 1. Through divine favor, he wants to create a compendium for students. The ethos of the text, then, is thoroughly pedagogical. "We are immediately reminded," the author continues, giving the opening of his work a sense of urgency, as though he were talking to a student cramming for an exam the night before it was to be given. The reference to the task of memorizing is telling as well: "we are reminded…."

The material to be memorized is characterized in three ways. At first, Bandinus speaks of "the general subject matter of all Scripture" (*generalis Scripturae totius materia*), suggesting that theology is really tantamount to an advanced form of scriptural commentary. It is legitimate

to regard this expression as synonymous with a phrase that occurs in the text from the *Sentences* which Bandinus is summarizing here, namely, "treatment of the sacred page" (*sacrae paginae tractatum*). *Sacra pagina* was the traditional term for what has, since the thirteenth century, come to be called "theology"—with this important difference, however, that "sacred page" stresses the close, inseparable connection between theological understanding and the reading, contemplating, and commenting of Scripture.[21] A few lines further into his text, Master Bandinus employs the fairly neutral term, "divine matters" (*res divinas*). It is found in Peter Lombard as well, who employs it somewhat later in the first chapter. Finally, Bandinus identifies the subject of his abbreviation as "teaching about God" (*doctrina Dei*). In this usage, he is following both the Lombard and Augustine, from whose treatise *On Christian Teaching* Peter Lombard derived his crucial distinction between things and signs. Nonetheless, the term *doctrina* is not unambiguous. Post-twelfth-century authors would prefer to speak of "sacred doctrine" (*sacra doctrina*), rather than of "sacred page," thus emphasizing the academic and "scientific" character of their discipline. There may already be a hint of this connotation in Bandinus.

The quotation from Augustine is abridged by comparison with the form in which it appears in the *Sentences*, and a careful distinction that Peter Lombard makes between two kinds of signs—those that merely signify grace, and others that both signify and confer grace—is obliterated in Bandinus's abridgment: "such as the sacraments of both Laws." An important nuance is lost here, to be sure; yet it would be unfair to say that Peter Lombard's teaching is distorted or seriously compromised.

Bandinus's faithfulness to the Master is confirmed in his abridged version of one of Peter Lombard's most controversial teachings, which most of his successors were to reject even though it was never formally condemned by the Church. The doctrine in question occurs in chapters 60 to 65 of Book I, where the Lombard maintains that charity is the Holy Spirit.[22] One may wonder what could have been so controversial about this teaching, given scriptural passages such as 1 John 4, where the identification of the Holy Spirit with the love of God and neighbor appears fairly straightforward: "Dearly beloved, let us love one another, for charity is of God. And every one that loveth, is born of God, and knoweth God. He that loveth not, knoweth not God: for God is char-

ity [7–8].… No man hath seen God at any time. If we love one another, God abideth in us, and his charity is perfected in us. In this we know that we abide in him, and he in us: because he has given us of his spirit [12–13]." Nevertheless, and despite the support that Peter Lombard found for his position in Augustine's treatise *On the Trinity*, subsequent theologians judged the identification of charity with the Holy Spirit to be threatening the distinction between nature and grace, the human and the divine: How can a human act, such as the act of loving God and neighbor, *be* the Holy Spirit?

Bandinus, however, states the Lombardian view in its full force: "The Holy Spirit is brotherly love"; "therefore, brotherly love is God."[23] He concludes his lengthy discussion of the issue—a discussion that summarizes not only the bare bones of the Lombard's position, but also many of the arguments in favor of and against it—in his own words, which render eloquent testimony to his commitment to the Master: "For this reason, having repelled the cold and jejune calumny of the enemies of the truth, we acknowledge freely that charity is the Holy Spirit. Let these people be enraged that it is God and God's gift by which many gifts are allotted to each and every individual as his own."[24] To lend strength to this declaration of loyalty, Bandinus even deploys the tools of Ciceronian oratory: "the cold and jejune calumny" is a well-worn rhetorical formula from the oration *Pro Caecina*.[25]

Bandinus, however, does not treat all of the *Sentences* with equal care. In the edition of the text printed in Migne's *Patrologia latina*, his abbreviation of Book I fills 57 columns; that of Book II, 42; but the abridged version of Book III occupies only 19 columns; and that of Book IV, 21. These numbers should, of course, be considered against the background of the corresponding books of Peter Lombard's work. Again, in the standard edition, Book I of the *Sentences* fills 274 pages; Book II, 251; Book III, 207; and Book IV, 330. While one notes the particularly detailed treatment of the sacraments in Book IV and the fact that Book III, devoted to Christology, is somewhat shorter than the rest, the work as a whole appears reasonably well balanced. This could hardly be said of Master Bandinus's abridgment, which gives short shrift to the final two books of the *Sentences*. Not surprisingly, then, the quality of his text deteriorates in Books III and IV. Whereas in Books I and II Bandinus is keen to reproduce not only Peter Lombard's opinions but also the

arguments through which he arrived at them (and occasionally, as we have seen, even a spirited defense is added), what we get in the final two books is closer to a mere summary of the Lombard's "positions." Much nuance—at times, crucial nuance—is lost.

Bandinus's treatment of the hypostatic union illustrates this defect. In Book III of the *Sentences*, Peter Lombard offers a notoriously ambiguous and hesitant discussion on the relationship between human and divine elements in the Incarnation. If God became man, then did he become other than himself? Did he leave his proper nature behind in Christ? If not, was Christ perhaps not fully human? The *Book of Sentences* attempts to answer these questions in a painstaking analysis of three contemporary theories, "the single most extended treatment of a particular point" in the entire work.[26] At the end of this examination, we do not find an endorsement of any one of the three theories, but rather a humble admission of the weakness of the human mind before the divine mysteries: "What has been said above," Peter Lombard wrote, "does not suffice to understand this question."[27] Bandinus, however, transforms the Lombard into a decided adherent of one of the three theories, the so-called *habitus* theory:

> But when we say, "God is man," a "having" (*habitus*) is implied while a nature or person is predicated, such that the meaning is: "God is man," that is to say, God is *having* man (*habens hominem est Deus*). If, however, the word "made" is placed in the sentence—as in, "God was made man"—then you should understand: that is, God began to *have* man (*Deus coepit habere hominem*)....[28]

Admittedly, some of his contemporaries, including his students, understood the Master as subscribing to the *habitus* theory, according to which, in the Incarnation, God assumed a human soul and human flesh in a way similar to how a person would wear a piece of clothing: God "had" a human soul and body.[29] Nevertheless, this is not an accurate summary of the Lombard's argument in the *Book of Sentences*. It is a distortion.[30] Thus, medieval readers who were introduced to Peter Lombard through Bandinus's abridgment would have ended up attributing teachings to the *Book of Sentences* for which there is no foundation in the text.

Our verdict on Master Bandinus, then, has to be mixed. While for the most part his compendium provides an intelligently condensed and reliable account of the theology of the *Sentences*, its second half is significantly weaker than the first. A study of the manuscript tradition of Bandinus's work would reveal whether the defects of Books III and IV are only an accident of the transmission of the text. Until this study has been undertaken, we will have to reserve our final judgment on the matter.

Filia Magistri

"Daughter of the Master," *Filia Magistri*, is a later abridgment of the *Book of Sentences*—in fact, one of the last representatives of the genre. It is an anonymous composition, but the fact that it borrows heavily from the *Sentences* commentary of Hugh of St. Cher—a Dominican who taught in Paris in the 1230s—allowed Raymond Martin to trace the work to Hugh's school. He assigned it a date around 1232–45.[31] Another work on which *Filia Magistri* relies in its reading of the *Sentences* is the "Golden Summa" (*Summa aurea*) by William of Auxerre, which is not exactly a *Sentences* commentary though it is patterned after Peter Lombard's great manual.[32] Unlike the abbreviation by Bandinus, *Filia Magistri* did not survive the transition into modern times: the work was never printed, despite the fact that its rich manuscript tradition extends into the fifteenth century.[33] In the Middle Ages, "Daughter of the Master" was so popular that many libraries owned multiple copies. The length of the work in these copies varies, as students of the *Book of Sentences* added and dropped material in view of their own interests and contemporary priorities. This phenomenon of an unstable, dynamic text is not at all unusual in the Middle Ages. Before the printing press was able to freeze authoritative versions of texts on the typeset page, transmission by users and professional scribes subjected literary productions to a process of rereading that was also, frequently, a rewriting.

One of the earlier, thirteenth-century copies of *Filia Magistri* was prepared at the Cistercian abbey of St. Mary at Cambron (in modern-day Belgium). After an odyssey of several centuries, the manuscript resurfaced in the library of one George Dunn of Maidenhead, England, from which the John Rylands University Library of Manchester purchased it

no mich t. primu de rebz: postea de si

gnis disseremus.

de istis uerbis
fru. vn

¶ Frui est amore inherere [santis] alicui rei propter seipsa uente ati q isti uia. q̇ul
ad sm pren t pha. re aut

¶ Vti uero: id quod in usum uenerit
sole fruend̄

referre ad obtinendū illud q̇ frueri

dū t. Abuti abum est si uti. Jt aug. vn

T assumie aliquid in facultate uolun

tatis. frui aute t uti cui luue ipsa. t at q̇ t

gaudio. si adhuc spei: s̄z iam fruit̄ u nu ptē. lua aliqch

ut. Hec sic determinamus. dicemus nos

hic et in futuro frui. qr sume q̇ ad oste iuuet q̇

alla uue uacua ert gaudio.

s̄z ibi q̇e t p ptē t plene. hic au si adeo

plene. potest t dici q̇d q̇ frut̄ in hac

uita si eu h̄t gaudiū spei: s̄z t rei.

q̇a ta delectat in eo q̇d diligit t cta

ram uu aliquatenus tenet.

sed non per
fecte.

in 1913. Raymond Martin discovered it there a couple of years later.[34] This manuscript is written in beautiful, perfectly neat Gothic script. The large initials that mark the beginnings of chapters are illuminated, and chapter headings appear in red ink (see Figure 3). Evidently, great care was taken in the preparation of this copy, which in the Middle Ages always indicates that the text thus treated was held in high esteem.

Filia Magistri is composed of two distinct elements: the main text, appearing in large characters, and notes—both interlinear and marginal—which are written in smaller letters. The notes, however, are not of an occasional, haphazard nature, added by this or that individual reader. Rather, the fact that the scribe provided spaces corresponding to the precise length of particular notes indicates that they were considered an integral part of the work. In order to understand the function of the notes, and indeed the conception of *Filia Magistri* as a whole, we should turn to the prologue—for, unlike Bandinus's compendium, this abbreviation does have a prologue. It is brief and to the point:

> Since, like the four rivers of paradise [see Gen. 2:10–14], the *Books of Sentences* water the gardens of the Church copiously, it is doubtless expedient, for the sake of those who delight in brevity, that their flow be restrained by a compendium—one through which the mother of disgust, prolixity of language, might be avoided, yet the order of books and their content somehow come to be known by those who are not aware of them. Therefore, in approaching the following work in the name of Jesus Christ, I shall add some magisterial notes, so that the excerpts may shine forth more clearly.

Division of the Books

> Sacred Scripture treats of two things, namely, the Creator and the work of the Creator. The work of the Creator, however, is divided into the work of creation and the work of recreation, and the work of final retribution. Again, the work of recreation is subdivided into the work that was performed in a particular person (such are the Incarnation, the Passion, etc.), and the work of the Church, recreating through the sacraments. Appropriately, then, the Master divided his work into four books, such that, in the first one, he treated of the Creator; in the second, of the work of creation; in

Figure 3: *Filia Magistri* in MS. Manchester, John Rylands University Library, Latin 203, fol. 76r

the third, of the work of recreation that was performed in a particular person; in the fourth, of the work of recreation that was
performed through the mediation of the Church—that is to say,
[he treated] of the sacraments. Finally, he ends his work with the
work of final retribution.[35]

The prologue opens with a well-chosen simile likening the *Sentences*,
with their four books, to the life-giving waters of the four rivers of para-
dise from the Book of Genesis. The simile reminds the reader of the
relevance of the theologian's work to the growth of the Church; but
it also alludes to the continuity between the *Book of Sentences* and the
Book that, ultimately, all Christian theology serves to elucidate (namely, Scripture). The following lines, however, adopt a much more sober,
pedagogical—one could even say, utilitarian—tone: some people de-
light in brevity, whereas wordiness engenders their disgust. Do we have
to imagine a certain type of student here, who for the sake of efficient,
painless study prefers unambiguous statements of doctrine to subtle theological disquisitions? It is, in fact, precisely such short and easy answers
that *Filia Magistri* provides. The work eliminates the dialectical character
that is so central to Peter Lombard's *Book of Sentences*: its relentless to-
ing and fro-ing between possible answers to deep theological questions,
the constant movement that often leads only to admissions of ignorance.
In its level of sophistication, then, *Filia Magistri* is far removed not only
from the *Book of Sentences* itself, but even from an earlier abbreviation
such as the one by Bandinus. It testifies to a streamlining of theological
studies that occurred in the decades separating the two works, a simplification no doubt due to the pedagogical needs of beginning students.

The author of *Filia Magistri* draws special attention to the "magisterial
notes" (*notulas magistrales*) that he added in order to elucidate the main
body of the abridgment. The word "magisterial" needs to be taken literally here. These are the notes "of a master"—a teacher—for the use
of his students. Their principal purpose is to update Peter Lombard's
teachings, that is to say, to add contemporary terminology and theological positions.[36] For instance, where the main text states, following the
Lombard, that "the treatment of the sacred page is primarily concerned
with things or signs," a note explains, "that is to say, essences and sacraments."[37] "Essences" is a more precise philosophical term than "things"
and reflects the influence of Aristotelian terminology upon theology.

The "division of books" is an important feature of our prologue. Neither Peter Lombard himself nor Bandinus provided a straightforward statement of the logic holding the four books of the *Sentences* together; they were not yet able to articulate the logic of theology as a system, at least not with rigor. In this regard, *Filia Magistri* is very different. It offers a didactically highly useful, lucid and logical derivation of the contents of the four books (see Figure 4). Interestingly, the terminology used in this derivation is not Peter Lombard's, but bespeaks the influence of Hugh of St. Victor, who organized his theology in terms of creation and recreation, or restoration.

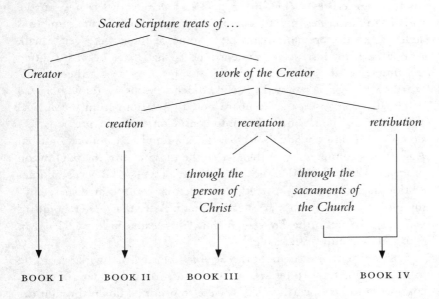

Figure 4: The structure of the *Sentences* according to *Filia Magistri*

Filia Magistri's treatment of controversial material confirms the impression that we have formed of it so far as a didactic tool without much aspiration to theological depth. The reader looking for Peter Lombard's controversial thesis on charity in Book I will find ... absolutely nothing! It has been omitted. Such subtle problems—controversial teachings that require thoughtful deliberation rather than simple memorizing—are too hard to digest for the student-audience of the work.

Glosses on the *Sentences*

Earlier on, I pointed out that in the earliest stages of its reception, the *Book of Sentences* was both condensed and expanded upon. Having examined two significant examples of condensation, let us now turn to the expansions.

The first author to gloss copies of the *Book of Sentences*—that is to say, to place notes in the margins of the text—was none other than Peter Lombard himself. The Master released a first version of the *Sentences* in the academic year 1156–57, after composing the work as a manual for his theology classes. When in 1157–58 he once again lectured on the basis of the *Sentences*, his students noticed that he had made numerous additions to the previous year's text. Some of these were very small. In one case, for instance, a student reports that Peter Lombard jotted the simple word *cave*—"Be careful!"—in the margin of a theologically tricky passage, concerned that his students might overlook a crucial detail. In other cases, the Lombard noted quotations from theological authorities that he had not taken into consideration in the previous version. One manuscript advises us that the Master placed a quotation from Augustine's commentary on Kings "in the margin after the publication of the book." At the end of the academic year 1157–58, however, another edition of the *Sentences* was made available that incorporated these "flying glosses," as contemporaries called them. After that, Peter Lombard was never to teach the *Sentences* again. He became bishop of Paris in 1159 and died only a year later.[38]

Each generation of users of the *Sentences* glossed the work according to its own questions, interests, and concerns. Moreover, certain glosses considered to be especially helpful were transmitted down through the centuries, so that it is not uncommon to find particular glosses recurring in different manuscripts of the *Sentences*. Although the gloss is not a genre whose use was limited to the twelfth century, marginal glosses antedate more elaborate forms of commentary. The thousands of glosses that we find in the margins of Peter Lombard's magnum opus range from the comical to the theologically deeply serious.

One weary student annotates his copy of the *Sentences* with words of exasperation: "Patience wears out every virtue!"[39] A Cistercian monk's thoughts wander; somehow, studying the *Sentences* brings to

mind his profession: "I promise stability and the conversion of my conduct according to the Rule of St. Benedict in this place which is called
Foucarmont…." Frequently, glosses highlight Peter Lombard's sources,
even when they are already identified in the main text. Others draw attention to parallel passages in contemporary theologians like Hugh of St.
Victor, Gratian, or Gandulph of Bologna. On occasion, they do so with
indignation at a debt unacknowledged by the Lombard: "outrageously
(*prepostere*) [these words] are taken from Hugh." Furthermore, it is not
rare to find glosses that correct or complete quotations provided by Peter
Lombard, in order to ensure accurate documentation. And every reader
of medieval manuscripts has come across the *manus quae indigitat*, the index finger of a little hand pointing to a portion of text that the glossator
judged to be especially worthy of attention—like this: ☞. In order to
make it easier to follow the thread of Peter Lombard's argument, its steps
are often indicated in the margins: formulae such as, "here he asks," "solution," "here he objects," are therefore frequent, as are glosses drawing
attention to the beginning of new chapters. These would later develop
into *divisiones textus*, that is to say, short marginal summaries of sections
of text that were designed to bring out their logical structure. Schematic
drawings served the same purpose. Finally, despite the great authority
that Peter Lombard enjoyed throughout the later Middle Ages—"the
Master," he was simply called—his theological views did not always
draw unanimous support. In such cases, we encounter glosses such as,
"Here the Master should not be followed" (*hic non tenetur magister*).

The next step in the development of the *Sentences* glosses is worth
some attention, since it sheds light upon larger structures of how textual traditions evolve. Already in the 1160s or early 1170s, some of the
marginal glosses on the *Sentences* began to detach, as it were, from their
main text and migrate onto pages of their own, where they formed continuous texts.[40] In other words, students of Peter Lombard such as the
mysterious Pseudo-Peter of Poitiers (about whom more in a moment)
decided to transform marginal glosses into keyword glosses. The text
that a marginal gloss annotates usually appears immediately opposite
the gloss; where necessary, a sign placed within the text and repeated
before the gloss helps render the reference unambiguous. In keyword
glosses, however, the original text has been omitted, except for brief
quotations—lemmata—at the beginning of each section of commen-

tary. Moreover, lemmata are incorporated into the running text, as in the following example. In the manuscripts, underlining makes it possible to distinguish the lemmata from the glossator's own words. I have used italics for the same purpose:

> *What, however* etc.... *any ... gradation*, such that one person would be greater than another, *but the entire godhead*, that is, the Trinity, that is, each of the persons *is equal to* the others *through its perfection*, since each one of them is perfect, *so that, with the exception of the words* etc. Understand this to be said....[41]

It is clear that the first keyword glosses could not—and were not designed to—be used without the *Book of Sentences* by their side. Keyword glosses, however, had a high potential to be developed into more independent commentaries, which were meant to be read as self-contained compositions. Such commentaries, in turn, gave rise to perfectly autonomous works of theology. We shall examine these developments in detail in the following chapters.

Of course, at each of the stages just described, the glossing game repeated itself as readers adapted texts for their own use. Therefore, we find manuscripts with keyword glosses that carry marginal annotations; in a later manuscript of the same work, some of these marginal glosses may have been incorporated into the main text, while others may have been jettisoned. The permutations are almost infinite, which makes it difficult to reconstruct the textual history especially of the earliest glosses—those that have not yet been tightly woven into self-contained texts, with a characteristic coherence that reduces the possibility for interpolations.

As we follow the transformation of marginal texts into central ones in the tradition of the *Book of Sentences*, it bears pointing out that the history of Christian theology as a whole can be viewed as having taken its origin in the margins of Scripture—metaphorically and, in many cases, literally so. In the history of Christian thought, the *Book of Sentences* is one of those marginal texts that turned into centers themselves—only to be displaced eventually by their own margins.

The Pseudo-Poitiers Gloss

Given the fluidity of the earliest glosses that were composed at the cathedral school of Notre Dame—Peter Lombard's immediate students and successors worked on the *Sentences* in a close-knit group in which manuscripts circulated to be copied and expanded upon by different people—it is not surprising that the first known continuous gloss on the *Sentences* should not have one identifiable author. It is commonly referred to as the Pseudo-Poitiers gloss, a designation which reflects the fact that the work used to be attributed, incorrectly, to Peter of Poitiers.[42] It was composed in the 1160s or early 1170s, but certainly before 1175 since it does not mention authors known to have been active in the last quarter of the twelfth century.[43] While there are only three surviving manuscripts that contain the work in its entirety, it spawned numerous other glosses into which its text was partially incorporated.[44] In this way, the Pseudo-Poitiers gloss exercised considerable influence on the early reception of the *Book of Sentences*.

The prologue to the gloss by Pseudo-Peter of Poitiers is elaborate. It employs the *accessus* format, a standardized form of introduction whose purpose is to answer certain basic questions about the text: who wrote the book, what is it about, why was it composed and in what manner, where, when, and by what means?[45] Our prologue does not address all of these questions, limiting itself to the subject matter of the work, its audience, division, and intention. Despite its considerable length, it is worth quoting in full, since it casts much light upon the way early scholastic theologians thought and wrote:

1. The whole of the Divine Page consists in things to be believed and things to be done, that is to say, [it consists] in the assertion of the faith and the strengthening of morals. This was not unknown to the prophet who said, *My mouth shall speak wisdom: and the meditation of my heart understanding* [Ps. 48:4]. Explaining this [verse], Cassiodorus wrote: "Wisdom consists in the contemplation of that which is above, and understanding in the strengthening of morals." Of these [matters], then, the Master treats in his work, but in general and in detail. In general, [he treats] of things to be done, in detail of things to be believed. For many disagree with him con-

cerning the objects of belief, but few or no people [disagree with him] concerning the objects of action. For example: the Master says that there is one God in the Trinity and that the same [God] is three persons, that the properties of the persons are several, and that they are the persons. Others contradict [that]. Therefore, in this book the Master treats of matters pertaining to the faith, introducing a large number of authorities that have been stated at length and diffusely by others, but which he summarizes in a short compendium.

2. Now the Master composed this book for three kinds of people, namely, for the faint-hearted (or those fleeing), for the lazy ones, and for the blasphemers. All of those are sufficiently prefigured in the Old Testament [see Ex. 19; 24; 32]. In fact, according to the commandment of the Lord limits had been established by Moses round Mount Sinai, which it was not lawful for the people to cross, lest they see the Lord and perish. When the Lord called and Moses ascended the mountain, Ur, Aaron, and Joshua followed him right to the limits, as well as the seventy who were to receive of his spirit. However, as Moses was staying with the Lord on the mountain, Ur, Aaron, and the seventy went back, fatigued by the tedium of the divine waiting. Only Joshua remained by the limits, anxious for the return of his master. The following could have occurred, [although] it is not reported that many of the people perished after crossing the limits.

3. The mountain that Moses ascended is mystically understood as Sacred Scripture, which exists in the immovable stability of both Testaments. It is protected so that it is not lawful to contradict it. The limits set around the mountain are mystically understood as the explanations of the saints, whose footsteps we are obliged to follow, lest we cross the limits that our Fathers have set. By Moses, who ascended the mountain when God called, those are mystically understood who in the early Church ascended through great divine inspiration to the eminence of the Sacred Page—such as Paul and the other apostles, who as the Holy Spirit dictated [to them] penetrated the profound and obscure [dimensions] of Sacred

Figure 5: The Pseudo-Poitiers gloss in MS. Naples, Biblioteca nazionale, VII C 14, fol. 3r

Scripture. Besides them, however, there are those who ascend right to the limits, yet neither cross them nor turn back out of lack of confidence—such as the eager doctors who apply themselves tenaciously to the thorough examination of Sacred Scripture. They are signified by Joshua. [Then] there are those who come right to the limits, but turn back tired—namely those who, considering the large number of books of the Sacred Page, lose confidence in themselves and therefore return to the other faculties, like dogs to vomit [see Prov. 26:11 and 2 Pet. 2:22]. Those are called faint-hearted or given to flight; they are indicated figuratively by Ur, Aaron, and the seventy. There are others who do not even reach the limits; who, *entangled with secular businesses* [2 Tim. 2:4], do not study or ask anything about Sacred Scripture. They are the lazy ones, signified by those who did not even venture to leave the camp. [Again,] there are others who cross the limits and perish, like the heretics who esteem the explanations of the saints less than their own inventions. They are the blasphemers, signified by those who perhaps perished after crossing the limits.

4. It is for these three kinds of people that the Master composed this book: for the faint-hearted or those given to flight, in order to call them back by means of the brevity of the work; for the lazy ones, to spur them on through the easiness of the work; [and] for the blasphemers, to refute them by the authorities of the saints.

5. Setting out, then, to discuss the Sacred Page compendiously, the Master considered that Sacred Scripture treats principally of two things, namely, of the Creator and the work of the Creator. The work of the Creator, however, is divided into the work of creation, the work of recreation, and the work of final retribution. Again, the work of retribution is subdivided into the work of recreation that Christ performs in [his] own person (the Incarnation, the Passion, etc. are of this kind) and the work of the Church, which recreates through the sacraments.

6. Appropriately, then, the Master divided his work into four books, so that it might have some agreement with the teaching of

the Gospels. Thus, in the first book he treated of the Creator; in the second, of the work of the Creator; in the third, of the work of recreation that Christ performed in [his] own person; in the fourth, of the work of recreation that the Church accomplishes, that is, of the ecclesiastical sacraments. Finally, he ends his work with the work of final retribution. For, in the first [book] he treats of the sacrament of the Trinity, of the persons and their properties. In doing so, he introduces authorities that appear contrary to each other, removing all contrariety from them by means of a suitable explanation. In the second [book, he treats] of the creation of the angel, the human being, and the other things, and in the end of the same [book], of the Fall of both of them. In the third [he treats] of the reparation of the human being (and not of the angel). In the fourth [he treats] of the sacraments of the Old and New Law and of their difference, and at the very end of the orders and the resurrection and of Christ, who will come to judge. This, then, is the subject matter of the Master, which pertains to theology in general, namely, the Creator and the work of the Creator or, if you prefer to say so, things and signs.

7. The intention is threefold. For he intends to call back those who are faint of heart, spur on those who are lazy, and refute the blasphemers. But he refutes the heretics in the following manner: first, he shows what is to be held regarding the faith; after that, [he shows] what needs to be spoken against in this regard; then [he shows] what it is better to hesitate about than have the temerity to define.

8. One could, however, object to the Master this [word] of Solomon: *Of making many books there is no end* [Eccles. 12:12]. Therefore, lest among such a large number of books this one appear superfluous, the Master precedes his work with a preface, in which he defends himself satisfactorily against the charge of arrogance, and his book against that of being superfluous. Moreover, in that [preface] he lays out three causes that discourage him from embarking upon such a large work, as well as three others that encourage him—causes through which, as though through stronger nails, the other three are driven out.[46] The first discouraging cause is the tenuousness of

knowledge; the first encouraging one the commendation of the widow [see Mark 12:41–44]. The second discouraging [cause is] the difficulty of the hard work; the second encouraging one the promise of the Samaritan [see Luke 10:33–35]. The third discouraging [cause is] the disparagement of those who are envious; the third encouraging one the profit and repeated request of his associates. See! the three encouraging causes cancel out the three discouraging ones. For although the tenuousness of knowledge discourages the Master from writing, nonetheless the commendation of the widow spurs him on even more and encourages him to write. For if the widow is to be commended because she cast into the treasure according to the measure of her ability, he will be commended wonderfully by the Lord since he casts into the treasure of Sacred Scripture according to the measure of his ability. The difficulty of the hard [task] also discourages the Master: if indeed it is hard to compile so much material into a unity, the difficulty lies not so much in the compilation as it does in the orderly arrangement—something that appears easy to someone who has not tried but difficult to someone attempting to do it. However, although the difficulty of the hard work frightens the Master, the promise of the Samaritan spurs him on even more since he said, *whatever thou shalt spend over and above, I will repay thee* [Luke 10:35]—which is why the Master paid him over and above. The disparagement of the envious, too, discourages the Master: for truly, over this work very many people have envied him and [continue to] envy him to this day. The profit and repeated request of his associates, however, cancel out this cause: for, repeatedly begged by his associates, the Master undertook the work. Intimating, therefore, the first encouraging cause he begins thus, saying:

9. *Wishing* etc. As is the wont of writers, the Master starts with a proem. And this is the content of the proem: first, he lays out the encouraging and discouraging causes....[47]

The text is a prime example of what the literary theorist Julia Kristeva has called "intertextuality." It is constructed as a "mosaic of quotations," all of which, in the author's—or, rather, authors'—imagination, evoke,

refer to, and clarify each other.[48] First of all, Peter Lombard's own prologue to the *Sentences* is cited and alluded to continually; often specific terms from it are woven into the Pseudo-Poitiers text. Thus, "assertion of the faith" (*fidei assertione*) in the first paragraph calls to mind "assertion of the truth" (*veri assertionem*) in paragraph three of the Lombard's prologue; the phrase "the lazy ones" (*pigros*) in paragraph two takes up the "lazy" person (*pigro*) from the fifth paragraph of the prologue to the *Sentences*; in the third paragraph, the expression chosen to describe the mountain as protected by the limits around it, *a deo munita est*, recalls Peter Lombard's term for the fortification of the faith, *fidem munire*, in paragraph two; and so forth throughout the text. And as the Pseudo-Poitiers prologue adopts and adapts terms and themes from Peter Lombard's preface, it imports with them the complex mixture of references to Scripture and the Fathers of which the latter is itself composed.

Even with these literary debts recognized, however, it would be a mistake to regard the Pseudo-Poitiers prologue as an "original" composition. With the exception of the first paragraph, it is closely modeled upon a *Sentences* prologue by Peter Comestor, who was one of Peter Lombard's most influential students, and indeed the author of another standard textbook of scholastic theology, the *Historia scholastica*. The Pseudo-Poitiers proem paraphrases and expands upon Peter Comestor's text rather than citing it literally, but the dependence is clear.[49]

Turning to the first paragraph, we note the division of *divina pagina*, of the Divine Page, into what we would term dogmatic and moral theology. This explicit definition of two distinct theological spheres was new in the twelfth century; one commentator believes that the Pseudo-Poitiers gloss is the first text in which it is found.[50] The division speaks to the fact that, in the urban schools of the twelfth century, theology has come to be dissociated from the monastic setting, but also from more immediate pastoral concerns. It is now reconstituting itself as a "theoretical" discipline in which the objects of belief are investigated, certainly not without personal commitment, but nonetheless with a certain professional detachment. At the end of the paragraph, there occurs the first of three brief reflections on Peter Lombard's method: the Master has created, we are told, a brief compendium of "things to be believed" (*credenda*), which is based upon authorities. These authorities, as the prologue further explains in paragraph six, often appear contrary

to each other, so that the task of the scholastic theologian becomes that of "removing all contrariety ... by means of a suitable explanation." In paragraph eight, another aspect is added to this lucid characterization of scholastic method: it may be hard, our author remarks, to gather so many authorities together into a unity but, in truth, "the difficulty lies not so much in the compilation as in the orderly arrangement" (*in ordinatione*). This, then, is dogmatic theology in the latter half of the twelfth century: a theoretical statement of the objects of faith, logically structured, which is based upon recognized authorities whose "sentences" are brought into harmony through suitable strategies of interpretation.

Paragraph two takes us to the heart of the Pseudo-Poitiers proem: its allegorical interpretation of the Exodus account of Moses' ascent on Mount Sinai.[51] What we can observe here is that, despite all his theoretical aims, our author's imagination is still deeply steeped in scriptural narrative. For him, the most appropriate manner to classify possible attitudes toward the study of the Sacred Page is by reflecting upon the way in which different people acted at a crucial moment in salvation history. Indeed, I think it would be mistaken to imagine our author as fusing, for the sake of literary effect, a taxonomy already existing in his mind with a biblical narrative. Rather, Scripture serves as the conceptual framework that furnishes him with the fundamental categories to structure reality.

The brief summary of the scriptural narrative in paragraph two is followed, in paragraph three, by the interpretation itself. This is worth dwelling upon, as it will allow us to come to a more profound understanding of the "onion" of the Christian tradition from our Introduction. According to the allegory, the theological tradition grows around a center of meaning—Scripture itself—which is out of bounds for the ordinary interpreter: for the interpreter, that is, who is not either a mystic, summoned by God, or divinely inspired. The bounds originate in a divine commandment that was first implemented by Moses, the father of the Israelites, whose action was repeated in a different way by our own Fathers, that is to say, the first interpreters of Scripture who could not rely upon divine inspiration. All interpretation, all theology, then, originates in a dark and obscure center, access to which is mediated by a hierarchy of messengers: the Holy Spirit, Moses, Paul and the apostles, the Church Fathers. Theology requires turning around this center, as it were, and to do so at a respectful distance. Even with the mediation of

the various layers of messengers, however, the center frequently remains dark for ordinary mortals—which is why, in paragraph seven, our author emphasizes the wisdom of hesitating in teaching certain aspects of the faith. Those who fail to respect the distance of Scripture die, having rashly and overzealously transgressed the bounds. Yet if there is mortal danger in keeping insufficient distance, the attitude of those who are too "busy" for theology deserves censure as well. So does the behavior of students who, overwhelmed by the difficulties of the Sacred Page, return to lesser objects of study—such at those taught at other faculties,[52] which our authors likens, not very flatteringly it must be said, to vomit. The metaphor takes up an image from Proverbs 26:11 ("As a dog that returneth to his vomit, so is the fool that repeateth his folly") and illustrates the fact that the study of theology requires prior acquaintance with the liberal arts—subjects such as grammar and rhetoric. Those returning from theology to the arts are therefore seen as regurgitating intellectual food that had already been digested.

Modifying our previous "onion," we could summarize the classification that emerges from the Pseudo-Poitiers prologue in Figure 6.

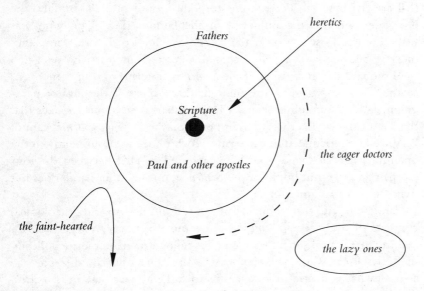

Figure 6: Classification of attitudes toward the Sacred Page from the
Pseudo-Poitiers gloss

Next, in paragraph four, the prologue addresses the question of the audience for whom Peter Lombard composed the *Book of Sentences*. Interestingly enough, the eager doctors of Sacred Scripture are not mentioned at all. Rather, it is those in need of correction—the faint-heated, the lazy people, and the heretics or blasphemers—for whom the Lombard wrote, according to our text. From a slightly different angle, paragraph seven repeats the same point. For the early school of Peter Lombard, therefore, the task of the theologian was not to comment upon or to create textbooks; rather, the study of Sacred Scripture and the Church Fathers remained at the center of attention, at least ideally. A textbook, even one as revered as that of the Master, was regarded as merely a remedial tool. We shall have to see whether this attitude was to change over the history of the *Book of Sentences*.

Paragraphs five and six do not require much commentary, since we are already familiar with the way in which they explain the structure of the *Book of Sentences*: the schema is the same as the one presented in *Filia Magistri* (see Figure 4 above). Like the allegorical interpretation of the Exodus passage, it is derived from remarks upon the *Sentences* that are attributed to Peter Comestor. Thus, both *Filia Magistri* and the prologue evidence the influence of the famous theologian who was Peter Lombard's successor at the cathedral school of Notre Dame and, in 1168, became its chancellor. It is also Peter Comestor who relegated the Lombard's own division of the *Sentences* in terms of things and signs to the kind of awkward afterthought that occurs at the end of paragraph six. Our prologue seems a little embarrassed about the fact that the Victorine schema that it has imposed on the *Book of Sentences* cannot very well be articulated in the terms which figure so prominently in the opening pages of that work. The suggested parallel between the four Gospels and the four books of the *Sentences*, on the other hand, does not stem from Peter Comestor.

Paragraph eight introduces an objection, not to the theological contents of the *Book of Sentences* but rather to its very existence: "Of making many books there is no end," as Solomon writes melancholically in Ecclesiastes. While the response to this objection could strike one as somewhat pedantic in its excessive detail, the fact that an objection should appear toward the end of the prologue is significant. It foreshadows the future development of the *Sentences* literature, in which simple

glossing was quickly to be complemented by a question-and-answer format.

Leaving behind the prologue, let us finally ask how faithful a follower of the Lombard the author of the Pseudo-Poitiers gloss really is. The Master's controversial identification of charity with the Holy Spirit in Book I is useful as a test case. Our author explains it in considerable detail; yet he makes no secret of his reservations. On Peter Lombard's interpretation of the assertion from the First Letter of St. John, "for God is charity," he writes: "This was not said of the love with which we love our neighbor." The Lombard's apparent statement to the contrary he finds *dissonans*, dissonant and confused. His commentary is hesitant.[53] Thus, we must conclude that even Peter Lombard's earliest followers were uneasy with a teaching that was quite dear to the Master himself.

Conclusion

During the first decades of its reception, the *Book of Sentences* was abridged and elaborated upon—both, it seems, for didactic reasons. The abridgments emphasize brevity and ease of memorization, whereas the glosses go beyond Peter Lombard's own theology, in more or less modest ways. Sometimes, they seek to explain a difficult passage; in other places, a glossator might note a parallel passage from another author, correct a quotation, or indeed cast doubt upon an aspect of the Master's teaching. Therefore, the glosses appear to shape the reception of the *Sentences* more actively than the abbreviations; yet it would be a mistake to regard the latter merely as small-scale reproductions of the *Book of Sentences*, containing the Lombard's thought in a nutshell. Small gestures such as an omission can produce significant effects. Thus, when *Filia Magistri* chooses to remain silent on the topic of charity as the Holy Spirit, it effectively prevents discussion of a controversial topic.

How were the abbreviations and glosses used in pedagogical practice? Unfortunately, this is a question to which the only answers are speculative. It is natural, however, to imagine them as complementary in a system of education in which mastery of the basics of the Sacred Page laid the foundations for more critical and detailed discussion of theological problems, and in which the *Book of Sentences* gradually established itself as the most valuable starting point for such discussion.

The analysis of the prologue to the Pseudo-Poitiers gloss enables us to understand how masters of the Sacred Page conceived of the theological project in the latter half of the twelfth century. Interestingly, at that point the *Book of Sentences* itself was considered an ancillary tool of instruction. The theologian's task was certainly not to study the *Sentences*, but Scripture itself—or rather, Scripture within the bounds of meaning established by the Fathers. In this manner, tradition served as the necessary mediation between the individual interpreter and the ultimate mystery at the heart of the word of God.

Chapter Two: The Thirteenth Century
Age of the Commentary

IN THE figure of Socrates in Plato's *Symposium*, we find a rare fusion of the ideals of the philosopher and the teacher. In a dialectic of mutual attraction, the teacher and student are together drawn toward the Form of Beauty and Goodness, which ultimately remains mysterious, located as it is "beyond being and knowledge." It can be talked about only in mythical terms. Thus, as they ascend to Beauty, the educator and the educated are confronted with their finitude. A student like Alcibiades, who craves to take possession of wisdom (by sexually possessing the teacher), is gently rebuked.[1]

More often than not, however, wisdom and pedagogy are not so beautifully reconciled. The previous chapter already hinted at some of the ways in which the *Book of Sentences* came to be short-changed as it underwent the first stages of didactic adaptation. Peter Lombard may have wanted to teach a spiritually most edifying conception of charity, but an influential abbreviation didn't let him. He may have wanted to declare himself incapable of formulating a convincing metaphysical account of Christ as God-man; Master Bandinus transformed him into an adherent of the *habitus* theory. From the point of view of a certain pedagogy—one oriented to the efficient communication of knowledge—*Filia*

Magistri and Bandinus pursued a completely rational strategy. Yet from the vantage-point of a contemplative approach to the mysteries of the divine, their changes were less fortunate.

Throughout the later Middle Ages, pedagogical pressures increased in the schools of Western Europe. The historian of ideas Walter Ong described the situation in the following terms:

> In the university context ... the role of the teacher thus had two aspects. His role was, first of all, still personal. He maintained knowledge in the personalist context in which it had been born in antiquity and from which, of course, it can never be entirely removed. But in the university, the teacher was also part of a corporation which was uncalculatingly but relentlessly reducing the personalist, dialoguing element in knowledge to a minimum in favor of an element which made knowledge something a corporation could traffic in, a-personal and abstract.[2]

Ong wrote these words on scholasticism retrospectively as it were, from the perspective of developments that came to full fruition only in the sixteenth century, especially in the work of the logician Peter Ramus. The emergence, in the thirteenth century, of the university as a formally recognized body of masters, organized after the model of the trade corporations and increasingly regulated by statutes, did not all at once transform deeply lived Christian spirituality into an object of abstract knowledge that was taught for money in the schools. However, the tendencies toward greater efficiency and rationalization are undeniable.

Stephen Langton (ca. 1150/55–1228) occupies a prominent place in the adaptation of Christian texts to scholastic use. Until the twelfth century, there existed no uniform system to divide the books of the Bible into chapters. Rather, a very large number of different systems of division had developed over the centuries.[3] Some books, especially most of the Prophets, were not cut into chapters at all. This confusion made it impossible to provide generally accepted references, a practice that became increasingly important with the growth of professional theology. Moreover, the traditional divisions were often of unequal length, rather than presenting the text in teachable "lessons," and did not mark off units of thought and meaning. Rather, they treated the biblical text like a play,

breaking it up into scenes according to the arrival or departure of a particular character or a change of location.[4] Stephen Langton was the Parisian master who devised the more academic chapter divisions of the Bible that have survived to the present day. Langton's new divisions were incorporated into the Paris Bible, which reached its standard form around 1230, including all the canonical books of Scripture handily in one volume.

Langton's Commentary on the *Sentences*

Stephen Langton, the famous archbishop of Canterbury who was to be closely associated with the creation of the Magna Carta, taught theology in Paris between around 1180 and 1206.[5] As a master lecturing on the *Book of Sentences*, he placed notes in the margins of his copy of Peter Lombard's work. These marginal notes were then—when and by whom, we do not know—extracted from the *Sentences* and transformed into keyword glosses. The whole has, sad to say, come down to us only fragmentarily in a single manuscript.[6] The fact that Langton's text provides scriptural references according to the new chapter divisions places its completion in the first years of the thirteenth century.[7]

Although Stephen Langton's work on the *Sentences* was born from ordinary marginal glosses, it contains elements that have earned it the reputation as the first commentary on Peter Lombard. In other words, it marks the beginning of a new genre within the literature on the *Sentences*.[8] The author's principal goal is no longer the literal exegesis of Peter Lombard's text. The keywords of the commentary generally serve as markers that indicate the beginning and end of entire sections, only certain points from which are taken up and examined. A general grasp of the subject matter is presupposed. Moreover, the vast majority of Langton's text does not consist in straightforward explanations—"the phrase x means such-and-such"—but rather in discussions of theological difficulties. These discussions do not all follow one rigid form, but usually consist of several arguments in favor of and against a certain position, with a solution by Stephen Langton. The beginning of the commentary provides a good example:

> "Of the old" ... "not in justifying." *Note*: All sacrifices in accordance with the Law signify the Passion of Christ. *But* from this

it appears that the works of the Law did not justify. *Solution*: The accomplished work (*opus operatum*), that is, the effect undergone by the thing accomplished, does not justify; neither does the thing that was done; rather, what justified was the work being accomplished (*opus operans*), that is, the action along with faith. But some actions founded upon the Law (*legalia*)—such as circumcision—take away sin but do not confer any grace. On the other hand, the sacraments of the Gospel—such as baptism—both take away the offense and confer grace. *Against that*: Virtue naturally precedes the remission of sins. For virtue is the cause of the remission of sins in the human being and circumcision takes away the offense, the cancellation of which is the effect of virtue. Hence it confers virtue, which precedes the remission of sin. *This does not follow. Comparison*: Condemnation brings about the suffering of hell. But badness is the cause of suffering; and yet condemnation does not bring about badness, nor is it its cause. For it is not because God condemns someone that this person is bad.[9]

The extract elaborates upon a question that arises in the *Book of Sentences* itself: namely, what is the difference between signs of grace in the Old Testament and in the New? Quoting Augustine, Peter Lombard stated that the former only signify grace, whereas the latter both signify grace and justify, that is to say, release the sinner from his guilt. In the given context—the opening chapter of the *Sentences*, a chapter that does not attempt to work out a sacramental theology—this remark appeared sufficient. Langton, however, is not satisfied with this degree of precision, wanting to dig deeper, so to speak. After all, since the composition of the *Book of Sentences* some fifty years have elapsed; theological reflection has become more sophisticated and demanding. The fact that the beginning of the *Sentences* is not the place to discuss issues of sacramental theology does not deter Langton. He formulates the following objection: From the text of the *Sentences* as it stands, it would appear that the religious practices of the Old Law did nothing to improve the state of the sinner before God; that they were in fact pointless and superfluous. In response, Langton offers a distinction that postdates Peter Lombard's theology, namely, that between the accomplished work (*opus operatum*) and the work being accomplished (*opus operans*). Justification requires not simply

the performance of certain rites, but faith in doing so. Moreover—and here Langton hearkens back to a distinction that is not foreign to Peter Lombard's own theology[10]—while certain rites from the Old Testament cancel sin, they do not confer any additional grace.

Our little dialogue continues, however, seeking more advanced discussion of the issue. It is agreed that virtue is a necessary condition for the forgiveness of sins. However, we just found out that circumcision does, in fact, forgive sins (if it is performed with the right disposition). But then, circumcision must bring about virtue, which is a grace.

Langton's response to the objection is significant. In fact, it draws attention to a logical fallacy in the argument just presented. Two things, he points out, which have the same effect should not be construed as causing each other. Thus, it is fallacious to claim that, because circumcision leads to the forgiveness of sins and virtue precedes the latter, circumcision also causes virtue. If this were correct, then one could equally argue that, since God's judgment of the sinner leads to suffering and suffering is caused by moral badness, God is also responsible for moral badness:

condemnation → suffering   circumcision → forgiveness of sins
moral badness → suffering   virtue → forgiveness of sins
?condemnation → moral badness   ? circumcision → virtue

This emphasis upon logical soundness in the context of dogmatic theology reflects the mounting influence that the approach typical of the arts faculty exercised upon theology. In the universities that were now constituting themselves formally, all courses of study in law, medicine, and theology required a prior master's degree in arts. That is to say, the arts faculty, with its emphasis upon grammar, logic, and rhetoric, trained the young students' minds before they went on to further study. It is useful to remind ourselves, therefore, that medieval scholasticism was "more arts than theology," to use the words of Walter Ong: "Arts scholasticism was important not only because it framed the mentality of those who governed the university and because it seeped through the whole university, but also because the great majority of arts students and teachers pursued it" in their subsequent careers.[11]

The mentality of the arts is captured very well in a text with which we are already familiar: the Pseudo-Poitiers gloss. On Augustine's classic

definition, "all teaching is about either things or signs," the gloss remarks: "There is some difference between the signs (*signa*) of theology and the signifiers (*significantia*) of the liberal arts; for in the latter utterances are called 'signifiers,' in the former things [are called] 'signs.' In fact, in the sacred page any thing is called 'sign' by which something is signified in it, but any thing whatsoever can have as many significations as it has internal or external properties, or harmonies (*convenientias*) with another thing."[12] The author of the Pseudo-Poitiers gloss has indeed put his finger on the difference between the *signum* of the theologian and the *significans* of the logician: a sign is an element of a world that can still be "read," because it is full of meaning. Everything points beyond itself, to other things, to the harmony of the whole, and ultimately to God.[13] A signifier, by contrast, is a sign that has been bent back onto itself, as it were; it no longer transcends itself but points only, self-referentially, to its own materiality. That is why "signifier" is synonymous with "utterance" (*vox*): it is a manifestation of speech to be analyzed according to the intrinsic laws of speaking—that is to say, grammar and logic.[14]

It is not difficult to see why theology must enter into a profound crisis when signs are systematically transformed into signifiers within its own domain. On the other hand—as Augustine already realized when he composed a work such as *De magistro* (*On the Teacher*)—occasionally grammar and logic can be quite useful to the theologian. Here is an example that will lead us back to our consideration of Stephen Langton's *Sentences* commentary.

Toward the end of Book I of the *Sentences*, Peter Lombard discussed the old theological problem of how God's omnipotent will is compatible with the existence of the evil deeds of human beings. One argument of the devil's advocate runs like this:

> Everything that is true ultimately comes from the Truth that is God.
> It is true that people do evil.
> Therefore, that people do evil ultimately comes from God.[15]

The Lombard was disgusted by this argument, which he found sophistic, offensive to God, and unworthy of a response. In the *Book of Sentences*, it is not rare to encounter theological issues that Peter Lombard takes up

with avowed reluctance, for the sake of his students, while considering them beneath the dignity of serious theological inquiry. For him, the sacred page is not a language game.

Stephen Langton's attitude differs subtly but significantly from that of the Master. In his commentary on the passage just summarized, he amiably reproaches the author of the *Sentences* for setting too little store by the objection: there is real difficulty in resolving it! "If God wills that this ['people do evil'] is true, he wills the connection of this predicate with the subject."[16] What is the solution, then? It consists in a precise logical distinction that was not available to Peter Lombard.[17] In the syllogism above, which concludes that God wills people to do evil, a confusion occurs between object language and meta-language, between language "about the thing" (*de re*) and language "about the utterance" (*de enuntiabili*). If all truth comes from God, then we may legitimately conclude that God wills the truth of the *statement*, "People do evil." It does not follow, on the other hand, that God wills the *fact* that people do evil.[18]

The distance that separates Stephen Langton's commentary on the *Sentences* from a simple gloss finds further confirmation in the frequent doctrinal disagreements between the Master and his commentator.[19] On the identification of charity with the Holy Spirit, for instance, Langton offers a meager one-sentence summary of the Lombard's position, only to conclude, "We are not of this opinion, since charity is a virtue just like faith, [a virtue] by which we love."[20] On numerous occasions, Langton also refers to his own works, using words such as "The solution is outside [this text]," "on this [issue], more outside," "what it is capricious to insert into these readings may be looked for outside," and so forth.[21] The references "outside" (*extra*) appear to indicate that the *Sentences* commentary is conceived as forming part of a larger system of thought, namely, the author's own.

Stephen Langton's prologue to the fourth book—no prologues to the other books have survived—furnishes the reader with an overview of the structure of the *Sentences* which consistently applies the things–signs distinction to the contents of the four books: the first book is devoted to things to be enjoyed (God and the Trinity), the second to things to be enjoyed and used (the human being and the angels), and so on.[22] This fact certainly shows that fifty years of reading and glossing the *Book of Sentences* have enabled the tradition to come to an accurate understand-

ing of Peter Lombard's approach, and to distinguish it from Victorine conceptions of the theological project. This improved understanding of the Lombard's thought underscores the significance of Langton's deliberate deviations from it. Let us now see how the new genre of the *Sentences* commentary developed in the decades after Langton.

Alexander of Hales

From the surviving *Sentences* literature of the twelfth century, it is clear that the *Book of Sentences* quickly came to play an important role in the teaching of theology at Paris and other rising centers of study. But what role exactly? The Pseudo-Poitiers gloss seems to suggest that the *Sentences* were initially regarded as nothing more than a study aid for those not quite able to engage in theology proper. If this was indeed the case, then the status of the work was to see a dramatic upturn early in the thirteenth century. Alexander of Hales (ca. 1185–1245) is credited with this development—or blamed for it.

The Sentences *as University Textbook*

Alexander was the first Parisian master of theology to base his "ordinary" lectures upon the *Book of Sentences*, rather than upon Scripture. To understand the nature of these lectures, it is useful to remind ourselves that a lecture is literally a "reading" (*lectio*). The medieval system of higher education distinguished between reading a text—in class, together with a teacher—"ordinarily" (*ordinarie*) and "cursorily" (*cursorie*). The ordinary lectures occurred in the mornings and were delivered by the masters. They involved the close in-depth study of an authoritative text. The cursory lectures, by contrast, were scheduled later in the day and given by graduate students (the so-called "bachelors"). They were of an introductory nature, providing a more rapid overview of the same material.[23] Until Alexander of Hales, it was not customary for a master of theology to lecture ordinarily upon any text other than Scripture; but Alexander changed that, deciding to devote his morning lectures to the *Book of Sentences*. Alexander of Hales taught as master of theology in Paris from 1220/21 until his death in 1245, with an interruption between 1229 and 1232. Over this period of twenty-five years, he shaped the subject in

a lasting and decisive manner.[24] He—not Albert the Great, Bonaventure, Thomas Aquinas, or some other theologian—was for a long time regarded as the most acclaimed master of the thirteenth century.

Alexander's move from Scripture to the *Sentences* as his basic textbook reflected and contributed to a number of concurrent tendencies: the transformation of *sacra pagina* into theology as a system of doctrine; the distinction between moral and dogmatic theology; the increasing emphasis upon pedagogic needs. The consecration of the *Sentences* as the standard textbook of theology would probably not have been possible, however, without an unusual step that the Fourth Lateran Council took in 1215—in defining orthodox Trinitarian doctrine, it mentioned Peter Lombard by name: "We however, with the approbation of the sacred Council, believe and confess with Peter Lombard that there is one highest entity, incomprehensible and ineffable, who is truly Father, and Son, and Holy Spirit...."[25] The Fourth Lateran Council was among the most significant for the definition of doctrine in the history of the medieval Church; for example, it was at this council that the theory of transubstantiation was officially adopted to describe the conversion of bread and wine into Christ's body and blood in the Eucharist. Fifty years earlier, in the 1170s, Peter Lombard's status as the embodiment of orthodoxy had still been less assured, to say the least, when Pope Alexander III twice condemned an aspect of the Lombard's Christology known as "Christological nihilianism": the strange theory according to which Christ, as human, is "not something."[26]

Alexander of Hales's decision to adopt the *Sentences* as the textbook for his ordinary lectures was not uncontroversial; neither was it completely successful. When a similar move was made at the University of Oxford in the 1240s, Robert Grosseteste, who as bishop of Lincoln had jurisdiction over the university, protested vigorously in a letter to the faculty.[27] After the masters appealed to the curia, however, Rome sided with them. The controversy seems to have resolved itself through the following arrangement, which existed in similar ways both at Oxford and at Paris. The *Book of Sentences* did indeed become the standard textbook of the theology faculty. University regulations stipulated that lecturing upon the *Sentences* was an integral part of the work of the bachelor; no one could acquire the licentiate (the permission to teach as a member of the body of masters) without having taught Peter Lombard. Moreover, the

regulations were quite precise about the modalities of these courses: their beginning, their duration, and the need to focus upon theological issues without lengthy philosophical and logical digressions were just some of the issues taken up by the statutes that embodied the regulations. Special care was taken in ensuring a certain solemnity in the way in which each course on the *Sentences* opened; indeed, the beginning of each of the four books was accorded special treatment. On these occasions, the bachelor was expected to deliver a formal inaugural address. Since these *principia* were to be attended by the entire body of undergraduate students and bachelors, they had to be arranged successively on different days for the various colleges of the university: we know, for example, that at Paris the Carmelites were to come first and the Dominicans last. No lectures started in the faculty of theology before the entire series of *principia* was complete. Considerable importance, therefore, and indeed pomp were attached to the task of lecturing upon the *Sentences*; yet these lectures were defined as the bachelors' duty, not the masters'. Their main responsibility remained the ordinary courses on Scripture.[28]

The Sentences *Restructured: The Distinctions*

Apart from helping to anchor study of the *Sentences* firmly within the theology curriculum, Alexander of Hales was responsible for another innovation, this time in the structure of the *Book of Sentences* itself. Peter Lombard, as we already know, divided his magnum opus into four books, and each book further into chapters. One rationale for the chapter divisions was ease of reference, because they made it possible for the reader to scan the work for specific topics without perusing the text as a whole. The table of contents further increased the usefulness of the chapters and chapter headings. Yet the Lombard's chapter divisions were not merely a technical device, like numbered pages and lines in a modern book; they also marked off units of meaning. The latter, however, they did rather imperfectly.

Peter Lombard's treatment of the invisible mission of the Holy Spirit, for instance, occupies chapters 60 through 65 of Book I. It is in these chapters that the Master formulates his doctrine of the Holy Spirit as charity. Thus, these chapters possess a definite thematic unity: they treat one clearly circumscribed theological question. In addition, chapters 60

through 65 also form a literary whole. At the beginning of chapter 60, he remarks, "Let us now come to specify the mission of the Holy Spirit by which It is sent invisibly into the hearts of the faithful." A few lines later, he states his main thesis: "this same Holy Spirit is the love or charity with which we love God and neighbor." After a critical examination and defense of the thesis in chapters 60 to 65, the discussion closes with words that are manifestly intended to wrap up the topic: "Charity, then, truly is the Holy Spirit. Whence Augustine says ... that there is nothing better than charity. Charity therefore is the Holy Spirit, who is God and the gift of God or given [by Him]." The next chapter, number 66, indicates the transition to a fresh topic by starting with the words, "Here is it asked...."[29]

Alexander of Hales had the genius to bundle such thematic units as we find them in chapters 60 to 65 of Book I systematically into what he called *distinctiones*, "distinctions."[30] By thus inserting another level of division between the levels of the books and the chapters, he managed to render the overall composition of the *Book of Sentences* considerably more perspicuous. After Alexander's innovation, a particular point made

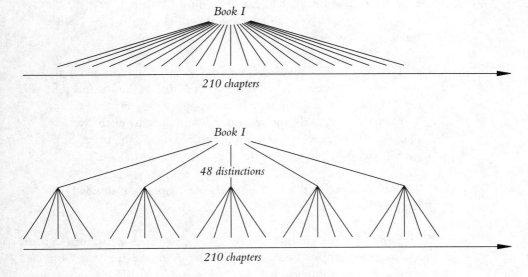

Figure 7: The structure of the *Book of Sentences* before and after the introduction of distinctions

within the pages of the work could be situated on at least three levels. A theological insight now no longer occurs as part of a narrative that is, to a large extent, horizontally structured: "having treated x we now turn to y and after that z will be addressed...." Rather, it is assigned a place within a methodically organized edifice that emphasizes the vertical, "logical" dimension (see Figure 7).

Divisiones textus *and Prologues*

Alexander of Hales most fully exploits his newly refined articulation of the *Sentences* in the beginning of Book III of his commentary. Here we find nine pages that are devoted to a detailed and exhaustive derivation of the contents of the book:

> 1. In the third book, there is discussion of the Redeemer, of the gifts through which the reparation is effected, and of the precepts in the fulfillment of which merit is had according to the state of first perfection. The first part, which is on the Redeemer, extends right to distinction 23, which begins thus: "But since above"; the second extends right to distinction 37, which begins thus: "Since there are two precepts of charity."

> 2. The first part is divided into three parts. The first is on the Assumption, the second on the union, the third on the Passion. The first of these extends right to distinction 5, namely: "Moreover, it is necessary to ask"; the second extends right to distinction 15, namely: "This, however, is not to be passed over"; the third, however, [extends] right to distinction 23.

> 3. Now the first part, which is on the Assumption, is divided into five. In the first, ...[31]

This *divisio textus* or "division of text," as it is called, does not require much commentary. Its ethos is already far removed from that of the twelfth-century prologues, which employed highly allusive and poetic language. In the *divisio textus*, the theological project is no longer defined by means of a scriptural allegory but, instead, through its internal me-

thodical coherence. Theology is clearly on the way to becoming science. Its dry language is purged of "signs" in the old Augustinian sense.[32]

If we stopped here, however, having examined only the first pages of Alexander's commentary on Book III, our characterization of his work would remain incomplete and, indeed, misleading. The general prologue at the beginning of Book I exhibits an entirely different style. It is, in fact, precisely the flowery style, larded with biblical allusions, with which we are familiar from the Pseudo-Poitiers gloss and, to a much lesser extent, even from *Filia Magistri*. It would appear, then, that the prologues to the *Sentences* literature developed distinctive conventions. The particular form these took in Alexander's general prologue was to set the standard for the thirteenth century: he "draws," as he puts it himself, all the contents of the four books from one well-chosen biblical passage. This procedure serves to underline the continuity between the Bible and the *Book of Sentences*, as well as stressing the primacy of Scripture: Peter Lombard does not, in fact, state anything that is not implicitly contained in the Word of God.

> 1. The contents of this first book can be drawn from what the Lord says in Exodus 3:14–15:[33] *God said to Moses: I AM WHO AM. I am the God of Abraham, the God of Isaac, and the God of Jacob, and this is my name for ever.* The contents of the following books are taken from what immediately precedes in the same chapter: *And the Lord said: I have seen the affliction of my people that is in Egypt and the rigor of them that are over the works. Hearing their cry and knowing their sorrow, I am come down to deliver them and to bring them into a land that floweth with milk and honey* [Ex. 3:7–8, condensed].

> 2. The Master, however, makes the following distinction, by means of a statement taken from Augustine, in the book *On Christian Teaching*: "All teaching is either about things or about signs." And he does not deny that signs are things. But there are some things that are to be enjoyed only, some that are to be used only, [and] some to be enjoyed and used. The first book is about things that are to be enjoyed, namely, the Trinity and unity. The second book is about things to be used, namely, created things. The third is about both [kinds of things], namely, about Christ, the virtues and

precepts. The fourth is about signs, namely, the sacraments of the Church.

3. Alternatively, [the books] may be distinguished by means of the aforesaid authorities, in the following manner: When he says, *I AM WHO AM*, the Trinity is indicated here, together with the unity of essence. Whence Dionysius [says], in the book *On the Divine Names*, "If they say that there is no praise of the entire Godhead when it is said, *I AM WHO AM*, but rather venture to define [it] according to one part, how do they understand, *Who is, and who was, and who is to come, the Almighty* [Apoc. 1:8]?" And John Damescene [says]: "The principal name among those that are predicated of God substantially is, *WHO AM*, just as he himself said through the revelation of Moses, *I AM WHO AM*." And although [the name] is common to the individual [persons], it can nevertheless be appropriated. *I*, in fact, belongs to the first person, and without qualifier indicates the first person in the Trinity. *Who*, which is an article-noun (*nomen articulare*), indicates the identity of the substance with the first person in the mode of another person, and in this manner indicates the Son. By *am* the Holy Spirit is indicated, who proceeds from both. For, *am* indicates the substance as act, and thus as proceeding from the substance of the preceding persons. In this manner, it is united with both.—Now, in this book there is a twofold discussion of the Trinity: either in itself and absolutely, or insofar as it is related to the rational creature, as for example [in the place] where the manner of the Holy Spirit's mission is discussed, etc., so that [the rational creature] may be perfected. And this is what the Lord signifies by what follows: *the God of Abraham, the God* etc. And since he was not God from eternity but only in eternity, this follows: *and this is my name for ever* (*in aeterno*), not from eternity (*ab aeterno*).

4. [Now] there follows the distinction of the contents of the other [books] by means of the preceding part of the authority. By *Egypt*....[34]

It is worth noting that Alexander acknowledges the thing-sign distinction that Peter Lombard himself regarded as the central structuring principle of the sacred page, but then moves on to offer his own biblical derivation of the contents of the four books.

Whereas Book III opens with a technical, very "scientific" *divisio textus* and Book I is preceded by the biblical prologue that we have just seen, Book II has no introduction at all. Book IV, by contrast, furnishes us with another example of the biblically inspired approach. Could these inconsistencies be due to the extremely poor manuscript tradition of the work? The text has come down to us in numerous manuscripts, but all are replete with omissions and mistakes. Moreover, only two of them contain the entire work (the rest being fragmentary). The editors explained this disappointing state of affairs with the fact that the textual tradition stems from lecture notes rather than from an "official" copy released by the author.[35] On the other hand, when Alexander of Hales prepared his *Sentences* commentary, both the literary conventions of the genre and the academic regulations concerning the manner in which the work was to be taught were still fluid—as we were, in fact, able to gather from Alexander's decision to lecture on the *Sentences* "ordinarily." By the 1240s, such a decision would have constituted a breach of university statutes. It is quite possible, then, that there were no firm expectations yet concerning the form of the prologues when Alexander lectured on the *Sentences*, most likely between 1223 and 1227.[36]

Title and Characteristics of Alexander's Commentary

A word on the title that the modern editors have given to Alexander's commentary is in order here. They decided to publish the work under the title of *Glossa*, following the usage of one of the two complete manuscripts.[37] Its literary form is, however, too far removed from the twelfth-century glosses for this title to appear entirely appropriate. Alexander's treatment of the *Sentences* comprises little in the way of literal exegesis; he evidently expected his students to be familiar with the letter of Peter Lombard's work. There must therefore have been prior instruction on the *Sentences* to prepare them for Master Alexander's ordinary lectures—no doubt by bachelors. Most likely, too, the students

availed themselves of study aids such as abbreviations before (or while) attending the ordinary course. To judge from the lecture notes that have been transmitted to us as Alexander's commentary, the latter took almost exclusively the form of questions. An example:

> **All teaching is about signs or things.** What a sign is, is defined in the beginning of [book] four. Or otherwise: A sign is something that offers itself to the senses, leaving the rest aside for the intellect.—But an objection is made about the body of Christ, which is a sign and a thing; hence, all theological speculation is not about things or signs.—I respond: This conjunction *or* should be taken subdisjunctively. Therefore, the division is made here according to opposed shades of meaning, not according to the things [themselves]. For a sign properly exists in knowledge, a thing according to nature. In the third book, then, there is discussion about the body of Christ insofar as it is a thing, in the fourth insofar as it is a sign.[38]

The structure of this brief extract epitomizes the rhythm of the entire work. Alexander of Hales extracts a key passage from the *Book of Sentences*, perhaps offering a brief explication or drawing a conclusion that appears to follow directly from the Lombard's thesis. Then he articulates an objection or problem that arises from the thesis. The master's resolution follows. Both the objection and the solution may be more or less elaborate; on occasion each part consists of several arguments, usually introduced by the conjunction *item*, "again." Alexander's commentary is sophisticated in terms of grammatical and logical analysis, but it invokes non-theological terminology judiciously, not placing excessive emphasis upon it. The work is, however, extremely detailed, filling four volumes of about 500 pages each in its modern edition.

What does Alexander of Hales have to say about our test case for fidelity to the Master, the identification of charity with the Holy Spirit? It is not surprising that he is not willing to go along with this thesis, central as it may have been to the *Book of Sentences* itself. Several Parisian masters—perhaps a majority—had rejected it before him. Yet he is discreet about this disagreement, avoiding overt criticism. Rather than repudiating Peter Lombard's teaching on the matter, Alexander defus-

es it in the typical scholastic way of introducing multiple distinctions. The principal one is between created and uncreated charity—with this distinction in place, our human love of God and neighbor is recast, almost automatically, as falling into the category of created charity. The Lombard's thesis then becomes untenable in its original form, for the Holy Spirit can no longer be identified with charity as such: that would make it a creature! Therefore, the Spirit comes to be conceived as the uncreated charity that functions as the efficient and exemplary cause of the created charity which is in us.[39] As his use of the concepts of efficient and exemplary cause shows, Alexander freely draws upon the resources of Aristotelian metaphysics that were becoming available in the first decades of the thirteenth century.

From Secular to Franciscan Master

The adoption of the *Sentences* as the textbook of his ordinary lectures; the division of the work into distinctions; the elaborate *divisiones textus*; the comprehensive commentary in the form of questions; the progress in doctrinal precision by comparison with the Master—these factors, especially in their conjunction, make the *Sentences* commentary by Alexander of Hales one of the most formative examples of the genre. However, not only is his work of great significance for the course that the *Sentences* literature was to take in the thirteenth century and beyond; Alexander himself was one of the pivotal figures in the development of scholastic theology. For, in the academic year 1236–37, he decided to become a Franciscan.

Once again, we must turn our attention for a moment to the institutional structures of the emerging universities. The schools of the twelfth century were largely run by secular masters; Peter Lombard is a typical example in this respect. The old monastic orders, based in the countryside, were not able to satisfy the educational needs of the growing urban centers—not only because of their location, but also due to their inward-looking spirituality, which did not encourage intercourse with the world beyond the cloister-walls. The newly founded orders of St. Dominic and St. Francis, on the other hand, made the cities the very focus of their missions. Furthermore, the Dominicans, in particular, had a strong affinity to higher education: they were founded as an order of preachers,

whose primary goal was to disseminate sound theological teaching in the face of heretical challenges to the Church. "Hence it was natural," Hastings Rashdall comments in his classic work *The Universities of Europe in the Middle Ages*, "that Dominic should have looked to the universities as the most suitable recruiting-ground for his order: to secure for his preachers the highest theological training that the age afforded was an essential element of the new monastic ideal."[40] Although the Franciscans were slower in embracing advanced learning, they too began to send their novices for study to the theological schools, establishing study houses at all the major universities. After initial tensions between the old secular masters and their new mendicant colleagues, the association of the friars with the universities was to become one of the hallmarks of European intellectual life over the next two hundred years.

One could say that the early tradition of *Sentences* commentaries by secular masters reached its completion in Alexander of Hales, who then became one of the founders of Franciscan theology. Bonaventure and Thomas Aquinas were two influential thinkers who developed the mendicant tradition of theology further.

Bonaventure and Thomas Aquinas

In preparing the critical edition of the works of Bonaventure (1217–74), the founder of the project, Father Fidelis da Fanna, and his team visited more than 400 European libraries and sifted through approximately 52,000 manuscripts.[41] In one of these, da Fanna discovered a curious text that, more than one hundred years after its discovery, scholars continue to find enigmatic.[42] It has found its place, not inappropriately, at the beginning of Book II of Bonaventure's *Sentences* commentary:

> By the Savior's helping grace, out of which it has been possible to complete the first [book], it is necessary to begin the second one, after equally urgent requests of the Brothers. And just as in the first book I adhered to the authoritative teachings (*sententiis*) of the Master of the *Sentences*, the common opinions of the masters, and—above all—of our father and teacher of good memory, Brother Alexander, so in the following books I shall not depart from their footprints. For I do not strive to invent new opinions,

but to weave the common and approved ones together anew. No one should consider that I wish to produce new writing; for I feel and confess that I am a poor and feeble compiler.[43]

Throughout the text, of which we have just read the first lines, Bonaventure speaks in a personal tone that is seldom heard in scholastic theology. He fervently insists that those who have accused him of departing from the teachings of his predecessors—in particular in regard to Trinitarian theology, the subject matter of Book I—have thoroughly misunderstood his intentions. Again and again, Bonaventure assures his audience, "I departed neither from the position of the Master nor from the way of truth"; "I did not disagree with him on the power to generate"; "if someone understands this correctly, I did not disagree with him [i.e., Alexander of Hales] on either the first or the second point"; "I did not contradict the Master but failed to say there and now add...." Frankly, the Seraphic Doctor (as the medievals came to dub Bonaventure) sounds almost desperate in defending himself against the accusation of having transgressed the bounds that were set by his predecessors, Peter Lombard especially. The *Book of Sentences*, it seems, served the theological community of the mid-thirteenth century as its ultimate standard of orthodoxy. It represented the limits drawn around the scriptural core of the tradition, limits that all theological discourse had to respect under pain of heresy (in this context, remember Figure 6).

There is, however, an exception to the extraordinary status accorded to the *Book of Sentences*—or, rather, there are eight exceptions. For in the course of his self-defense Bonaventure identifies several points of doctrine "in which the Master is not commonly supported; indeed, common opinion holds the opposite [view]. These [points], however, are eight, such that in each book there are two of these positions." The very first consists in the opinion that "charity, which is the love of God and neighbor, is not something created but rather uncreated, like the Holy Spirit."[44]

The name of "Brother Alexander" is invoked twice in our text as a guarantor of orthodoxy, in both instances with the same formula, "our father and teacher of good memory, Brother Alexander." Perhaps "our" (*noster*) refers to the entire community that Bonaventure is addressing; but it is also possible that he himself studied under Alexander of Hales

during the last years of the great master's life, that is, between 1243 and 1245. Be that as it may, the repeated invocation of *frater Alexander* renders impressive testimony to the esteem in which Alexander and his seminal work were held.

When I referred to the text that we are currently studying as being "enigmatic" I meant the fact that we know very little about the precise circumstances in which Bonaventure delivered this oration. Who had expressed unease about his fidelity to the *Sentences* and to Alexander of Hales? Why did Bonaventure see the need to take the step of prefacing the prologue to Book II of his *Sentences* commentary with a personal statement? Several turns of phrase both at the beginning and the end of the text suggest that it was read as part of the *principium* ceremony for Book II, that is to say, to a large segment of the university community. Moreover, the *principia* included a part called "protestation of faith" (*protestatio fidei*), in which the speaker assured the audience of his orthodoxy.[45] This is what one could interpret Bonaventure as doing in our text. The *protestatio* could have occurred while Bonaventure was lecturing as bachelor on the *Sentences*, in the early 1250s. There is a problem, however. Recent research has established that the Seraphic Doctor changed the order of books in his lectures on the *Sentences*, starting with Book I, but then treating Book IV before moving on to II and III.[46] If this is so, the self-defense may not have been written as a speech at all but rather as a letter.[47] Yet even this hypothesis is not completely satisfactory, given the fact that the text refers so clearly to a lecture setting: "By the Savior's helping grace, out of which it has been possible to complete the first [book], it is necessary to begin the second one...." Further research on this interesting text will perhaps be able to ascertain the precise circumstances of its composition.

The Prologue to Bonaventure's Commentary

The prologue that follows the *praelocutio*, as the modern editors have styled Bonaventure's self-defense, is modeled after Alexander of Hales's paradigm—no doubt the prevailing one in the 1250s—attempting as it does to derive the contents of Book II from a biblical quotation. Each of the four books is preceded by such a biblical derivation of its contents, in addition to a detailed *divisio textus*. As we remember, Alexander of

Hales's work was inconsistent in this regard, sometimes offering a prologue, sometimes a *divisio textus*, and sometimes nothing at all.

The prologue to Book I is of a general nature, introducing the work as a whole. Its theme is Job 28:11: "The depths also of rivers he hath searched, and hidden things he hath brought forth to light." Bonaventure comments, "More careful consideration of this word, which is taken from Job 28:11, opened the way for us to foresee the fourfold kind of causes in the *Book of Sentences*, namely, material, formal, efficient, and final."[48] The juxtaposition of the old biblical approach with the terminology of Aristotelian metaphysics is striking: in his proem, Bonaventure attempts to weave these two strands together. Is this the kind of novelty that caused scandal? His strategy consists in identifying a particular word from the biblical text with one of the four causes, and then demonstrating by means of four properties that belong to the entity which the word signifies, how the causality under consideration manifests itself in each of the four books of the *Sentences*. An example will serve to illustrate this ingenious procedure.

The word "rivers," Bonaventure decides, hints at the material causality that is at work in the *Sentences*—in other words, the contents of the four books. Now a river possesses four principal characteristics: it is of perennial duration (unlike, say, a creek that swells up in the rain, only to disappear during a dry spell); it is broad, unlike a small stream; its flow is circular (as attested by Ecclesiastes 1:7, "unto the place from whence the rivers come, they return"); and finally, it brings about purification. These four characteristics map easily onto the four books of the *Sentences*, in that

1. the emanation of the persons of the Trinity—the subject matter of Book I—is like an eternal flux;

2. the creation of the world, of which Book II treats, is appropriately "foreseen" in the broadness of the river;

3. the Incarnation, to which Book III is devoted, unites the first and the last parts of creation—the eternal God with the human being, fashioned from mud on the sixth day—just as in a circle, the beginning and end of a line are conjoined;

4. the cleansing qualities of the river symbolize the power of the sacraments, which are the focus of Book IV.

And so forth for each of the four causes.

In analyzing the structure and development of traditions, Alasdair MacIntyre suggested that at certain crucial junctures in the history of a tradition—namely, at points where one tradition encounters another, "rival" one—it may become necessary for its members to speak two "first languages."[49] Only such bilingualism enables those working within the tradition to evaluate it over against its challenger and to "weave it together anew" by incorporating new elements that have proven superior. This is exactly what we have seen Bonaventure do in his *Sentences* prologue. He speaks both the language of traditional Christian thought—the language of signs, of a "symbolic space"[50]—and the language of the liberal arts, inspired by Aristotelian logic and metaphysics. This is a language composed of signifiers. The way in which the two meet in the Bonaventurian prologue, and indeed in Bonaventure's thought more generally, is quite remarkable.

The Questions on the Prologue

After the general prologue, we find four questions that take up and deepen its insights. First, the Seraphic Doctor asks what the subject matter of theology is.[51] Before examining his answer, let us note that Bonaventure does not ask what the subject matter of Scripture or of the sacred page is; he defines his project as *theologia*, "theology." Once the inquiry is framed in these terms, the question of its subject matter becomes significantly more pressing than it was in the preceding tradition. The sacred page, in fact, possesses its own unity, which is a narrative one. To be sure, the *Sentences* and its earlier commentaries were no longer structured like biblical stories—as I have pointed out many times. Nevertheless, as long as this literature saw itself as remaining on the same page, as it were, with Scripture, the problem of its subject matter could not become urgent. The sacred page, understood as the inquiry of the theology masters, partook of the unity of the Sacred Page (that is, Scripture). Thus, Peter Lombard spoke of a division in terms of things and signs, but quite

vaguely and without much rigor. His successors came to a better, more methodical grasp of the structure of the work; even they, however, were not interested in determining what its *one* subject was.

Bonaventure's answer still sounds somewhat tentative and hesitant. The subject of every science, he explains, is able to be envisaged in three ways: as the principle of the science (*principium radicale*), as that which constitutes its concrete content (*totum integrale*), and as that which constitutes its content from a more general point of view (*totum universale*). Theology, then, conceived as scientific inquiry (*scientia*), can be said to have three subjects corresponding to these three vantage-points: God, Christ, and the objects of belief.

If the direction that theology is taking in Bonaventure is not yet entirely clear, a comparison with Thomas Aquinas's position on the same issue will remove any doubts. Aquinas (1224/5–74) taught the *Sentences* in Paris between 1254 and 1256, a couple of years after Bonaventure.[52] Unlike the latter, however, he was a Dominican. The questions following his *Sentences* prologue are still more methodology-conscious than those of his Franciscan colleague.[53] First, Aquinas asks whether the human being needs any other branch of knowledge besides the "philosophical sciences."[54] This question affords the Angelic Doctor (as Aquinas is often called) the opportunity to situate theology within a general system of knowledge and to distinguish it from philosophy. He then moves on, in the second question, to address explicitly the problem concerning the unity of theology. For, if its unity is no longer the one stemming, ultimately, from the narrative coherence of the Sacred Page, where does it originate? Answer: in knowledge. The unity of theology as a science is a result of the kind of knowledge obtained in it:

On this [question] one should note that any knowledge is higher in proportion as it is more unified and extends to more things: thus, the understanding of God, who is the highest, distinctly contains the knowledge of all things, through the One that is God himself. So, both because this science is the highest and because it has its efficacy through the very light of divine inspiration, it contains the consideration of all things—while remaining unified, non-multiplied....[55]

Theology is a science, *scientia*; as such, its unity is epistemological. Yet—and here Thomistic theology differs crucially from modern conceptions of science—the epistemological unity of the theological science is not *simply* generated by its internal logical coherence and methodical structure, but primarily by its participation in the unity of God's knowledge of himself.

Against this background, we will not be surprised that Aquinas offers a much less hesitant definition of the subject matter of theology: "we can say that the divine being knowable through inspiration is the subject matter of this science."[56] Things and signs have disappeared entirely from the picture. It is no longer the properties of individual things that point to the Creator, but the unity of a field of abstract knowledge.

Bonaventure's second question attached to the general prologue is devoted to the formal cause of the work or, as he also puts it, to "the mode of proceeding." Taking inspiration, once again, from Job 28:11 ("The depths also of rivers he hath searched"), he decides that the appropriate method for the task at hand is "thoroughly searching" (*perscrutatorius*). To clarify this term, he introduces two synonyms: *ratiocinativus sive inquisitivus*, "ratiocinative or of the nature of an inquiry." The adjective *inquisitivus* connotes methodical, rigorous procedure—the noun *inquisitio*, "inquisition," already carried a juridical meaning in Roman times. Bonaventure acknowledges that Scripture itself proceeds "by the narrative mode."[57] But this is not a valid objection, in his opinion, for what he is doing in his *Sentences* commentary is quite distinct from Scripture. (Is it necessary to point out that this dissociation of theology from Scripture constitutes a radical departure from the way in which the *Book of Sentences* viewed itself?) Bonaventure invokes the theory of subalternation, from Aristotle's *Posterior Analytics*, in order to elucidate the relationship between the theological project and the Bible: "this book is related to Sacred Scripture by the mode of a certain subalternation, not [by the mode] of a principal part." Aristotle's standard example of a subalternated science was that of optics in relation to geometry: optics, being interested in the behavior of light, applies the laws of geometry without being able to account for them.[58] Analogously, theology derives its principles—the objects of belief as such (*credibile ut credibile*)—from Scripture, but uses these principles as the basis for further research. In this process, it transforms the objects of belief as such into objects of belief rendered intelligible (*credibile ut factum intelligibile*).

Question three, on the final cause or end of theology, is worth considering as well. Although he carefully weighs up the implications that are entailed in his conception of theology as a science, Bonaventure's final answer is unambiguous: "We concede, therefore, that [this book] exists so that we may be made good." The ultimate moral goal of theology is due to the fact that the knowledge it conveys is not of the purely abstract kind; rather, it is wisdom, which has both a contemplative and a practical side, with the latter predominating. Again, the comparison with Aquinas is illuminating. As was the case with the subject matter of theology, Aquinas seems slightly "ahead" of Bonaventure, in the sense that he fully embraces and works out a position which, in Bonaventure's thought, was but a possibility. For according to the Angelic Doctor, "since every science should be considered principally from [the point of view of] its end, the final end of this body of teaching, however, is the contemplation of the first truth in the fatherland [that is, in heaven], therefore [this science] is principally speculative."[59] In Aquinas's thought, theology has fully constituted itself as a subject appropriate for university study: it is unified, situated within a larger system of disciplines yet distinct from them, thoroughly scientific, and intellectual.

On the face of it, Bonaventure's fourth and final question appears jejune: "What is the efficient cause or the author of this book?" Peter Lombard, of course! That is, indeed, the conclusion Bonaventure reaches, but only after careful reflection upon the meaning of authorship. To appreciate the significance of this question and of Bonaventure's answer to it, we must consider it against the backdrop of the slow dissociation of theology from the sacred page. For as long as theology occupied the margins of Scripture, metaphorically speaking, there could be no question of the theologian as "author" of ideas. On the other hand, once the sacred page turned into a methodically structured science called "theology," the human writer had to be assigned a more constitutive role. This is precisely what we find Bonaventure doing. His thesis, however, must have been controversial. Writing in the late 1250s, his Oxford colleague Robert Kilwardby begged to differ in his own questions on the *Sentences*: "Although one may say that the Master is the compiler or publisher of this book, nonetheless God must be said to be its author."[60] This clearly was the traditional view.[61]

The Structure of Bonaventure's Commentary

Bonaventure's commentary is structured in accordance with the distinctions that Alexander of Hales introduced into the *Book of Sentences*.[62] The treatment of each distinction follows a rigorous three-step rhythm:

1. First, a *divisio textus* explains the plan that can be discerned in Peter Lombard's argument.

2. Then, a section with advanced questions follows—advanced in the sense that they go beyond any issues directly addressed by the Lombard himself. For example, the first question in the first distinction of Book I asks whether "using" is an act of the will or of reason.

3. Finally, "doubts concerning the letter" (*dubia circa litteram*) take up concerns that arise more immediately from Peter Lombard's text.

The "doubts concerning the letter" reflect and prolong an earlier stage in the reception of the *Sentences*, when the work was still useful as a reasonably up-to-date account of the theological debate. By Bonaventure's time, however, the literal doubts have been reduced to a kind of appendix to each distinction. The center of the commentary is occupied by the author's own questions, the sequence of which still mirrors the organization of the *Book of Sentences*, although their content no longer bears any direct relation to the Master's original theses. The *Book of Sentences*, one could perhaps say, now functions like the skeleton of a body that has grown up: all the parts are still in the same place in relation to each other, yet each individual part has increased in size and matured.

The internal articulation of the central question part—no. 2 in our list above—is fairly complex. First, a brief prologue explains the succession of the questions. These usually fall into several groups, called articles; each article, in turn, will be composed of a number of subquestions. Each of these micro-questions is arranged in the dialectical format that has become standardized at this stage in the development of scholastic thought:

i. Is such-and-such the case?

ii. It appears that it is (or is not). Several arguments follow.

iii. On the contrary ... (arguments for the opposite opinion).

iv. Response and resolution of the problem by means of one or several distinctions: on the one hand, on the other ...

v. Return to the arguments presented under (ii).

A graphic representation of the typical structure of each distinction appears in Figure 8.

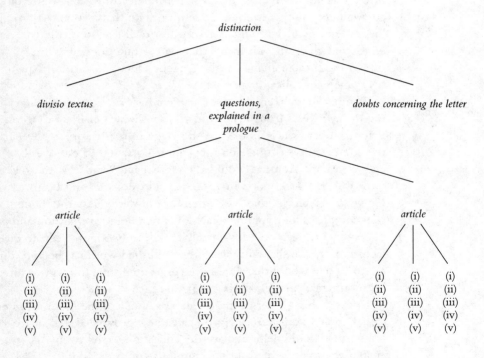

Figure 8: The arrangement within each distinction of Bonaventure's commentary

If we mentally fuse Figure 7 (p. 63) and Figure 8, the resulting structure will give us an idea of the literary architecture of Bonaventure's *Sentences* commentary—with one caveat: Peter Lombard's original division of his work into chapters has disappeared entirely. Still, even after the removal of one level of division, the structure remains impressively involved. Theological science presents itself to us as a ramified system in which meaning is no longer generated through a flow of ideas on a relatively straightforward, horizontal narrative plane, but rather through the logical place which each element of doctrine occupies in a hierarchy that unfolds complex pieces of knowledge into their smallest constituent parts.

Thomas Aquinas's Failed Coup

From the point of view of its structural features, Thomas Aquinas's commentary on the *Sentences* is identical with that of Bonaventure: prologues, commentary divided according to distinctions, the three steps of textual division, advanced theological questions, and literal questions—in all these elements, the Angelic Doctor's work mirrors that of his Franciscan colleague perfectly.

Thomas most likely did not complete his *Sentences* commentary during the two years from 1254 to 1256 when he was charged to lecture on Peter Lombard's four books. At this stage in the history of the Parisian theology faculty, a course on the *Sentences* was spread out over two academic years;[63] Aquinas would therefore have "read," as the technical term was, Books I and II in 1254–55, and Books III and IV in 1255–56. However, given the massive dimensions of the work—the modern edition comprises four volumes, each of which holds over a thousand pages of densely printed text—it probably took him two more years to give his lecture notes the shape in which the published work has been transmitted to us. He would therefore have committed time to this task after his appointment as master, during the years 1256 to 1258.

In 1265, the chapter of the Roman province of the Dominican order called upon Thomas Aquinas to head a new provincial *studium*, or study house, that would help improve the education of the young friars in the area. It was to be located at the community of Santa Sabina in the Eternal City. Faced with this task, Thomas immediately turned to the textbook

with which he was familiar from his studies in Paris, and upon which he had commented so painstakingly. Seeing a need for improvements, however, he set about to revise his Parisian commentary. The result was a new, second *Sentences* commentary, which is preserved on the guard leaves and in the margins of an Oxford manuscript whose body contains the Parisian version.[64] Structurally, Thomas's Roman *Sentences* commentary differs from his earlier one in that it omits the *divisio textus* and *expositio textus*—an omission which, in the words of the commentary's modern editor, "may indicate that Thomas is less interested in commenting on the *Liber sententiarum* itself and more interested in addressing the theological substance of the book."[65] But Thomas's dissatisfaction with the genre of the *Sentences* commentary was even more profound than this remark suggests for he gave up the project, leaving his Roman commentary on Peter Lombard unfinished. The work covers only distinctions 1 to 17 and 23 to 24 of Book I. Thomas must have concluded that the skeleton of the *Sentences* was no longer able to accommodate his mature thought.

A new manual of theology was needed. This is why he started the composition of the *Summa theologiae*, a work that must be understood as having grown out of the *Sentences* tradition. The famous prologue to the *Summa* still rings with his frustration over the *Book of Sentences*:

Since the teacher of Catholic truth must not only instruct those who are [already] advanced, but [since] it is also incumbent upon him to educate beginners—according to this [word] of the Apostle, "As unto little ones in Christ, I gave you milk to drink, not meat" [1 Cor. 3:1–2]—the main point of our intention in this work is to hand down what pertains to the Christian religion in a way that is appropriate for the education of beginners. We have, in fact, weighed the fact that those who are novices in this [field of] teaching are greatly hindered in those [works] that have been written by various individuals: on the one hand, [this is] because of the multiplication of useless questions, articles, and arguments; on the other, because those [points] that are necessary for them to know are handed down not according to the order of the discipline (*secundum ordinem disciplinae*), but according to what was necessary to

the explication of books, or according to what the occasion of disputing allowed; finally, [this is] because the frequent repetition of the same things engenders distaste and confusion in the souls of the listeners. Striving to avoid these and similar [problems], we have attempted, with the confidence of divine assistance, to address what pertains to sacred doctrine briefly and lucidly, as the subject matter permits.[66]

Thomas's principal objection to the continued use of the *Sentences* genre lies in the fact that any *Sentences* commentary, as advanced as its theological content may be, remains tied to the structure of the original work. Peter Lombard's *Book of Sentences*, however, does not flow from one unifying principle able to generate a complete system of theology, without gaps or overlaps. Rather than deriving theology scientifically from one intrinsic principle, the *Sentences* still reflect the influence of factors extrinsic to the "order of the discipline." The work in fact betrays its distant origins as commentary upon Scripture: it embodies the idea of *sacra pagina*, not *sacra doctrina*. One can understand why, for Thomas Aquinas, this defect was exacerbated, not alleviated, by the *Sentences* commentaries: they attempted to build a system of theology upon a foundation unable to support such an edifice. The result was such redundancy and confusion that students were completely put off. This pedagogically highly unsatisfactory situation, Thomas argues, calls for a fresh approach.

A brief remark may be appropriate to explain Thomas's reference to "the occasion of disputing." Disputations were the second major form of instruction at the medieval universities, besides lectures. These disputations, it appears, were born from questions that first arose in the reading (or lecturing upon; the medieval Latin word is the same, *lectio*) of authoritative texts—such as the Bible, Peter Lombard's *Sentences*, or works by Aristotle. The questions gradually detached themselves from the texts, which afforded the intellectual community greater opportunity to explore issues in the liberal arts or in theology according to their own logic. The result was the institution of the public disputation, of which there were several kinds: ordinary, quodlibetal, "Sorbonic" (pertaining to the Sorbonne, one of the colleges of the University of Paris), etc. In all their variety, the disputes had this in common: they followed the dialectical format that we have already discovered in the *Sentences*

literature (articulation of a problem, arguments in favor of one position, arguments for the opposite position, solution—also called "determination," and finally response to the initial objections).[67] The disputes were crucial in training the medieval student to think scholastically, that is to say, dialectically, open-mindedly, but always with a view to a solution that would be defensible before the academic community. Yet—to return to our interpretation of Aquinas's prologue—the disputes provided an occasion only for the exploration of individual issues, or groups of individual issues. They did not lend themselves to the elaboration of entire theological systems.

Thomas's bold move to replace the *Sentences* commentaries with a new manual, his own *Summa theologiae*, did not succeed. Not only did the tradition of commenting upon Peter Lombard continue unabated for another 250 years, but until the early fifteenth century, even his own followers would look to his *Sentences* commentary as the authoritative source of Thomistic theology, rather than using the *Summa*. Thomas's attempted coup failed; the Master continued to reign.

Ancillary Literary Forms

The development from *sacra pagina* to *sacra doctrina* suggests, naturally enough, that theology in the thirteenth century took place at an increasing distance from its sources, and in particular, from its Source—that is, from Scripture itself. This impression is correct, inasmuch as the literary forms that functioned as the vehicle of the new theological science strove to articulate the objects of the Christian faith as intelligibly as possible: in Bonaventure's words, the "objects of belief as such" from Scripture (*credibile ut credibile*) were transformed into the "objects of belief rendered intelligible" that belong to theological science (*credibile ut intelligibile*). In order to give the "credible" the form of the "intelligible," in order to make it appear *as* intelligible, theology deployed sophisticated dialectic and didactic tools, such as the *divisio textus* and the question. These tools served to recast the narratives of Scripture into the form of professionally teachable knowledge.

The same pedagogical impulse, however, which impelled the theologians of the thirteenth century toward increasing abstraction in their presentation of the Christian faith also drove them back toward their

sources—to Scripture, certainly, but also to the Fathers and even to the newly available corpus of Aristotelian writings. These sources needed to be made amenable to the new methodology of *scientia divina*.

Among the works of Thomas Aquinas, there is a little-known text which, astonishingly, had never been printed before the Leonine Commission—a working group of scholars first appointed by Pope Leo XIII to create an authoritative edition of Aquinas's writings—brought it to light in 1971, by including it in its critical edition of the Angelic Doctor's works.[68] Its manuscripts have transmitted it under the title *Tabula libri Ethicorum*, "table of the book of the *Ethics*." The reference is to Aristotle's *Nicomachean Ethics*, of which Thomas and his secretaries prepared this alphabetical index, most likely around the year 1270, in preparation for Thomas's commentary upon Aristotle's work. The *Tabula* summarizes the principal points of Aristotle's ethical teaching under alphabetically arranged headings, from *accio* ("action") to *visus* ("sight"). References are provided by means of book and chapter numbers, plus letters from A to G. Such letters had come to be used, not only in Aristotelian literature but more generally, to indicate further subdivisions of chapters. At the end of the *Tabula*, we find a list of the chapters of the *Ethics*, together with the words with which they begin. Before being forgotten in the fifteenth century, the *Tabula* had a history that was not all placid. When on March 7, 1277, the bishop of Paris, Étienne Tempier, censured 219 propositions to counter doctrinal developments that, in his eyes, threatened the orthodoxy of the university, he included an entry from Thomas's alphabetical index—namely, one of the five that occur under *mors*, "death": "That death is the end of fears and terrors, since it is the limit. III XI c." To Tempier, this statement seemed to exclude the terror of hell.[69]

Thomas Aquinas's alphabetical index of the *Nicomachean Ethics* was not a project of extreme originality. Devices to facilitate the study of integral authoritative texts multiplied since the end of the twelfth century; by the end of the thirteenth, they had become common. The first text to be indexed alphabetically was Scripture itself, when the need was felt for a fresh approach to the composition of sermons. The so-called biblical "distinctions"—another use of the word *distinctio!*—listed all the allegorical meanings of a particular scriptural term. This procedure enabled the preacher to base an entire sermon on a brief biblical

passage, in such a way that the sermon could be developed according to the multiplicity of meanings of a central term. However, the use of indexing techniques—alphabetical and otherwise—quickly spread to more academic contexts, especially since, at the medieval university, all the theology masters were also preachers, and their students, potential preachers.[70]

Robert Kilwardby's Tables on the Sentences

The English Dominican Robert Kilwardby (ca. 1215–79) was a particularly ambitious indexer and tabulator. From around 1256, when he became master of theology at Oxford, he devoted himself to the systematic study of the Fathers, especially—but not exclusively—Augustine. His approach to open up their original texts to contemporary study entailed three levels of study aids. First, he prepared brief summaries, section by section, of dozens of Augustinian texts, in addition to some works by other patristic and medieval authorities, including—most importantly for us—the *Book of Sentences*. On the basis of these *intentiones, conclusiones*, or *capitula*, as the summaries were called, he then created alphabetical subject indices (*tabulae*) for most of these texts. Finally, the project culminated in a large-scale alphabetical concordance that synthesized the individual indices from the previous stage, resulting in a kind of encyclopedia of the tradition.[71]

Kilwardby's study aids on the *Sentences* must have been very popular, for they have come down to us in numerous manuscripts.[72] One complete set of three levels of tables upon the *Book of Sentences* is contained in MS. London, British Library, Royal 9.B.VI, fols. 2r–24v. The set illustrates Kilwardby's working method very well. The collection opens with the announcement, "Here begins the division of the first book of the *Sentences*, first generally regarding the four books, then [there follows] the division particularly regarding the first [book] alone."[73] The incipit is slightly misleading, suggesting as it does the existence of a general index or table concerning the whole of the *Sentences*; in fact, the collection begins with a table of the prologue before moving on to Book I. Therefore, the prologue is what the scribe must have had in mind when speaking of a division "generally regarding the four books."[74] In any case, the first couple of folios (2r–3v) of the manuscript contain

complex synoptic tables of the contents of the prologue and of Book I. The method Kilwardby employs in these tables could be dubbed "ramification," following a term that appears in the *Sentences* commentary by Richard Fishacre, a confrere of Kilwardby's and one of his predecessors in the Dominican chair of theology at Oxford. In lieu of the *divisiones textus* with which we are familiar from Paris—that is to say, texts verbally explaining the structure of Peter Lombard's line of thought—Fishacre made use of *arbores ramificatae*, "ramified" or "branched trees," which summarize large sections of the *Sentences* visually in complex line drawings. These ramifications are a major feature of Fishacre's approach, appearing consistently throughout his commentary.[75] Robert Kilwardby did not use ramifications in his own writings on the *Sentences* (which consist of questions loosely attached to the original text; there is no element of literal commentary). Some such diagrams were, however, added by a later user of Book IV.[76] Moreover, we have an alphabetical index for all four books of Kilwardby's *Sentences* questions, though this does not seem to have been prepared by the author himself.[77]

But back to Kilwardby's "ramified trees" in the manuscript from the British Library. After the prologue, the division proceeds distinction by distinction. The distinctions are counted in the margin; thus, to the left of each ramification, the appropriate distinction number appears: D. 1^a, D. 2^a, D. 3^a, etc. The first words of the distinction being analyzed, underlined, form the starting point of the ramification, which moves from left to right on the page (see Figure 9). After the lemma, Peter Lombard's argument is broken down, step by step, into its smallest elements. For example, according to Kilwardby's analysis, distinction 17 of Book I is composed of three major parts: an initial statement of Peter Lombard's own position, a solution of objections raised by advocates of the contrary view, and a final section in which the Lombard makes an addition to his original statement. The first section can be divided further, into a part where Peter Lombard states his own intention and provides authorities, and another part where he raises questions. And so forth. As the ramification develops, it moves further and further to the right-hand side of the page, until it finally reaches its destination: chapter numbers. In the case of distinction 17, Kilwardby lists fifteen chapters—which is curious, since distinction 17 corresponds to chapters 60 through 65 of Book I, according to Peter Lombard's original chapter numbers. When

Alexander of Hales recounted the chapters after he introduced his division into distinctions, distinction 17 naturally fell into six chapters. We must conclude, then, that Kilwardby restructured the chapters as part of his ramification.

In MS. Royal 9.B.VI, the ramification of the four books of the *Sentences* is broken up into two parts: the divisions of Book I fill folios 2r through 3v, but those pertaining to Books II to IV appear at the very end of the collection, on folios 19v through 24v. This is no doubt an anomaly, due to some kind of scribal oversight.

In between the two parts of the ramification, two further tables complete Kilwardby's study aid on the *Sentences*. First, on folios 4r to 16v, we find *conclusiones* for all four books—summaries that attempt to capture the gist of each distinction in one sentence per chapter. Most of these one-sentence summaries include an underlined lemma, making it possible to correlate them easily with the original text. We must note that the chapter divisions correspond to those that Kilwardby arrived at in the preceding ramifications, not to Peter Lombard's original chapters. Thus, if we look up distinction 17 of Book I, we will find brief summaries for fifteen chapters, not six.

This second table is equipped with a sophisticated multilevel numbering system. First, the user had of course to be given a tool to locate books and distinctions. The books are indicated by means of rubrics that are written within the two columns of text. For instance, after the "conclusions" pertaining to Book I, we read (fol. 7r): "Here the summaries of the first book of the *Sentences* end. Here the summaries of the second book begin." The distinctions are indicated outside the columns of text, in the margins. Also in the margins, to the left of each column of text, the entries of this second table are counted continuously. With each of Kilwardby's new chapters constituting one entry, at the end of the table we reach 1,870. Furthermore, to the right of each column, chapter numbers appear, counted within each distinction according to Kilwardby's new system.

Now to the third element of this impressive array of keys to the *Sentences*. Copied onto folios 17r to 19r, a series of alphabetical tables appears. Its principle of organization is not completely clear. To be sure, there is an alphabetical element, but the order is not what we would expect from an "alphabetical" table. The first one begins with *Adam;*

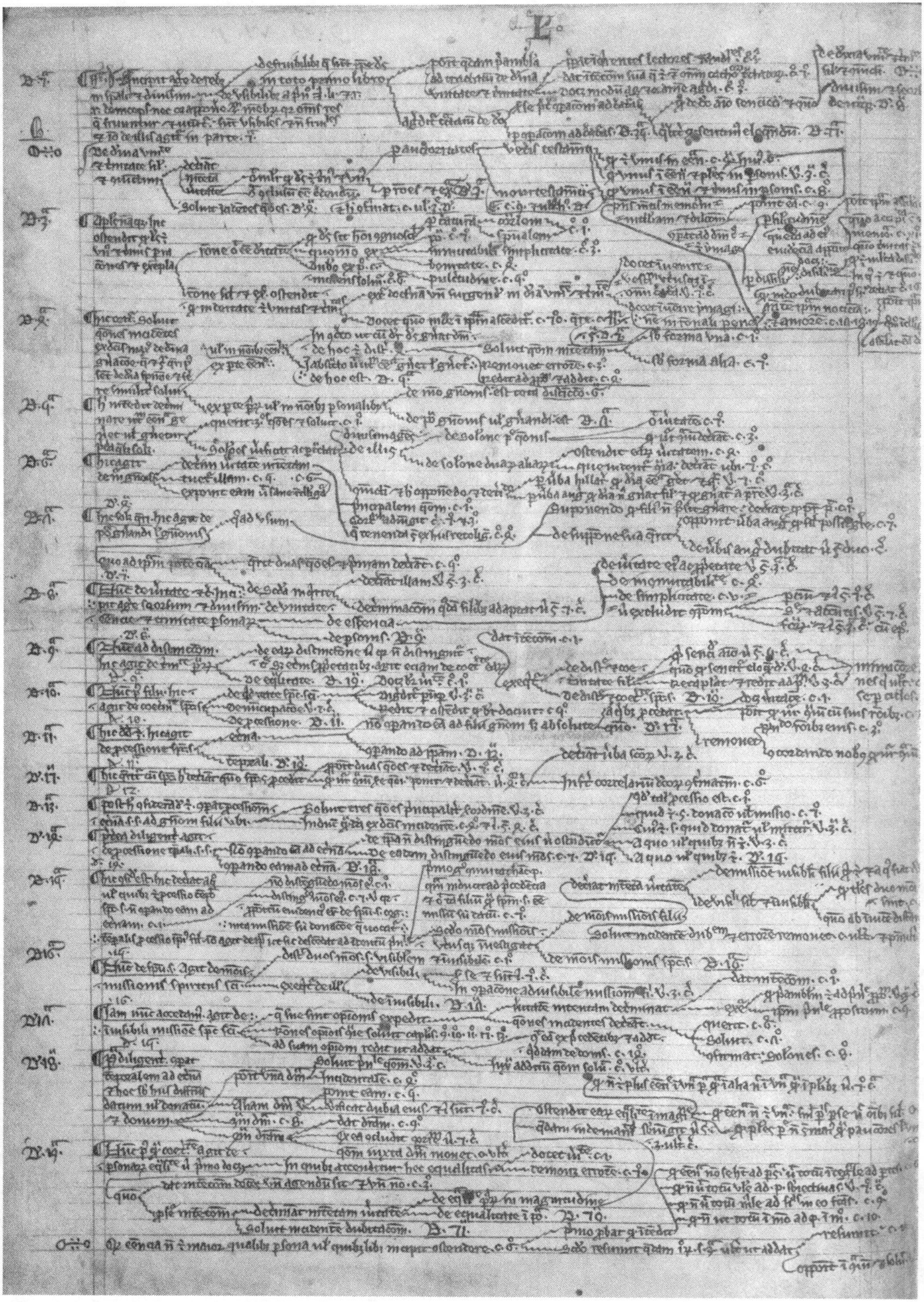

twenty-nine lines later, it has already reached *vates*, "prophet," having quickly moved through *aer, agnus, amor, aqua, auctor, avis, aurum, chaos, claves, cantor, cato, causa, datum, factor, Iacob, lapis, malum, manna, magus, mane, mare, nasa* [?], *papa, plato, panis, pater,* and *sanctus.* Beside each entry, to its right, we find one or several chapter numbers that refer to the preceding summaries. For instance, the entry on Plato sends us to chapter 478, where the summary informs us that in Book II, distinction 1, chapter 2, Peter Lombard, in discussing the creation, "shatters Plato's error concerning the principles" (fol. 7r). Sure enough, the *Book of Sentences* mentions Plato in precisely this context at the beginning of Book II. Kilwardby's tables work!

All in all, there are 29 such alphabetical tables. Either the scribe or Kilwardby himself has made an attempt to arrange their first words sequentially in accordance with the order of the alphabet. Thus, after a few tables that begin with an "a" word, we find several "e" tables, then there are "i" tables, and so forth. Within each table, the procedure that we encountered in the first one repeats itself; that is to say, its entries do not all start with the same letter but, instead, quickly move through the entire alphabet, or a large part of it. Toward the end of the series, however, the alphabetical order—if there ever was one—breaks down. For instance, on folio 18v, a table that starts with *obstinacio* goes on to list *omnipotencia*, then *bonitas*, followed by *cogitacio* and several more "c" words before reaching *similitudo.* Similarly, on folio 19r a table that begins with *unus* and *uti* continues with *cultus* and *crux.*

Kilwardby's (or the scribe's) inability to handle competently an alphabetical system of order points to a fascinating intellectual phenomenon. In the thirteenth century, the alphabetical order was still new; scholars were not generally accustomed to it. There was resistance as well. Thus, Robert Grosseteste, the bishop of Lincoln whom we already encountered in the struggle over the place of the *Sentences* in theological instruction, designed a table of references to authoritative texts in which he deliberately arranged the topics in a logical, or indeed cosmological, order. His *Tabula* begins with entries on God, continues with topics concerning the Word, and then moves on to a group of entries *de creaturis,* "on creatures," and so forth.[78] In contradistinction to Grosseteste's approach, the arrangement of words according to the order of the alphabet, such that *Adam* is followed by *aer* ("air") rather than by *Eva* ("Eve"), requires

Figure 9: Robert Kilwardby's ramified tables on the *Sentences* in MS. London, British Library, Royal 9.B.VI, fol. 2v

that they be ripped out of the order of the cosmos, that they be stripped of their function as signs and be reduced to signifiers. Furthermore, the cosmic order reflects a divine design, so that by "reading" the world of signs with open spiritual eyes, the human being is able to trace it back to its Maker, the ultimate Thing. The order of the alphabet, on the other hand, is completely arbitrary and conventional; there is no bond that ties "a" to "b" and dictates that this must be followed by "c." Or rather, there is one, but this bond is the human mind itself.

The move from signs to signifiers, and from the cosmic to the alphabetical order, constitutes a Copernican turn—to use a Kantian expression here—of immense epistemological consequence. In the world of the sign, the human being was primarily a reader: his task was to "read" the order of the world and to represent it faithfully in his writings so as to enable a return from signs to the Thing. In the new world of the signifier, the human being is primarily a writer: faced with a jumble of words arranged in no intrinsic, natural pattern, he himself has to create a "cosmos," an ordering scheme, that will make sense of it all. Moreover, as historians of medieval manuscript culture Mary and Richard Rouse have perspicaciously pointed out, "the use of alphabetical order was a tacit recognition of the fact that each user of a work will bring to it his own preconceived rational order, which may differ from those of other users and from that of the writer himself."[79] In other words, whereas signs bind together the community that reads them, signifiers require a much more active act of ordering that enables individuality. It is not a coincidence that the thirteenth century saw the rise of the pocket Bible, of complete texts of Scripture that could be carried around by the individual student or master. The Bible "descended from the communal altar to become the private property of the priest, a personal possession of the friar."[80]

It would take centuries for all these developments to come to full fruition. There can be little doubt, however, that the seeds of modernity were sown in the thirteenth century.

Abbreviations of Sentences *Commentaries*

In the first chapter, we saw that, from the earliest stages of its career, the *Book of Sentences* was abbreviated for pedagogical purposes: the condensed versions were easier to "cram." Since the commentaries of

the thirteenth century moved theological reflection beyond the letter of Peter Lombard's original text, a need was felt for abridged versions of these commentaries as well—especially of the most influential and respected ones. Thus, we know that Bonaventure's *Sentences* commentary was abridged a number of times. The characteristics of these abbreviations reflect their pedagogic aims: tables of content and clear textual divisions make them highly suitable as study aids. Interestingly, the Bonaventure abridgments display a characteristic liberty of their authors with regard to the Seraphic Doctor's original teaching; frequently, they feel quite free to diverge from his views and develop independent lines of thought. Abridgments of Thomas Aquinas were quite different in that regard, showing great fidelity and commitment to Thomism as a "school."[81]

Not all the abbreviations, however, pursued academic goals. Some of them returned the *Book of Sentences*, in a rethought and condensed form, to the monastic life in which Christian reflection had been so firmly rooted in the centuries before the twelfth. This phenomenon teaches us an important lesson: it may be possible to discern a fairly clear direction in the development of the *Sentences* literature; yet beneath these large-scale currents there are significant countercurrents that complicate the overall picture, warning us not to rush to conclusions.

A good example of such a countercurrent is the abbreviation that the English Dominican William de Rothwell composed around 1270–80 of the *Sentences* commentary by his French confrère Peter of Tarantaise.[82] William de Rothwell's abridgment is not the only such work that was devoted to Peter of Tarantaise's commentary on Peter Lombard.[83] Doubtless it is Peter's accession to the papacy, in 1276, that explains why his commentary was abbreviated several times: he was an important and influential man of the Church, and the first Dominican ever to become pope. Peter's commentary was not devoid of originality, attempting to mediate between the positions of Bonaventure and Thomas Aquinas. Perhaps surprisingly, the future pope frequently sided with Bonaventure rather than with the member of his own order—which indicates that, toward the end of the thirteenth century, there existed no "fixed party lines" yet between the Franciscans and the Dominicans.[84]

As was the case with the abbreviations that we examined in the previous chapter, William de Rothwell's abridgment is not simply a small-scale reproduction of its original. Although William rarely voices

his own opinion, the manner in which he selects and omits material from Peter of Tarantaise's commentary—occasionally having recourse to other sources as well—shows his own theological preferences. Most importantly, however, William chooses not to retain the dialectical format of the typical *Sentences* commentary of the late thirteenth century, with its constant movement between opposite positions. Rather, in abbreviating Peter of Tarantaise's commentary, William distills "sentences" from it. These sentences, according to the author of a recent study of the abbreviation, seem to have been aimed at contemplation of certain fundamental aspects of the faith.[85] The fact that most of the manuscripts of William de Rothwell's work were owned by monasteries comports well with this hypothesis.

Chapter Three: The Fourteenth Century
The Movement away from the *Sentences*

JEAN-LUC MARION, a contemporary French philosopher whose thought draws on the traditions of phenomenology and Christian negative theology, has recently produced remarkable work that is aimed at overcoming some of the critical limitations of modern philosophy. According to such modern thinkers as Kant and Husserl, experience can take place only within a horizon of presuppositions that keep any given phenomenon within the limits of what is "possible." In other words, whatever enters human experience does so within a framework of expectations against which it is measured and evaluated; indeed, all experience is necessarily reduced to the parameters of such a framework. On this account, there is ultimately nothing that could challenge human thought, forcing it to reconstitute itself fundamentally so as to be able to accommodate an extra-ordinary experience. In this scenario, thought is comparable to a myopic set of eyes that are able to perceive only what is given to them within a limited range of vision; whatever is further removed becomes so blurred in its features as to be unrecognizable. Marion asks us to consider the possibility of a horizon that adjusts to what appears within it and is constituted by it (rather than vice versa). Could certain "saturated" phenomena, such as epoch-making historical

events, shatter existing horizons of what is considered possible, forcing thought to regroup around literally mind-blowing phenomena? Maybe the events of September 11, 2001, constitute an example of a saturated phenomenon. They shattered previous beliefs about the invulnerability of American soil, the nature of war, and so on. Existing categories of thought proved insufficient to grasp the full import of the attacks; and as it was impossible to think 9/11 on the basis of conventional ideas, a new ideological universe arose around it. "We live in a different world now," it is often claimed.

For Marion, the saturated phenomenon *par excellence* is revelation, Christian or otherwise—an event that explodes the assumptions of an entire culture, subsequently becoming the center and starting point of a new one.[1] When God's own voice makes itself heard in human civilization, through prophets or—as is Christianity's claim—through his own son, humanity has to reconsider all of its beliefs in a fundamental manner. Take the person of Christ, for instance: was he God or was he human? If one takes Christianity seriously, this basic distinction between the human and the divine breaks down, as Christ was both fully God and fully man. Human thought falters in the face of the challenge of the Incarnation.

Peter Lombard's controversial identification of charity with the Holy Spirit could be interpreted along similar lines: charity transcends the limitations of fallen human nature to such an extent that it cannot be understood according to human parameters; it must therefore be thought of as an irruption of the Holy Spirit into the human realm. To love—truly and fully love—God and neighbor, to love even one's enemies, Peter Lombard is suggesting, is no longer human: it is a manifestation of the presence of the Divine within human nature. As such, it can never become fully comprehensible. The difference between revelation and charity, on the one hand, and an epoch-making event, on the other, is that human thought can never do complete justice to the former, whereas the latter merely requires a fundamental reconfiguration of ideas previously taken for granted.

It is not surprising that Peter Lombard's doctrine on charity met with little enthusiasm among the theologians following him. In our attempt to trace the reception of the *Book of Sentences* in the twelfth and thirteenth centuries, we have witnessed the awakening of the power of systematic

theology. In this *scientia divina*, revelation is increasingly received according to the parameters of a methodically constituted realm of scientific inquiry—"according to the order of the discipline," as Thomas Aquinas puts it in the prologue to his *Summa theologiae*. In Robert Kilwardby's sophisticated tables, the tradition is broken down into alphabetically ordered units, ready to be reassembled into a system by a creative author. This author now shapes original theological writings, no longer content to place annotations in the margins of the Sacred Page. In this manner, revelation stands in danger of being domesticated, as it were, instead of being recognized for the saturated phenomenon that it is.

These and similar developments are both continued and given a new direction, radicalized as well as challenged, in the *Sentences* commentaries of John Duns Scotus.

John Duns Scotus

Note the plural: "commentaries." Scotus (ca. 1266–1308) was not the first thinker to revise his commentary upon the *Book of Sentences* and produce several versions; we have already seen Thomas Aquinas attempt the same. Aquinas, however, abandoned his revision because his new theology could not be articulated adequately within the literary structure of the *Sentences*. This was no longer a problem that worried Duns Scotus and his contemporaries. For them, the *Sentences* commentary ceased to serve the function of engaging the thought of Peter Lombard. Rather, their lectures on the *Sentences* and the corresponding literary genre became the major vehicle for the exploration and defense of their own theological ideas. Not only is there rarely any serious discussion of Peter Lombard's theology in the "commentaries" of the fourteenth century; authors of *Sentences* commentaries feel free to treat even the topics suggested by the work of the Master in a very selective manner, according to contemporary emphases: "theologians in this later period discussed the 'hot' topics (or at least the ones that interested them most) and ignored the others."[2] The *Sentences* commentary, then, survives only in an ironic way—by ceasing to be a commentary in any proper sense of the word. On the other hand, the fact that in the fourteenth century the genre casts off the shadow of Peter Lombard allows it to grow exponentially; for now theologians employ it throughout their careers to develop

and refine their ideas, leaving behind entire series of revised versions.[3]

Such is precisely the case of Duns Scotus, who "read" the *Sentences* at least three times: at Oxford, in the academic year 1300–01; at Paris, in the year 1302–03; and again at Oxford, in 1304–05. In addition, Charles Balić, the leading expert on the literary history of Scotus's *Sentences* commentaries, considered it possible that the Subtle Doctor's first reading of the work of Peter Lombard occurred at Cambridge, between 1297 and 1300. This hypothesis would force us to admit at least three layers of revision in Scotus's works on the Lombard.[4] To complicate matters further, none of these commentaries is complete, each bearing upon only one or two books of the *Sentences*; some of them exist only in the form of student notes (*reportationes*); and the manuscripts present a veritable jungle of additions and deletions, some of which may be due to the author himself, while others must be attributed to his students. On the upside, however, during his final years at Oxford, Scotus himself created an "ordered" synthesis of his teaching in the various versions of the *Sentences* commentary. This so-called *Ordinatio*, albeit itself incomplete, has come down to us in a very reliable manuscript that is the result of an attempt by Scotus's own disciples to prepare an authoritative text, indeed something like a medieval critical edition. The editors based their work on the version of the *Ordinatio* that was most commonly used among his students, but they compared it carefully with Scotus's own copy. They indicated passages that could not be verified "in Scotus's book" (*in libro Scoti*), additions and deletions by the master, and even blank spaces that he intended to fill later.[5] Our following discussion will be based upon the modern edition of this manuscript.

The Literary Form of the Ordinatio

The literary structure of the *Ordinatio* is quite recognizably modeled after the five-step dialectical format that we already encountered in the commentaries of Bonaventure and Thomas Aquinas: question, arguments for one side, arguments for the opposite position, solution, return to the initial arguments. Scotus's work is, however, considerably more difficult to follow than the productions of his predecessors, on account of the fact that the Subtle Doctor is in the habit of embedding multiple sub-questions within a larger question, a bit in the manner of Russian

nesting dolls. In the following outline, I have schematized the form of the opening section from Scotus's *Sentences* prologue:

> Question: Does the human being need supernatural teaching?
> Arguments con (nos. 1–3)[6]
> Arguments pro (4)
> Digression: the opinion of the philosophers (denying the need for the supernatural)—several arguments (5–11)
>> Two arguments against the philosophers (12–18)
>>> Counterarguments (*instantiae*) by the philosophers (19–27)
>>> Response to these counterarguments (28–39)
>> A third argument against the philosophers (40–41)
>>> A counterargument by the philosophers (42–44)
>>> Response to this counterargument (45–48)
>> A fourth and fifth argument against the philosophers (49–52)
>>> Response to these arguments (53)
>> A further argument in support of the first three (54–56)
> Scotus's solution, by means of a distinction (57–65)
> Authorities supporting the first three arguments against the philosophers (66–69)
>> An objection from the philosophers (70)
>> Response to this objection (71)
> Response to the original arguments by the philosophers (72–89)
> Response to the initial arguments con (90–94)

Frequently, the sections distinguished in this schema will themselves possess a sophisticated internal structure. Most notably, Scotus likes to break down arguments into their syllogistically relevant parts of major, minor, and conclusion, providing separate reasons to support the major and the minor premises.

One may already be able to understand why Scotus received the epithet "Subtle Doctor" from his contemporaries: his positions are often far from easy to define. In the *Sentences* commentaries of the mid-thirteenth century, it sufficed to turn to the central portion of a question or article in order to find the author's solution to a given problem, a solution that typically relied upon one or more relatively straightforward distinctions. By the time of Scotus, scholasticism had produced complex doctrinal

syntheses that had acquired lives of their own, at several removes from Scripture, which they were originally meant to elucidate. An author was expected to situate himself vis-à-vis these systems of thought, in detailed and painstaking discussions. This is why he now developed "his solution gradually—in fact, dialectically—in contradistinction to the various opinions presented and critically considered."[7] In the question whose schema I have sketched out above, Scotus's solution emerges step by step as he carefully weighs the individual arguments in favor of and against those who deny the need for revelation in the human quest for happiness. It is easy to get lost in these drawn-out debates, with their relentless movement back and forth; even a veteran Scotist such as Father Balić often found it difficult, "because of the many opposing viewpoints, to know whether Scotus or his opponent is speaking. This difficulty is increased by the fact that Scotus often refers back to what he had already said in relation to the question at issue."[8]

Scotus's *Sentences* commentary in the *Ordinatio* dispenses with the traditional, biblically inspired prologue, instead delving immediately into technically framed issues of epistemology and method. The old prologue, we may remember, served as a bridge between the metaphorical language of Scripture and the conceptually more precise theology of the *Sentences* commentaries. In the *Ordinatio*, this connection is severed. Its prologue is something like a short work in its own right, filling over two hundred pages in the critical edition.

Scotus's Conception of Theology

At first sight, Scotus's understanding of the theological project gives the impression that his thought stands in unbroken continuity with the tendency, so strong in the thirteenth century, to conceive of theology as an Aristotelian science. Indeed, in his response to the first question from his *Sentences* prologue—"whether it is necessary for the human being, in his present state [i.e., in this life], to have some teaching supernaturally breathed into him"—Scotus denies that as an object of knowledge the supernatural, or revelation, can ever exceed the bounds set by human nature, that is, of reason. For the supernatural to be known, it has to submit to the horizon of human knowledge in which it is received:

To the question, then, I respond by first distinguishing in what way something is said to be supernatural. For a receptive power can be compared to the act which it receives or to the agent from which it receives [this act].… Applying [this distinction] to the issue at hand, then, I say that when we compare the possible intellect to the actual knowledge in it, no cognition is supernatural to it, since the possible intellect is perfected naturally by any cognition whatsoever and is naturally inclined to it. Speaking in the second sense, however, such [cognition] is supernatural which is generated by an agent in whose nature it is not to move the possible intellect to such a cognition naturally. For the present state, however, according to the Philosopher [i.e., Aristotle], it is in the possible intellect's nature to be moved to cognition by the agent intellect and a sense image; therefore, only such cognition is natural to it which is impressed [in it] by those agents.[9]

There is no room for a "saturated phenomenon" here! While Duns Scotus does not rule out God as a source or agent of supernatural cognition, as soon as such revelation enters the (possible) intellect, it has to conform to the nature of human intellection.[10]

Following the same logic, Scotus maintains that the theological virtues of faith and charity presuppose naturally acquired faith and natural love. The differences between the infused and the acquired acts are merely accidental, being due to the agent that brings them about. Thus, the faith infused by God cannot err, for example, unlike naturally acquired faith, with its sources in tradition or the witness of individual people.[11] In his commentary on distinction 17 of Book I—one of the rare passages of the *Ordinatio* where a teaching of Peter Lombard's is seriously examined—Scotus reinterprets the Master as holding that charity is, in fact, a supernatural habit created in the soul (which is precisely the position that the *Book of Sentences* disputed so vigorously), because it is identical with grace itself.[12] To love God and neighbor means to be in the state of grace; therefore, it is not necessary to posit a habit of charity in addition to grace itself. This is an original attempt to save the Master's teaching, but it lacks textual support in the *Sentences*. The important point here is that a supernatural habit created in the soul (whether the habit be charity or grace) is structurally analogous to a natural habit—to a state,

that is, which the soul acquires naturally. Peter Lombard, by contrast, regarded charity as a radical reconfiguration of human existence, almost as a kind of deification.

Strictly speaking, there can be no "proof" that the human being stands in need of revelation. By strongly emphasizing this point, Scotus underscores the autonomy of philosophy and theology in their respective fields. Since revelation is received within the bounds of nature, theology needs to have recourse to metaphysics and other branches of philosophy; but the latter cannot do the theologian's job. It cannot prove the truths of the faith. In an important marginal note that the medieval editors of the *Ordinatio* found in Scotus's own copy, the Subtle Doctor cautions:

> Note that nothing supernatural can be shown to exist in the wayfarer [that is, in the human being here on earth] by means of natural reason or can necessarily be required for his perfection; neither can even the one who possesses [a supernatural attribute] know that it is within him. It is therefore impossible to use natural reason here against Aristotle: if one argues from matters of belief (*ex creditis*), this is no argument against a philosopher, since he does not concede a premise based on faith. This is why the reasons advanced here against him have a different [non-philosophical] premise that is based on or proven from faith; therefore, they are but theological persuasive arguments, [proceeding] from matters of belief to something believed.[13]

What occurs in Scotus's thought is a somewhat paradoxical development: on the one hand, we find in him the strongest respect for the autonomy of nature and, hence, of philosophy, which is the domain of natural reason. As a consequence, the impact of the supernatural upon human nature seems to be minimized: in the passage just quoted, Scotus maintains that a person is unable to tell whether his faith or love is of natural or supernatural origin. It is impossible, in this life and without the invocation of faith, to distinguish between a love of God and neighbor that has been acquired naturally, through habituation, and the supernatural charity that accompanies grace. The impossibility to tell the difference between the two is precisely due to the fact that grace can be received only within the bounds of human nature, to whose capac-

ity it is thus reduced. On the other hand, however, Scotus's emphasis upon the autonomy of nature also serves to free theology from the yoke of philosophy and its methods. For the Subtle Doctor, the necessity of revelation, the supernatural, and theology are not primarily matters of metaphysics but rather of faith, trust, and the covenant between God and his people. Scotus writes:

> Beatitude is conferred as a reward for merits that God accepts as worthy of such a reward, and therefore it does not follow by natural necessity from any of our acts but is given contingently by God, who accepts some acts as being meritorious in relation to him. This is not knowable naturally, as it appears, since here even the philosophers erred, positing that everything which comes from God comes from him necessarily ... for it cannot be known by means of natural reason what the divine will accepts insofar as it accepts contingently such-and-such [acts] as being worthy of eternal life, and that they also suffice; this depends entirely upon the divine will concerning those [acts] to which it relates in a contingent manner.[14]

It is in this context that a distinction arises which is key to an understanding of later medieval thought: the distinction between God's ordered and absolute power. As Scotus explains, "it is possible for God, on account of his absolute power (*de potentia absoluta*), to save anyone whatsoever," even a non-Christian who completely lacks faith. However, "on account of his ordered power (*de potentia ordinata*), [grace] is not given without a preceding habit of faith."[15] The term *potentia ordinata* expresses the fact that God has freely entered into a relationship with the world that is "based on covenant and self-commitment."[16] God, who is omnipotent, could in principle act in utterly unpredictable ways, had he not committed himself to his people. But he has, and we can trust that commitment, the principal features of which we know through Scripture. Such trust is what faith is all about. Philosophical theories about natures and their causality, by contrast, fail when it comes to grasping the covenantal relationship between God and his people.[17]

The distinction between *potentia ordinata* and *potentia absoluta* constitutes the root of late medieval "nominalism"—a doctrine usually

understood, reductively, as the denial of the existence of universals outside the mind. On the standard account, a nominalist is a thinker who believes that only individuals truly exist while general concepts are mere abstractions that possess no reality: they are mere "names" (*nomina*; hence the term "nominalism"). Thus, for a nominalist, scientific systems are constructs of the human mind, related to the "world out there" only in a highly mediated fashion. Although Scotus was not a nominalist in this sense, he paved the way for it, precisely through the prominent place that the distinction between God's absolute and ordered powers occupies in his thought. For this distinction severs any necessary causal link between the Creator and creation: since God could have created a different world, the structures of creation cannot be traced back metaphysically to the Creator. Creation, consequently, needs to be understood on its own terms, for what it is in itself. From this conviction, it is only one further step to the denial of universals as a kind of meta-reality that exists in addition to the world of individual things.[18]

With regard to the relationship between theology and metaphysics, Scotus's position in the prologue to the *Ordinatio* articulates a complex "independence in interdependence."[19] As we have already seen, metaphysics is indispensable to theology so that it can grasp the natural structures in which revelation and grace are received; yet theology also transcends the purview of metaphysics decisively.

Scotus developed his thought in response to the condemnation of 1277 that was mentioned in passing in the previous chapter. In this condemnation Bishop Étienne Tempier censured 219 theses that he claimed were taught at the faculty of arts in Paris. The theses, taken as a whole, formulate a virulently anti-Christian system of philosophy that takes its inspiration from Aristotle and his Islamic commentators. The blacklisted propositions range from general attacks against Christianity, such as articles no. 152 ("That the discourse of the theologian is founded in fables") and no. 174 ("That there are fables and falsehoods in the Christian law, just as in others"), to specific philosophical doctrines; in our context, the theses that deny the possibility of a supernatural beatitude are most germane: articles no. 40 ("That there is no more excellent condition than to devote oneself to philosophy") and no. 176 ("That happiness is had in this life, and not in another").[20] It has been shown, however, that many of the condemned theses were taught by no Parisian "artist"

at all; rather, it was paradoxically Bishop Tempier himself who created a complete and coherent philosophical heresy upon the basis of certain tendencies that he perceived in the arts faculty. In other words, with the objective of suppressing a full-blown challenge to the Christian faith before it could constitute itself explicitly and systematically, Tempier drew consequences from contemporary positions that no one was yet prepared to defend or perhaps even think.[21] The Parisian condemnations were swiftly followed by a parallel move in England, where Robert Kilwardby, now archbishop of Canterbury, issued a similar document concerning thirty theses taught by masters at Oxford.[22]

The condemnations at Paris and Oxford were widely understood as indictments of the kind of Aristotelianism that, flourishing in the thirteenth century, gave rise to the theological syntheses of thinkers such as Thomas Aquinas. This is why, "from the moment of the condemnations of the 1270s, Aquinas could be read as a radically dangerous thinker,"[23] one whose positions required fundamental corrections. Indeed, it seems that, subsequent to the condemnation of 1277, Bishop Tempier planned an official inquiry into the orthodoxy of Thomistic thought; this plan, however, did not succeed.[24]

As I have said, the thought of Duns Scotus was meant as a response to this crisis, which it attempted to overcome by carving out a space where theology could reaffirm its autonomy. The clearest connection between Scotus and the condemnation of 1277 is the theologian Henry of Ghent, whose ideas have received much attention in recent scholarship. His theology served as one of the main inspirations of Duns Scotus, whose teachings took shape through what has been called "a passionate reading of Henry."[25] As it happens, Henry of Ghent was also the most prominent member of the commission of theologians that, at Tempier's request, drew up the list of errors to be censured by the bishop.

William of Ockham

William of Ockham (ca. 1285–1347) belongs to the same tradition as Duns Scotus: a fellow Franciscan, schooled at Oxford, Ockham frequently developed his positions in dialogue with those of the Subtle Doctor, whom he may in fact have known personally.[26] Like his older confrère, in his works Ockham endeavored to disentangle Christian the-

ology from the Aristotelian embrace that had led to the crisis of the late thirteenth century. Although the condemnations of the 1270s had no doubt lost some of their edge when Ockham lectured on the *Sentences* between 1317 and 1319, one can still hear their distant echo. Ockham must have prepared a first version of his *Ordinatio* on Book I in the years immediately following his Oxford lectures; however, the work underwent changes as Ockham's thought continued to evolve.[27]

Theology: Certain, but not a Science

Just like Scotus's *Ordinatio*, Ockham's work opens abruptly, dispensing with the old biblical prologue: "Is it possible for the wayfarer's intellect to possess evident knowledge of theological truths?"[28] This is the prologue's first question. The problem of the evidence of the teachings of theology has its origin in two propositions that were censured in 1277.[29] In thesis 37, Bishop Tempier construed the philosophers as maintaining that "nothing should be believed if it is not known in itself or can be asserted from principles that are known in themselves." Similarly, proposition 151 declares, "For someone to possess certainty with regard to some conclusion, it is necessary that he base himself upon principles that are known in themselves." Such is, in fact, the ideal of Aristotelian science: the principles of a conclusion must be self-evident, or must be derived from self-evident principles. But what does this mean for *scientia divina*? Bonaventure attempted to secure the scientific status of theology by means of an ingenious theory of subalternation, according to which theological ratiocination is based upon scriptural principles; we briefly touched upon the matter in the preceding chapter. Realizing that, in and of itself, such a scriptural foundation is still too weak to satisfy Aristotelian criteria of evidence, Aquinas then added the further explanation according to which theology is subalternated to God's self-knowledge and to the vision of God enjoyed by the blessed. This, clearly, is self-evident knowledge. God, however, chose to share this self-evident knowledge of himself with us, through the medium of Scripture.[30] Still, of course, the truths contained in Scripture are not self-evident to us, the poor "wayfarers" here on earth! The attempt, therefore, to construct a theological science *à la* Aristotle could easily backfire, producing the kind of skepticism whose germs Tempier presciently detected in the minds of the members of the Parisian arts faculty.

This is why Ockham follows a different path to secure the validity of the theological project. Still more clearly—and less subtly—than Scotus, he insists upon the autonomy of theology; while the theologian may, indeed must, employ the tools of philosophical reasoning, theology is not scientific in the Aristotelian sense of the term. There are two ways of looking at this move: it is both a defense of theology against illegitimate incursions of philosophical method, and an attempt to preserve the specific logical rigor of philosophical inquiry.[31] The Venerable Inceptor (as the schoolmen called Ockham, who after a heated controversy with the chancellor of the University of Oxford was never admitted among the ranks of the masters of that university, remaining forever someone awaiting his inception or graduation) offers the following uncompromising definition of science:

> What is science (*scientia*)? I say that science, insofar as it is distinguished from the other intellectual habits that the Philosopher discusses in Book VI of the *Ethics*, is evident knowledge (*notitia evidens*) of necessary truth, [knowledge] able to be caused by premises that are applied to such truth by means of syllogistic discourse.[32]

In the question concerning the scientific character of theology, it is not the use of logic and syllogistic discourse that presents a problem; in that sense, Ockham's theology could be characterized as being extremely, indeed aridly "scientific." (We are by now far removed from the spiritual atmosphere of Peter Lombard: "Longing to cast something of our want and poverty along with the little poor woman into the treasury of the Lord...." That is not the language of William of Ockham!) For Ockham, what is at issue is the notion of theological evidence. He spends the first seventy pages of his *Sentences* prologue on a technical examination of what evidence requires, distinguishing complex knowledge (involving a proposition) from its non-complex elements, and an intuitive grasp from an abstract grasp of these simple elements. A first conclusion follows in question 2: "I say that God, on account of his absolute power, is able to cause evident knowledge of some theological truths, although perhaps not of others, in the intellect of the wayfarer."[33] Of course, this conclusion is based upon the hypothesis of God acting by means of his absolute power; we are therefore engaged in a logical exercise more than in an examination of theological inquiry as it actually proceeds. However,

even upon the assumption that God would make evident knowledge of himself available to a created intellect in this life, such knowledge, Ockham shows in question 3, would give rise to science only to a very limited extent: for the simplicity of the divine essence prevents it from being approached syllogistically.[34]

This, however, is not the problem with theology as ordinarily under-stood—with theology "that can be obtained by theologians upon the basis of the common law" (that is, the law to which God has freely subjected his actions and which therefore defines his ordered power).[35] Such theology "is not a science properly speaking"[36] because it lacks the necessary evidence of its principles.

In Book VI, chapter 3, of the *Nicomachean Ethics*, Aristotle had pre-sented a list of five states or "habits" in virtue of which the soul can grasp truth: art (*technē*), science (*epistēmē*), prudence (*phronēsis*), wisdom (*sophia*), and intellection (*nous*).[37] Given Aristotle's definition of each of these habits, theology could reasonably be associated only with science. Ockham's denial of the scientific status of theology, therefore, deprives it of any place in the classification of veridical states of the soul—states, that is, through which access to truth is possible. This is a most troubling consequence, and Ockham, whose *Sentences* prologue refers to the rele-vant passage of the *Ethics* several times, is acutely aware of the difficulty. He resolves it rather simply: by proposing to expand Aristotle's list. Why not add a habit to the five that the Philosopher mentions?

When it is said that the veridical intellectual habits are only five, I say that there are only five kinds of naturally acquired veridi-cal habits, which the Philosopher enumerates in Book VI of the *Ethics*. This is because, according to the Philosopher, faith is not, according to its entire region, a veridical habit, because it can exist with regard to false as well as true [claims], according to him. Yet, beyond these habits there exists another veridical habit, because it cannot comprise anything false. Such is faith with regard to the theological matters of belief, whether it be acquired or infused.— In another way one can say that the Philosopher only speaks of evident and certain habits, and theology is not of such a kind with regard to matters of belief, because it is not evident, although it is certain.[38]

... faith can be a non-evident veridical habit, and such is theology for the most part.[39]

In these passages, Ockham speaks as a Christian. An Aristotelian who considers faith from the outside might think that it resembles mere opinion, which is sometimes true and sometimes false. The Christian, by contrast, believes that matters of faith are certain—not, to be sure, evidently certain but rather certain in virtue of the authority of Scripture and of the Church. Such authority serves as the starting point for all theological reflection: "one must never concede contradictory statements about one and the same matter, unless they are obtained from Scripture or from a determination of the Church, or are evidently and by means of formal conclusion inferred from such [sources]."[40]

Ockham's emphasis upon the foundational role that Scripture and the dogmatic decisions of the Church play in theological inquiry put him at odds with the dominant currents at the University of Oxford, which at the beginning of the fourteenth century (in 1310 or 1311) enacted statutes that required all bachelors of theology to lecture upon the *Sentences* before lecturing on Scripture.[41] Combined with the now prevalent custom for masters to continue working on the *Sentences* commentaries that they had first delivered as bachelors,[42] the statutes contributed to a strong shift of emphasis from biblical to speculative theology. The Franciscans and Dominicans resisted these developments for years, even appealing to the papal curia over this "perversion of the order of teaching," but ultimately lost the battle—an ugly and bitter battle, it must be said, in which more lowly motives than strictly theological ones played an unfortunate role, for the secular masters of the university acted in order to protect their system of study against the parallel but different one of the mendicant orders. Indeed, there may have been resentment over the fact that the mendicant colleagues offered their lectures for free, drawing students away from the secular masters' courses and thereby encroaching upon their business interests.[43]

In his theory of theological method, then, the Venerable Inceptor was in agreement with the position of his Oxford confrères. His practice, however, hardly gave much weight to the kind of biblically based theology that Peter Lombard had espoused in the *Sentences*. The prologue to the *Ordinatio*, which comprises 370 pages in its modern critical edition,

contains exactly one quotation from Scripture![44] Moreover, the style of the work is dry, focusing as it does upon issues of logic and epistemology. Robert Guelluy, author of a monograph that patiently examines the argument of the entire prologue, sounds exasperated at the end of his study. "No breath of air, no spirit, no inspiration in these arid and dense texts," he complains in his conclusion.[45] In other words, in Ockham we witness a complete dissociation of speculative theology from spirituality. He appears to have forgotten what Peter Lombard knew, namely, that theology is about salvation, including that of the theologian himself. It is striking that, at one point in the prologue, Ockham envisions the possibility of a theologian completely lacking faith:

> Thus, I say on this article that, with regard to the matters of faith, the theologian increases his habit of acquired faith—if acquired faith precedes his studies. If, on the other hand, [such acquired faith] does not precede [his studies], then he acquires it, if he has [infused] faith. And such a habit is not in someone who lacks faith. Beyond this habit and, in fact, for the most part, the student of theology—whether he have faith, be heretical, or lack faith—acquires many scientific habits that can be acquired in the other sciences.[46]

What is appearing on the horizon here, as a possibility, is the study of theology as an object of intellectual curiosity. Ockham does not endorse this possibility, but it becomes conceivable. It is an unintended consequence of Ockham's project of reaffirming the specificity of theology, of rejecting the universal validity of Aristotelian ideals of science, while at the same time applying rigorous logical analysis to the principles of faith—logical analysis that draws on the same Aristotelian heritage. Theology now is no longer a work of piety that requires the lived commitment of the theologian; but neither is it a science. Its status has become deeply ambiguous.

The Literary Structure of the Ordinatio

One of the paramount concerns of Peter Lombard's commentators in the twelfth and thirteenth centuries was to exploit the potential that the *Book of Sentences* had for the construction of a thoroughly system-

atic theology. Therefore, one of the main objectives of the prologues of that period was to derive the contents of the four books from a clearly articulated principle (such as the distinction between things and signs), or indeed from an appropriately chosen scriptural verse. Later, elaborate *divisiones textus*, inserted at strategic points of the work, ensured that the reader always knew where a particular discussion belonged in the over-all scheme of theological inquiry.

As we have already seen, no traditional prologues occur in the commentaries of Scotus or Ockham, nor are there any *divisiones textus*. The absence of the latter is an obvious consequence of the fact that Peter Lombard's own text has receded into the background as the "commentaries" have become an occasion for independent theological inquiry. However, the mutation of the prologue into a disquisition on theological method and epistemology, together with the disappearance of the textual divisions, also has to do with the fact that there no longer exists a systematic theology whose parts need to be held together by texts devoted to the structure of the field as a whole. Rather, in the fourteenth century theology fragments to the point that even major issues of Christian doctrine, such as the Incarnation and Christology, can come to be treated in passing, neglected in favor of questions that were of greater contemporary concern, such as the logical problem of future contingents.[47] Such is the case of Ockham's *Ordinatio*, which practices a very selective method of commenting on the themes addressed in the *Sentences*.

As far as the structure of individual questions within the *Ordinatio* is concerned, the Venerable Inceptor uses the same format that we already encountered in Scotus; that is to say, he adapts the thirteenth-century structure of argumentation to make room for detailed discussion of the philosophical and theological positions that have developed since. One could speak of a "position-centered approach" in the *Sentences* commentaries of the fourteenth century.[48] Question 7 of the prologue to the *Ordinatio*, which treats the scientific status of theology as actually accessible to us (not as hypothetically possible, assuming divine action *de potentia absoluta*), provides a representative example:

> Question: Is the theology that can be obtained by theologians upon the basis of the common law a science properly speaking?
> Arguments pro (182, 6–21)

Arguments con (184, 1–3)

Digression: three positions supporting the scientific status of theology

> Aquinas and Richard of Middleton (184, 7–185, 13)[49]
>
> A position cited by Scotus (185, 14–187, 2)
>
> Henry of Ghent (187, 3–14)

Refutation of these positions in general (187, 16–189, 15)

Arguments against each of the three positions

> Response to the first view (189, 17–190, 12)
>
> Response to the second view (190, 13–191, 3)
>
> Response to the third view (191, 4–192, 20)

Brief digression: two positions that oppose the scientific status of theology

> Position of the philosophers (192, 22–193, 4)
>
> Position of William of Ware (193, 5–9)

Ockham's solution: agreement with the latter two positions (193, 11–15)

> First part of the solution (on the theologian's habits in general; 194, 1–12)
>
> Second part of the solution (specific habits acquired by the theologian)
>
> > Peter Auriol's opinion (194, 14–195, 21)
> >
> > Refutation of Peter Auriol's opinion (195, 23–196, 18)
> >
> > Ockham's own opinion (196, 20–199, 7)

Return to the three positions favoring the scientific status of theology

> Response to the first view (199, 9–201, 3)
>
> Response to the second view (201, 4–205, 11)
>
> Response to the third view (205, 12–23)

Response to the initial arguments pro (206, 2–22)

The thoroughness of Ockham's discussion is quite impressive: he addresses the arguments of those who defend the status of theology as an Aristotelian science not once, but twice. The second series of responses is more nuanced than the first, profiting from the insights gained in the solution. The literary form of Ockham's questions can still be analyzed in terms of the dialectical format with which we are familiar from the

commentators of the mid-thirteenth century. We are still dealing with a dialectical structure of argument and counterargument; at the very end of each question, Ockham still returns to the initial arguments; and the author's solution is still located at the heart of the text. The central portion of the question, however, has ballooned, as a result of what I have called "digressions"—a term that is not completely appropriate, since these "digressions" are integral to Ockham's reasoning. The digressions, or mini-treatises within the larger question, examine positions that are more complicated than the simple arguments and counterarguments offered at the beginning and end of the question; these small treatises are themselves structured dialectically.

While Ockham composed his *Ordinatio* with contemporary positions in mind, situating himself constantly over against them, he still refrained from identifying by name the authors whose positions he repudiated, modified, or embraced. The Venerable Inceptor must have felt bound to the time-honored convention of naming only authorities of the distant past. The effect this convention produced was precisely to keep the debate centered on the issues and arguments under consideration. Between 1280 and 1320, however, we see the emergence of clearly defined schools—such as Thomism and Scotism, favored by the Dominicans and Franciscans, respectively—each with its own system of thought, and with adherents eager to defend it against other schools. A trend toward the identification of contemporary authors flowed naturally from this development. It seems to have started in the 1310s.[50] By the time of Gregory of Rimini, a couple of decades later, it would be customary to identify one's contemporary sources.

Charity and God's Absolute Power

We already know that even Peter Lombard's earliest commentators generally agreed that the Master's doctrine concerning charity was one of several points on which his teaching was not to be considered authoritative. Bonaventure codified this consensus, which remained intact until Scotus challenged it, through a somewhat unlikely reinterpretation of the Lombard's meaning. Ockham, too, believes that the Master's teaching can be saved. His strategy in so arguing, however, differs from that of his subtle predecessor. In fact, in his discussion of distinction 17,

Ockham invokes the key distinction between *potentia absoluta* and *potentia ordinata*.

Ockham's argument is simple and, once one has grasped the principles of his thought, predictable. He reminds his reader that the word "charity," *caritas*, is derived from *carus*, "dear." Charity, then, is the quality that makes us dear to God, rendering our acts meritorious. But what is it that makes us dear to God? Is there any act by which we could force God to save us? Of course, the answer is no. Therefore, in a sense charity, as dearness-to-God, is nothing but the divine will itself: "charity itself is the gratuitous will of God that accepts someone as being worthy of eternal life."[51] This, the Venerable Inceptor suggests, is what Peter Lombard must have had in mind when he identified charity with the Holy Spirit.

On the other hand, "in fact"—*de facto*—a person is not dear to God and capable of acting meritoriously in his eyes unless he or she possesses a created habit of charity.[52] This is the case simply "because God ordained it to be so,"[53] not because he would not be able to act otherwise. Therefore, considering the question from the point of view of *potentia ordinata*, Ockham aligns himself with the "authorities of the Saints," that is to say, with the consensus of the tradition.[54]

Gregory of Rimini

The *Sentences* commentary of Gregory of Rimini (ca. 1300–58) presents an excellent example of the state of the genre in the middle of the fourteenth century. Gregory was neither a Dominican nor a Franciscan, but rather an Austin Friar, which may have afforded him a certain independence vis-à-vis prevailing currents of thought. Moreover, although he was heavily influenced by the Oxford style of theologizing, Gregory's own education was continental, and his teaching career culminated in Paris. There, he commented on the *Sentences* in 1343–44, after several years of preparation, including various appointments as lecturer at Augustinian study houses in Italy, during which he had to teach Peter Lombard's work.[55] Since Gregory published only the first two books of his commentary, it is puzzling that these first two books in fact contain references to his lectures on Books III and IV; in distinction 3 of Book I, for example, he remarks that a particular point "will perhaps be seen

in the third book."[56] Other references sound less tentative; thus, still in the same distinction we are informed that the question of universals "will become clear in the third book."[57] Pascale Bermon suggested that, by the fourteenth century, it had become customary at the University of Paris to explain only Books I and II of the *Sentences*.[58] If this were so, however, why would any Parisian theologian refer his audience to his commentary upon a later book? Venício Marcolino submitted a more convincing hypothesis, which challenges any account that is exclusively based upon an author's published and circulated works.

First of all, Gregory must have "read" the entirety of the *Sentences* several times when lecturing at the Augustinian study houses of Bologna, Padua, and Perugia. It is reasonable to assume that he had notes for these lectures, notes possibly going as far back as his Parisian years of undergraduate study, in 1323–29. For, as Marcolino emphasizes, the statutes of the University of Paris required each student to bring a copy of the *Book of Sentences* along to the lectures upon this work. These copies were frequently prepared with broad margins in which students could take notes.[59] In other words, when lecturing upon a particular book or distinction, a fourteenth-century commentator upon the *Sentences* would most likely have relied upon material going back to his student days; he therefore had the whole text before him and could use it for references. Secondly, Marcolino shows that the university statutes which were in force at the time of Gregory of Rimini unequivocally required the *baccalaureus Sententiarum* to cover the entire work. This was normally done in two years, although the mendicant orders—and, since 1340, the Austin Friars as well—were allowed to discharge the task in only one year. This rule was extended to the entire university around 1350.[60] In any case, on Marcolino's account Gregory explained all four books of the *Sentences* in 1343–44, and then proceeded to prepare his lectures for publication. Book II was circulated in 1346, Book I probably somewhat earlier.[61] Gregory may have had the intention to rework Books III and IV for publication as well, but if such plans existed, they were not executed.

Marcolino's theses are compelling. At the same time, they complicate our picture of the fourteenth-century reception of the *Book of Sentences* considerably. While the published works of the commentators of this period evidence an increasing movement away from the original text, a much closer reading of the work may have prevailed at the level of

undergraduate instruction. The fourteenth-century commentators, however, no longer saw a need to publish their basic explanations of the *Sentences*, which, intended as they were for beginners, did not contribute significant insights to the advanced theological debates of the day.

Literary Features of Gregory's Lectura *upon the* Sentences

Like the *Sentences* commentaries of Scotus and Ockham, Gregory of Rimini's *Lectura*—or "reading," named thus after the title given to the work in a number of manuscripts—opens immediately with technical questions concerning the epistemological status of theological inquiry. As in the case of his Franciscan predecessors, these questions are formally tied to Peter Lombard's prologue: "About the prologue of the *Books of Sentences*, I ask...."[62] Gregory formulates five such questions:

1. Is properly scientific knowledge of the theological object acquired through theological discourse?[63]

2. Is it possible to have science of such an object, or [merely] opinion?[64]

3. Is the possession (*habitus*) of all the theological conclusions one in number?[65]

4. Is God, as God, the subject in our theology?[66]

5. Is theology speculative or practical?[67]

These questions obviously did not come out of thin air. Some, such as the question about the theoretical or practical character of the theological enterprise, remount as far as the twelfth century, when the Pseudo-Poitiers gloss first posited an explicit distinction between dogmatic and moral theology. Others, however, are of less distant origin: for example, the preoccupation with the scientific status of theology is more recent, as is the notion of "our theology" (*theologia nostra*). The latter reflects Ockham's distinction between theology as hypothetically possible *de potentia absoluta* and "our" theology as actually accessible *de potentia ordinata*.

Gregory breaks each question further up into articles. He does this in such a way that the articles come to be situated between the opening arguments pro and con, on one side, and the response to the initial arguments on the other. As a consequence, this old thirteenth-century structure is stretched to the limits of its viability. In the case of the first question, for example, fifty-five pages (in the modern critical edition) separate the initial arguments from the response they finally receive. It would seem that the center of gravity of the question no longer lies in the examination of these arguments, drawn without exception from ancient, patristic, and Islamic authorities (such as Aristotle, Augustine, or Avicenna), but rather in the critical assessment of contemporary positions (see Figure 10).

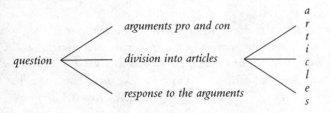

Figure 10:
Questions and articles in Gregory of Rimini's *Lectura*

Within each article, the literary structure favors detailed examination and comparison of opposing positions. The author's own solution occupies the central place; it appears in a series of "conclusions" that are accompanied by groups of supporting arguments. The following list of headings reflects the composition of article 1 of the first question:

Article 1: What, generally, is the object of a science?
Ockham's position
Three conclusions against Ockham
    Arguments for the first conclusion
    Arguments for the second conclusion
    Arguments for the third conclusion
Objections against the conclusions
Response to the objections
Response to Ockham's position as initially formulated

We can see that the movement from the argument-centered to the position-centered composition of the *Sentences* commentaries has reached a certain completion. The historical connection between the "new English essay-style"[68] that Gregory inherited from Scotus and Ockham, and the literary form of the thirteenth century is recognizable only to the well-trained eye; to all intents and purposes, we are dealing with a new literary form. Rather than moving by means of a rapid five-step (question, arguments for one side, arguments for the opposite position, solution, response to the arguments), it develops ideas by weighing up complex positions in extended essays.

As for Gregory's coverage of Peter Lombard's distinctions, his practice is very much in line with that of other fourteenth-century authors: he concentrates upon those distinctions that are of particular interest to him and his audience, treating others in passing. Thus, for example, he groups distinctions 14 to 16 of Book I together, asking but one question on their subject matter. To the famous distinction 17, by contrast, he devotes six questions, which he examines in over 260 pages.[69] Gregory's entire commentary, of course, circulated as a kind of "rump" theology, given the absence of Books III and IV. We may conclude that Gregory of Rimini's work continues the tendencies toward a theology that is highly speculative and rational but no longer systematic—certainly an interesting development, given the emphasis that the systematic character of theology received in the twelfth and thirteenth centuries.

Yet there are also significant new elements in Gregory's approach. I already hinted at the fact that he identifies all his contemporary sources. In addition, however, and more unusually, he displays firsthand knowledge of his older sources, in particular Augustine. Indeed, Father Damasus Trapp called Gregory "one of the best or the very best Augustine scholar of the Middle Ages."[70] Not content to repeat hackneyed quotations culled second-hand from the contemporary literature, Gregory is keen to provide a more positive foundation in the tradition for his highly speculative theology. His references are extremely precise: "According to Hugh [of St. Victor], *On the Sacraments*, Book I, part 10, chapter 2, faith is superior to opinion ..."; "I argue from the sense intended by Augustine, *Against the Letter of the Foundation*, chapter 9, who says ..."; "Augustine, in Book XIV of *On the Trinity*, chapter 1, says that...."[71] This emphasis on the sources of his theology is not a mere for-

mality, but enables Gregory to evaluate contemporary points of view in light of the tradition; it counterbalances the structural tendencies of his *Sentences* commentary, which favor more recent debates. Gregory's doctrine on grace in distinctions 26 to 29 of Book II, for instance, is firmly rooted in a rereading of Augustine.[72] The dynamics at work here are not unlike trends that we discovered earlier on in the thirteenth century: at the same time when authors such as Thomas Aquinas transformed theology from *sacra pagina* into a more abstract "science," a desire arose to build this *scientia* in close contact with the sources—hence the interest in elaborate tables and indices.

Whereas exact references to older authorities are incorporated into the main text of Gregory's *Lectura*, the quotations from more recent scholars are identified only in the margins; the main text continues the custom of referring to them rather vaguely, using phrases such as "one doctor" (*unus doctor*) or "one opinion" (*una opinio*).[73] Nevertheless, the fact that the manuscripts and early printings of Gregory's work all contain the marginalia very strongly suggests that they do not represent later additions, but were rather prepared under Gregory's own supervision.[74] To give an example, in article 1 of question 1 on the prologue (the structure of which we summarized above), the main text does not refer to Ockham by name in discussing his conception of the object of scientific inquiry. In the margin, however, the statement of Ockham's position, with the arguments supporting it, is identified as *Ocham q 9 prologi et in pluribus aliis locis*, "Ockham, in question 9 of the prologue and in many other places."[75] The response to Ockham's position is accompanied by the following marginal remark: *Ad rationes pro opinione Ocham*, "[response] to the reasons for Ockham's opinion."[76]

Indeed, the margins of Gregory's *Lectura* are full not only of notes that identify the author's sources, but also of structuring elements. Thus, the five arguments adduced in favor of Ockham's position in question 1, article 1 are counted marginally: p^m, 2^m, 3^m, 4^m, 5^m—first, second, third, fourth, fifth. Then the margin draws attention to the first conclusion against Ockham: *prima conclusio*. This conclusion, in turn, comes in two parts: p^m, 2^m. Then, as we move on to the second conclusion, the margin announces: *secunda conclusio*. And so on and so forth. The (excellent) critical edition has retained only the most important of these structuring elements; to get a more complete idea of the layout of the medieval text,

enūtiatiõe dicimus verā vel falsam ee: z sic pz afis: p̃ia
pbaf: qz in q̃ nõ eet ipse assensus: inutil z supflue ipsa po
neret in intellectu denfante:cū in quol3 tali intellectu sit
assensus q est enūtiatio idipsu3 sigñas q̃ sigñat z̃: z ipa
q̃ ad nihil valeat ad q̃ nõ sufficiat assensus. ꝰScda3 z̃-
nes pbo sic. q̃ mentalis demfatiõis elicita ex habituali
scia est actualis notitia eius q̃ habitualr scimus p̃sciam
ex q̃ p̃cedit. g̃ q̃ b̃z e actus cognoscẽdi sic ee: sicut sigñat
per ipsam:z vlterius. g̃ q̃l3 demfatiõis q̃ est actus cogno
scẽdi sic ee:sicut ipsa sigñat. Prima p̃ia pz: qm̃ per habi
tualē sciam scimus sic ee. v̄. g̃. per geometricu3 habitū: q̃
anguli trianguli valẽt duos r̃ectos. Scda p̃ia clara est:
añs pbo: qz q̃ b̃z nõ e aliud q̃ q̃dãbū: seu locutio q̃dã
mẽtalis q̃ dicim9 sic ee: sicut per habitualē sciam novim9:
s3 talis locutio est notitia ei9: q̃ scimus: sicut pz p̃ Aug.
is. de tri. vbi post q̃ pbauit q̃dã cogitatiões ee cõdis locutiões: subiūgit q̃ tales locutiões si ex scia oziantur sūt
quedã visiões seu notitie: vñ ait. Nec tñ qz dicimus locu
tiones cordis ee cogitationes:iõ nõ sunt et visiões exorte
de notitie de visionib9 qñ ve sunt:fozis. n. cū p corp9 hec
siūt:aliud e locutio aliud visio:intus aūt cum cogitamus
verũq̃ vñu est:ita audivio t visio.i. actualis notitia: z infra.
Necesse e ingt:cū verũ loquimur: i. q̃ scim9 loqmur: ec ipa
sapia quã memozia tenemus:nascat vbū: q̃ eiusmodi sit
oino:cuiusmodi est illa scia de q̃ nascitur. z in fine.i3.cap.
tūc ingt est vbū simillimū rei note de q̃ gignitur z imago
eius:qn de visione scie visio cogitatiõis exorit q̃ est vbū
lingue nullius. Ex qbus habet clare q̃ vbū z locutio in-
teriorez scia bitualis pcedens e visio seu notitia actualis
eius rei de q̃ habem9 sciã:eiq̃ scie a q̃ pcedit simillima.

cap.io.
B

cap.i2.

i3.d.tri.
cap p z
i2.

Nec pot dici q̃ Aug. sumat vbū vel locutionez p notitia
que e simplex intelligẽtia tm̃: qnimo:sic appet ibi.manife
ste loqui de cogitatiõib9 z locutiõibus enuciatiuis. ꝰ2°
cõtigit b̃e demfatioñ mẽtalē absq̃ vlla alia p̃pone que
sit notitia. g̃ q̃ metalis demfatiõis e notitia pz p̃ia: qm̃ nõ
cõtingit demfatiõn b̃ri sine z̃ne:añs pbaf: qm̃ si q̃s vbi
gra.cognoscat q̃ si aliq̃ sunt eidē eqlia iter se sunt eqlia:z

L

cogscat simul cū b̃ q̃ a.z.b.sunt eidem
v̄.g.c. eqlia ipse vn̄q̃ cogscit q̃ a.z.b.
sunt inter se eqlia: s3 demfatione pse
cta:nec alia p̃p̃ illud sciedū e necia hui9:
sed totū hoc e ipol9 absq̃ vlla p̃positio
ne alia ab istis notitijs: z q̃l3 eaq̃: sicut
experiẽtia docet in eo maxie q̃ ex p̃pria
inuẽtiõe z non aliena doctrina ad hāc
notitiã deuenerit. ꝰ3° p̃misse mẽtalis

t.

b.

a.

3ᵐ

demfatiõis sunt notitie qb9 cognoscit sic ee: sicut p̃ ipsas
sigñaf. g̃ z̃ q̃ metalis demfatiõis eiusdē roñis qua cogno
scit sic ee:sicut ipsa sigñat. p̃ia pz: qm̃ nõ e maioz necitas
ponẽdi z̃ne z notitia sibi cõforme obtiue a se distincta: q̃
ponẽdi p̃misas z notitias sibi cõformes ab eis distictas:
nec vtilitas aliq̃ et appet: cū ad babedū talē z̃ notitia suffi
ciant notitie p̃missaru.i.que sunt p̃misse:añs pbaf, z gfa
exẽpli sumo istā minoze demfatioñis assumpte in p̃cedẽti
roñe.v.3.a.z.b. sunt equalia. c.sint a.z.b.due linee ducte a
cẽtris duo9 circulo9 se secātiū ad pūctū sectiõis.que cẽ
tra sint extremitates linee.c. iuxta doctrina3 p̃me Eucli
dis.cõstat aūt q̃ ad cognoscēdū q̃ a.z.b. sunt equalia ipsi
c.sufficit cognoscere q̃ si linee aliq̃ trahunt a cētro cir
culi ad ei9 circuferẽtia:/sunt equales:z q̃ linea a.z.c.tra
bunt a cētro vnius circuli ad eius circuferẽtia:z sit̃ li
nea b.z linea.c.z totū B pot intuitiue cognosci absq̃ for
matione alterius p̃ponis vocalis vel metalis distincte ab
istis notitijs z q̃l3 earū: immo certe si aliq̃ alia forma
ret inutilis z superuacue fieret. z B dico in eo q̃ metalr in
seipso demfat. z idē est de maiore: z q̃buslibet p̃nijs no
tirijs cõplexis: qm̃ pter ipsas nulle alie propositiones vel

D

notitie sūt necessarie.
ꝰ4° B pbaf ex itẽ
tiõe p̃hi p̃ posterio
rū dicetis. q̃ demfa
tio e syllus apodecti
cõ.i. vt ipsemet expo
nit: s3 q̃e in b̃ndo ip
sum scim9: B aūt nõ
eet verūnisi vt ipsa
demostratio vel aliã
pars eius eet scia formalr:sicut nec in babẽdo aliquẽ co
loze essemus albi:nisi ille color eet albedo formalr. g̃ z̃.
ꝰ3° z̃ q̃ pz ex p̃cedētib9:qm̃ si eadē z̃ est assensus.z cogni
tio de sic ee:sic ipsa sigñat:nõ trib9 actib9 distictis:s3 vno
eodēq̃ q̃s enūtiat:cogscit: z creditseu assentit q̃ sic eet:ē
sigñat ipa z̃. B affirmat:qm̃ nulla expẽtia vel rõ:quātū
appet:cogit ad ponẽdū illā actuū multitudinẽ:nec et aliq̃
aucitas sacra:quapp rõnabili9 illa m̃ltitudo negat q̃ po
nit. ꝰPro sol̃one rõnū p̃mitto q̃ sic pz p̃ Aug.is.de tri.
z p̃ Ansel.in moñ.ac et p̃ expẽtia volẽti diligeter aduer
te:duplex est gen9 enūtiationū metaliū. Q̃dã.n.est earū
que sunt vocaliū enūtiationū imagines z vel similitudines
ab exterio1b9 vocib9 in aiaz deriuate:vel ip̃sa z̃ ficte:iux
modū q̃ i̅fra dis.3.declarabit de abstractiõe z fictiõe in aia
sp̃eu vel cõceptuū.z iste nõ sūt eiusdē rõnis in oib9 boi
b9.S3 alie sunt in greco:alie in latino:et idē3 sigñantes:
sicut alie sunt enūtiatiõesvocales q̃s pfert exteri9 grecus
ab bis q̃s idē sigñantes pfert latin9.bas in se pot aduer
tere:q̃s:cū taces ore:loquif corde:formādo vba filia b̃3
que si ore loquerem9 pferret exterius. Q̃dã vo genus est
enūtiationū mentaliū q̃ nullax sunt similitudines vocū:nec
s̃m illax diuersitate in boib9 b̃ntib9 diuersificar:sed eadē
sunt s̃m spēm apud oēs idipm nalr sigñantes:q̃ voca
les eis subordinate ad sigñandū ad placitu:z per institu
tiõe sigñant:z ille sūt illa vba que nullius lingue sunt:z
vacalia verba exterius soñatē:z metalia primo mõ dicta
pcedunt s̃m sniam Aug.Doc aūt genus 2ᵐ enūtiationuz
metaliū subdiuidif:qm̃ quedã imediate ex rõnis
notitijs incõplexis:tanq̃ ex partialib9 causis:vel ex alijs
complexis vel incõplexis:ex illis mediate vel imediate
causatis:em ex babiribus ex talibus notitijs cõplexis de
relictis cañr:vel fo1sitan etiã quedã nõ ex aliqbus icõple
xis notitijs cañr:sed sunt simpliciter prime venientes in
mẽte naliter:de quibus nescimus quando in nobis eri
stunt:aur vnde vel quomodo s̃m Lõm:in.3° de aia.h̃moi
sunt enūtiationes ille:quas q̃s absq̃ g̃latione exteriori
enūtiationū vocaliū:z interiori et formatiõe illis similiū
format.dū aliq̃ veritatē mẽte demfat:b̃ et essent q̃scū
q̃ formaret q̃ nalr surdus eet:aut nulla oino loquela lin
gue didicisset:dū aliq̃ veritatē mẽte demfarer. Quedam
vo sunt q̃ nõ ex talib9 p̃mis notitijs rex aliq̃ p̃dictous
modox cañr:cuiusmodi sunt enūtiatiões qb9 q̃s enūtiat
mẽte z iudicat sic vel sic ee:aut nõ ee:nõ cognoscēs:tñ in
tuitiue aut alia notitia p̃ vel ex intuitiua deriuata quesic
sit vel nõ sit:sicut enūtiat in mẽte q̃s dum credit vel opi
nat.Iste maneries p̃ponū metaliū sic se habent q̃ p̃po
nes p̃mi generis sic sunt enūtiatiões q̃ nõ sūt notitie fo
malr:neq̃ assensus:nõ plus q̃ enūtiatiõesvocales qb9
sunt sit̃es. Secūdi aūt generis p̃pones z enūtiatiões sūt
z notitie z assensus. Tertij aūt generis p̃pones z enūtia
tiões q̃dem sunt z assensus: q̃ b̃ notitie. Et bis aūt seq̃
tur q̃ dissensio nõ est aliq̃s act9 intellect9 a q̃libet assensu
distinct9:qnimo qliber est assensus q̃dã:q̃ pbaf,qm̃ cuz
assensus metalis sit enūtiatio: cū enūtiatio sui enūtiatio si
bi opposita:que erit et assensus sui sigñificati:q̃ est op
positū sigñato relique opposite. vñ sicut assensus quo q̃s
assentit seu credit diametrū esse symetrum:nõ est aliud q̃

p̃ sol̃o
ne nota
cap.j. z
xj.c. io.

F

B

Lõ.36.

D

it is useful to refer to one of the Renaissance printings (see Figure 11).

The marginalia are not the only consultation aid that accompanies the work from its earliest manuscripts onward right into the Renaissance editions. Each book is followed by a simple table of contents (*tituli quaestionum*) and by an alphabetical table (*tabula*); the latter is described as "a table, in alphabetical order, that gathers together, so that they can be found, all the notable contents in this first [book]."[77] If we look up a concept—"theology," say—in our *tabula*, we are offered a series of brief statements extracted from the *Lectura*. The first entry (in a series of entries) on *theologia, theologicus*, for instance, reads:

> That theological discourse proceeds from probable statements to conclusions that are the object of faith. Opinion: qu. 1 of the prologue, art. 2, at the beginning.[78]

When we look up the reference, we find that the statement reflects a position defended by Peter Auriol, a position, however, that Gregory rejects—hence the table's warning: "opinion"!

The tables are prefaced with detailed practical instructions for the user, who is urged to prepare his copy of the *Lectura* for efficient consultation, thus completing the work of the scribes. Some structural features of the work that could pose difficulties are briefly explained as well. In addition, the tables offer a methodological warning: they need to be employed with care, lest their necessary brevity and abridged character cause the user to misunderstand the author's genuine teaching. Here is the preface to the alphabetical table of the first book:

> In order that what is sought from this table may be found easily, the researcher should make sure to inscribe clearly in the margins of his book the principal arguments of a question, the articles, conclusions, and corollaries, the opinions of others and their motives, the doubts, and the principal objections to the conclusions or to a question. He should be aware, too, that sometimes a single question is asked of several distinctions together (such as, for example, of the nineteenth and twentieth), and in this case in the table only the first distinction is named (namely, the nineteenth). Also, when there is a single question concerning a single distinction, it is called

Figure 11: Marginal structuring elements and geometrical illustrations in Gregory of Rimini's *Lectura*

the "first" in the table—but improperly so. And it should be noted that the conclusions must be marked in the margin [at the place] where they are proven, since frequently all the conclusions are first stated together, then proven severally. Where the proof occurs, therefore, it should be marked "conclusion." Should any teaching (*sententia*) in the table be obscure, so that from the sound of its letter something could be understood that is not consonant with the truth, it should be looked up in the book. This is because, for the sake of brevity, the conclusions and other [elements] could not always be recorded in the table as they are set forth in the book; in some cases this is perhaps due to a mistake of the tabulator, who changed the meaning where he believed he was only changing the letter.[79]

The mention of a tabulator, who may inadvertently have misrepresented some of Gregory's positions, indicates that authorship of the tables should not be attributed to Gregory of Rimini himself. On the other hand, the *Lectura* appears to have been accompanied by these tables from the moment of its first publication. For the same reasons, therefore, for which it makes sense to assume that Gregory himself supervised the preparation of the marginal apparatus for his *Sentences* commentary, it is reasonable to attribute ultimate responsibility for the tables to him.[80] Gregory's *Lectura*, then, was designed from the very start as a powerful theological research tool, coming complete with exact references to traditional authorities as well as contemporary positions; with an alphabetical index to the principal statements contained in the work; with a sophisticated marginal apparatus throwing into relief the structure of the text down to the level of individual arguments; and with a "how-to" guide instructing the user on how to render his copy fit for the most efficient use and avoid basic methodological mistakes in consulting the work.

Theology as Knowledge of Significates

What is the subject matter of theology? For Peter Lombard, who of course spoke of *sacra pagina* rather than theology, the answer came in the form of the Augustinian distinction between things and signs; *Filia Magistri* in the same context distinguished between the Creator and the

work of the Creator; and the Pseudo-Poitiers gloss opted for the *credibilia* or objects of belief as the proper contents of theological inquiry. Later, in the thirteenth century, Bonaventure gave a more complex answer in assigning theology the threefold subject of God, Christ, and the objects of belief, while Thomas Aquinas used the definition "the divine being knowable through inspiration" to demarcate the field of inquiry of the "divine science." Let us now consider Gregory of Rimini's fourteenth-century position on this question.

Gregory's solution presupposes a distinction that he found in Ockham's *Ordinatio*. In discussing the problem of whether God, *qua* God, is the subject matter of theology, the Venerable Inceptor emphasized the difference between the object and the subject of a science: "the subject of a science," he explained, "is the subject of a conclusion, but the object of a science is that which is known and serves as the end of an act of understanding."[81] Ockham then went on to assert that God as God—put differently, God considered in himself—cannot possibly be the subject of "our" theology because God is knowable only mediately, through concepts; the notion of subject, however, suggests something "that serves as the immediate end of an act of understanding."[82] I can have an immediate grasp of my mother, but not of God. Yet the fact that God is not the subject of theology, in this precise terminological sense, does not preclude his serving as the object of (non-scientific) acts of understanding.

But what is the object of a science (or field of rational inquiry, such as theology)? Here Ockham and Gregory of Rimini part ways. According to the *Ordinatio*, "the object of a science is that which is known and serves as the end of an act of understanding"—and Ockham continues, "of such a nature, however, is the known conclusion itself."[83] Gregory's rejection of this thesis is unambiguous:

This opinion does not appear true to me, which is why I set forth three conclusions against it and in support of the response to the present article. The first is that the conclusion of a demonstration is not the object of a science acquired by demonstration. The second is that the extra-mental thing isn't either. [The] third [is] that the entire significate of the conclusion is the object of a science. From this, it is clear that the entire significate of a theo-

logical conclusion is the object of a theology acquired by means of theological discourse; and similarly, the object of a theology that is concerned with the theological principle is the entire significate of such a principle.[84]

According to Ockham, objective knowledge is knowledge of the conclusion of a demonstration, that is to say, it is knowledge of a proposition. This position amounts to nominalism, according to which universal concepts (which are the necessary building-blocks of scientific knowledge) exist only in the mind. To be sure, Gregory follows Ockham in rejecting the idea that the things themselves (*res extra*) can be the object of science. This is because he embraces Aristotle's conception of objective knowledge as being aimed at what is necessary and eternal—contingent, individual things are neither.[85] Rather, they are radically finite in their dependence upon God's free act of creation. Post-1277 thought refuses the Aristotelian hypothesis of universal essences existing within creation, since such essences would afford the created order a (semi-)autonomous rational ground immanent to it.[86]

Gregory's own position attempts to avoid the binary logic of the opposition realism/nominalism. In maintaining that it is the entire significate of a conclusion (*significatum totale conclusionis*) which is at the heart of objective knowledge, Gregory stresses two aspects of objectivity. On the one hand, the object of knowledge is not simply linguistic or conceptual, but is, rather, what the linguistic-conceptual order *signifies*. Objectivity thus remains mediately tied to reality: "science can be acquired precisely by means of non-reflexive acts that are aimed objectively at things outside the mind, where by 'things' the significates themselves are to be understood, whether they are signified by terms or by propositions."[87] In short, the object of knowledge is neither extra-mental reality nor a simple linguistic expression designating such a reality, but rather the reality itself *as designated*. The "Authentic Doctor"—as medieval thinkers liked to call Gregory of Rimini—seems to be hinting here at the irreducibility of the symbolic in the constitution of human knowledge.[88]

On the other hand, Gregory's claim according to which objective knowledge involves the *total* significate of a conclusion points to the need for a holistic understanding of reality. Scientific knowledge (or quasi-scientific knowledge, as theology is not a science properly speak-

ing) does not aim simply at a particular element of reality, such as God or the human being, but rather at a structured state of affairs. As Gregory explains, the proposition "a man is white" is not true because there is a man and there is whiteness but because a man is white, that is to say, because the state of affairs of a-man-being-white (*hominem esse album*) obtains.[89]

Gregory of Rimini's theory of the object of scientific knowledge has attracted an unusual amount of scholarly attention.[90] On the medievalist side, Gedeon Gál has been able to show that the Authentic Doctor borrowed the theory from the *Sentences* commentary of Adam Wodeham.[91] More spectacularly perhaps, in 1936 Hubert Élie offered a pioneering interpretation in light of contemporary philosophies of language, especially the theories of Alexius Meinong and Bertrand Russell.[92] The nominalist tendencies of fourteenth-century thought have made this period of medieval intellectual history generally attractive to analytic philosophy, due to the conviction of the latter that linguistic analysis is the only possible path to knowledge, since the "things themselves" are accessible to us only in and through language.

Gregory's attenuated nominalism epitomizes the development of theology in the first half of the fourteenth century. Finally, we witness the culmination of a movement that had been afoot for two centuries—I mean the slow shift, adumbrated already in the Pseudo-Poitiers gloss, from signs as objects of theological inquiry to signifiers taking on that role. Several factors contributed to this development: at first, simple pedagogical needs and impulses, then the rediscovery of the Aristotelian conception of science, and finally—quite ironically—the negative reaction to that conception. The result is a theological system that is not free from internal tensions. It is not scientific in the strict Aristotelian sense, yet it does not hesitate to adopt the most rigorous logical procedures. "Geometry," it has been observed, "becomes an ideal for theology."[93] In the case of Gregory of Rimini's *Lectura*, geometrical drawings occasionally illustrate his explanations of methods of reasoning (see Figure 11). Yet theology is unabashedly based upon scriptural, not philosophical, principles: "properly theological discourse is composed of statements or propositions that are contained in Sacred Scripture, or of [statements] that are derived from the latter or at least from others that are of the same kind."[94] But given the nature of theological discourse as an analysis

of signifiers—which acquire their meaning from the linguistic context, unlike signs, which are inseparable from the "things" they stand for—it can be practiced even by non-believers. Just like Ockham, Gregory of Rimini envisions this possibility reluctantly, but explicitly: as a method of reasoning, "theology can be acquired not only by the faithful but also by someone lacking faith, as is sufficiently clear."[95]

Essentially, between the twelfth century and the fourteenth, a thick layer of objectivity inserted itself between the sacred page and its reader. This mediating layer consists of all the methodical procedures that we have discovered in the two centuries under consideration, from simple study aids such as abbreviations to Ockham's sophisticated theological distinction between the subject and the object of science. In the twelfth century, the text of Scripture still retained some of the functions of a saturated phenomenon, drawing the reader into its circle and forcing him to think in terms of the language of the prophets and of the Gospels. When theology becomes a science, in the thirteenth century, it leaves Scripture behind, the contents of which it translates and absorbs into conceptual discourse. Once theology has in this manner left the sacred page, in the margins of which it originated, it cannot return. It is now the theologian who constitutes the text of theology. The thinkers of the fourteenth century, who find this consequence abhorrent, attempt to limit the purview of methodical inquiry through ingenious distinctions, such as the distinctions between *potentia absoluta* and *potentia ordinata* and between the subject and object of theology. These distinctions succeed in keeping God *qua* God outside the field of objectivity, but only at the price of rendering this field itself all the more rigidly methodical. There is now a split between methodically constituted objectivity and God, in himself, who has become utterly inaccessible (except by religious faith).

★ ★ ★

Not surprisingly perhaps, the second half of the fourteenth century was a period of decline in the reception of the *Book of Sentences*. This decline affected English theology in particular. William J. Courtenay pointed out that the "best-known theologians from the last part of the century ... left no *Sentences* commentaries and no scholastic work for the other traditional genre[s]."[96] A sense of skepticism, followed by disgust,

pervaded the English schools as theology increasingly separated itself from biblical and devotional interests. It became a kind of game without consequences, played in a realm of autonomous signifiers. The theological literature that has survived from the second half of the fourteenth century speaks eloquently to these trends. Father Damasus Trapp discovered a short *Sentences* commentary that is the work of an anonymous bachelor who read the *Sentences* at Oxford around 1384.[97] The approach that the young bachelor employed in commenting upon Peter Lombard's work is full of "linguistic casuistry ... the sensationalism of a terminology calculated to dazzle, to surprise, to make a point, a point indeed so thin as to break off."[98] In one context, for instance, our bachelor offers a conclusion according to which "Christ is [present] in the sacrament of the Eucharist not differently than in ordinary bread, in wood, or in a stone."[99] This statement is not heretical in intention, appearances notwithstanding. What the author means is that the "total Christ" (*totus Christus*) is present in the consecrated bread and wine, not through the power of the sacrament itself, but only concomitantly (in the sense that the presence of the Body and Blood entails the presence of the whole person of Christ). This is Catholic doctrine. Since, he further argues, the total Christ is also not contained in wood or in a stone, the presence of Christ in the Eucharist is no different from his presence in such profane substances. This reasoning is, of course, highly sophistical:

> Through the power of the sacrament, the total Christ is not present in the Eucharist.
> The total Christ is not present in ordinary bread, in wood, or in a stone.
> Therefore, Christ is present in the Eucharist not differently than in ordinary bread, in wood, or in a stone.

The stated purpose of such exercises was to train the minds of young theologians; the consequence, however, was to fuel deep skepticism. In the 1380s, a Carmelite by the name of Stephen Patrington studied at the University of Oxford. We know of him because of his distinguished later career: elected prior provincial of the English Carmelites in 1399, he was close to the royal family, serving as confessor to King Henry V, and played a notable role in the controversy with the Wycliffites. In 1415, he

was named bishop of St. David's in Wales. A year later, he was transferred back to England, where he occupied the see of Chichester. He died in 1417.[100] The notebook from his days as a student at Oxford has survived in three copies, no doubt due to the author's prominence. It is composed in a question-and-answer format, containing entries on over 500 different topics.[101] Many of the questions are treated perfunctorily, but the very first is answered at considerable length. Its title is symptomatic of the tone of the entire work: "That a wayfarer cannot by any act be certain of the existence of a thing distinct from himself in place and subject."[102] This sounds like Descartes, who two centuries later founded his entire philosophy on doubts concerning the existence of the external world. It is no wonder that a theologian such as John Wyclif (ca. 1320–84) reacted violently to these trends. His outcry against the "doctors of signs" (one should perhaps say "signifiers" instead) is well known:

> And thus, universality or metaphysical truth does not depend upon the created intellect, since it precedes the latter, but rather depends upon the uncreated intellect. From eternal intellectual knowledge, this [uncreated intellect] produces everything as its effect. It is the ignorance of this sense [of universality] that made Ockham and many other doctors of signs (*multos alios doctores signorum*) turn away from the real universal, out of a weakness of understanding.[103]

The situation was less bleak on the Continent. Here, *Sentences* commentaries continued to be produced and published in the second half of the fourteenth century. Yet the character of the commentaries reflects a certain tiredness with the genre: they emphasize the first two books, generally become shorter, and are frequently copied directly from other authors.[104] Trapp dubbed the latter phenomenon *lectura secundum alium*, "reading according to another." The phrase itself appears to be a neologism not attested in the manuscripts, although a bachelor such as Simon of Cremona (an Austin Friar who lectured upon the *Sentences* at the Parisian study house of the Augustinians around 1365–66) speaks of reading the *Sentences* following a particular author, *secundum Hugolinum*—that is, Hugolinus of Orvieto.[105] In addition to being a *lectura secundum alium*, Simon's work follows a most interesting "mathematical pattern of subdivision: 3 × 3."[106] That is to say, throughout the commentary Simon religiously adheres to a format whereby each question falls into three

articles; these articles in turn correspond to three principal arguments at the beginning of the question.

One must not underestimate the potential for innovation that was inherent in the "readings according to another." Even if authors more and more often opted to base their *Sentences* commentaries upon the work of predecessors, what they chose to include and to exclude, the arrangement of the materials, etc., still left some room for originality. In studying the question on the Eucharist from the *Sentences* commentary of the Cistercian James of Eltville (who read Peter Lombard at the University of Paris in 1369–70), Bakker and Schabel were able to demonstrate that James's text is much more than a simple piece of "plagiarism." Rather, James weaves his argument together from a number of different authorities, chosen deliberately and strategically at crucial points of the discussion. These authorities include the Austin Friars John Hiltalingen and Thomas of Strasbourg, the Dominican Robert Holcot, and the Carmelite Osbert Pickingham.[107]

Marsilius of Inghen

As we have seen, after the radical innovations that theological discourse underwent between the twelfth century and the first half of the fourteenth, in the second half of the fourteenth century a certain disillusionment set in. By the end of the century, theologians who published *Sentences* commentaries were rare.[108] Rarer still were those who covered all of the four books and composed commentaries that could rival the monumental productions of the older generations, whose prologues alone often filled thick tomes. Marsilius of Inghen (ca. 1340–96) was such an exception. Yet his commentary on the *Sentences* clearly reflects the changed intellectual landscape.

Marsilius, a secular priest, was a product of the University of Paris, where he became master of arts in 1362. While teaching, he also served his alma mater in various high-ranking administrative functions, even as rector and delegate at the curia. From 1366, Marsilius pursued studies in theology concurrently with his other duties. Having endorsed the election of Pope Urban VI in 1378, he appears to have left Paris quietly when King Charles V called upon the university to support the antipope Clement VII at the start of the Great Schism. In 1386, we find Marsilius at Heidelberg, where Prince-Elector Ruprecht I appointed him master

of arts and founding rector of the new university. Continuing his theological studies, Marsilius read Peter Lombard's *Sentences* in the academic years 1392–94, before receiving his doctorate in 1396.[109]

Marsilius died before he was able to complete revising his *Sentences* commentary for publication, that is to say, before he was able to prepare an *ordinatio* for the entire text. This is why the manuscripts contain a few blank folios, and portions of blank folios, in places where the author did not have the opportunity to supply relevant material. The first printed edition on two occasions explicitly attributes the lack of a particular portion of text to Marsilius's death in 1396. This edition, published by Martin Flach, Jr., of Strasbourg in 1501, in many places presents a significantly better text than the manuscript tradition: obscure passages have been clarified, arguments expanded upon, and grammatical peculiarities in Marsilius's late medieval Latin have been corrected in light of the rules of classical Latinity.[110] It is not unlikely that the printer had at his disposal a more recent, more thoroughly revised version of Marisilius's work than the one that the known manuscripts have transmitted to us. Yet it is difficult, if not impossible, to prove such a hypothesis and to distinguish authentic improvements from corrections that may be due to the printer or someone in his employ.[111]

Theology as scientia pietatis

Marsilius of Inghen belongs to the nominalist tradition. He takes it for granted that theology studies terms: "the subject of sacred theology must be a term standing for the Creator (*terminum supponentem pro Creatore*)."[112] Nevertheless, he renounces and denounces the nominalist excesses that had caused widespread disgust with the "doctors of signs." Keen to purge theology of perhaps well-meaning but nonetheless deeply irritating subtleties, he employs common sense in evaluating the soundness of doctrines. For instance, in discussing Gregory of Rimini's ingenious theory according to which the object of science is the total significate of a conclusion, Marsilius remarks:

> This mode concerning complex signifiables, [a mode] distinct from non-complex things, is subtle to the point of going beyond the imagination of common people, and especially mine, or perhaps it is introduced due to ignorance of logic.... For who is able

to conceive that "the fact of being God" [or "the fact of there being a God"] (*Deum esse*) is neither a substance nor an accident nor
these two together, and that it nonetheless exists?[113]

We may remember the opening lines from Peter Lombard's prologue
to the *Book of Sentences*: "Longing to cast something of our want and
poverty along with the little poor woman into the treasury of the Lord,
to scale the heights, we have presumed to undertake a work beyond our
powers, placing the trust for completion and the wages of the work upon
the Samaritan, who, having taken out two pence for the care of the half-
dead man, promised to repay all to the one spending over and above
that." During the two and a half centuries separating the *Book of Sentences*
from Marsilius's commentary, such a tone of humble piety had become
increasingly rare, having been drowned out by the self-confidence of
theologians armed with the latest advances in scholarly methodology.
In Marsilius, however, something of Peter Lombard's spirit of humility
returns—in the awareness that the ultimate measure for the "success" of
the theological project is not its theoretical sophistication but something
much simpler—its ability to nourish faith:

> *Corollary*: Someone wishing to make progress in sacred theology
> must first believe that whatever is expressed assertively in Sacred
> Scripture is true. Subsequently, he should investigate how these
> [truths] mutually defend each other, how they depend upon each
> other, and which other salubrious [truths] follow from them....
>
> Second *corollary*: The power of the Catholic faith is such that a
> simple faithful little woman has more numerous, more distinct,
> and more salubrious notions of the divine than all philosophers
> have had—indeed, can have—in the pure natural light [of rea-
> son]....
>
> The third *corollary* [is] that, through such faith, the faithful little
> woman has more assistance and more incentives for the virtues
> than all the philosophers can find through the natural light [of
> reason]....[114]

Maarten Hoenen, a contemporary Marsilius scholar, has shown that our
theologian from Heidelberg rejects the application of logical and philosophical methods in contexts where such a procedure might carry a risk

of doctrinal error.[115] His rationale is the fact that "the sacred science is not a science of presumption or of logical superstition but rather of piety (*sed pietatis*), which must not destroy simple [believers] but build them up."[116]

If logic cannot, in the last analysis, furnish us with reliable criteria of theological truth, what is it that guarantees the validity of doctrine? Here, Marsilius's strategy is twofold. On the one hand, he uses his vast knowledge of the tradition to select teachings that constitute consensus positions. Marsilius owned the largest known private library in four-teenth-century Germany: an imposing 237 titles.[117] The sources he quotes most often, both implicitly and explicitly, include Bonaventure, Thomas Aquinas, Henry of Ghent, Duns Scotus, Peter Auriol, William of Ockham, Thomas of Strasbourg, Adam Wodeham, John Buridan, Gregory of Rimini, and Hugolinus of Orvieto. However, among this multiplicity of sources, he has a pronounced preference for theologians whom he views as defending balanced, sound doctrine. Thomas Aquinas is particularly close to his heart, as can be gathered from the many in-stances where Marsilius aligns himself with the theologian whom he calls the "Holy Doctor." For example, in treating the standard question as to whether theology is of a practical or speculative nature, he writes, "First, the Holy Doctor says that it is partly practical and partly specula-tive; in the main, however, it is speculative. This is very probable, since I believe it should be said thus."[118]

The second aspect of Marsilius's method of securing the doctrinal soundness of his teachings consists in his emphasis upon the authority of the Church, and in particular upon the relevance of canon law as a source of systematic theology. Marsilius distinguishes four sources of theological truth: the Apostolic Creed; Scripture; chronicles of the lives of apostles and martyrs (insofar as the Church receives them as authen-tic), together with truths "divinely revealed to the Fathers"; and all the decrees and councils of the Church that stand unrepealed.[119] To the last point he adds that "all the decretals that have not been repealed can be called theological truths."[120] Marsilius's discussion of charity provides a good example of how he employs canon law as an authority in sys-tematic theology. The first argument he cites against Peter Lombard's identification of charity with the Holy Spirit, and the Master's rejection of the conception of charity as a created virtue, is quoted directly from

the decretals of Pope Clement V.[121] In his own response he repeats the argument, stressing its completely binding nature:

> These [points] having been made by way of introduction, the responding conclusion must be: A created charity, granted by God in this life, has to be posited.
> This is proven from the Clementine [decretals] previously adduced. Whence a Catholic is no longer allowed to have doubts concerning this [matter], since in the said Clementine [decretals], the holy Council and the authority of the Church come down in its favor [that is to say, in favor of the conclusion].[122]

In his pioneering study of Marsilius's thought, the German scholar Gerhard Ritter found evidence of what he dismissively called *ängstliche Kirchlichkeit*.[123] If there is indeed a presence of such "timid churchiness" in Marsilius's *Sentences* commentary, this must be understood against the background of the crisis of theological certainty in the latter half of the fourteenth century and the resultant distrust in philosophical and logico-semantic arguments. If theology cannot be founded scientifically, and if logical tools can be dangerously misleading in our attempts to grasp the structures that God, through his ordered power, has given to his relationship with creation, then the authority of God's Church functions as a last resort in the foundation of truth. This authority finds its most rigorous, because legally enforceable, expression in canon law. In the passage just quoted from Marsilius's discussion of charity, he could have referred to the Council of Vienne (1311–12), upon which the relevant part of the Clementine decretals is based. It is significant that he chose the decretals instead, in order to give his argument as juridical, and therefore firm, a foundation as possible.[124] The Great Schism may have been another factor in attracting Marsilius to the certainty of canon law, which he may have regarded as a last bulwark against human turmoil.

On certain points of doctrine, then, Marsilius of Inghen is completely unambiguous, namely, points that have been dogmatically defined by the Church. On other issues, however, our theologian remains surprisingly open and noncommittal. Thus, Marsilius proffers a long list of opinions on the famous question concerning the scientific character of theology; the authors represented range from Thomas Aquinas, with his

endorsement of the scientific nature of *sacra doctrina*, to Peter Auriol, who denies it. As Marsilius moves on to the next issue, he remarks in passing, "These [positions] having been listed so that anyone may choose the one he might like, the third conclusion shall be this: ..."[125] In other words, Marsilius doesn't care. The once burning question has lost its controversial character. Theological interests have shifted to other, now more pressing matters, where the faith itself is at stake.

It is the same with the problem of the subject of theology. Again, Marsilius draws up an extended list of possible opinions: we find the whole gamut of views represented, from Augustine's distinction between things and signs, through Bonaventure's threefold subject of theological inquiry (which Marsilius appears to have misunderstood), to the opinion of one Heilmann Wunnenberg, who was a fellow bachelor at Heidelberg and held that the subject of theology is God, "insofar as he is knowable by us by supernatural means and enigmatically."[126] All in all, the list contains ten different conceptions of the subject matter of theology. Having completed his catalog of positions, Marsilius asks the reader to choose:

> I have listed these opinions in detail, so that—given the fact that they are all probable in the minds of those positing them—anyone may choose the opinion which he deems more probable.[127]

He later proposes a solution of his own, but it is very tentative and, in his own words, "simple": "These fine statements of the masters and doctors having been noted without prejudice, we set forth [some] simple propositions."[128] Marsilius goes on to state his position according to which the subject matter of theology is a term standing for the Creator.

A New Structure

The form of Marsilius of Inghen's *Quaestiones super quattuor libros Sententiarum* matches its contents. There are still some traces of the old dialectical format preferred by his predecessors; these traces, however, are mere relics of what was once a living form of composition. The literary form of Marsilius's *Questions* is expository prose, and not a dialogical to-and-fro between objections and responses. The work has a clear first-

person speaker, Marsilius himself. The multiplicity of traditional voices, which had been at the center of the dialectical efforts of his predecessors, sinks into insignificance as Marsilius derives his positions directly from Church authority or, where no such authoritative decisions exist, declares that the reader may choose whichever opinion he deems preferable. Moreover, Martin Flach, whose press published the work in 1501, was quite right when he advertised it, in the incipit of Book I, as being arranged "in the best order, quasi-mathematical, [and] most certain."[129] The order is quasi-mathematical in that Marsilius develops his arguments in a linear manner, in series of propositions that form a continuous logical chain. The work thus completes the movement "from the art of discourse to the art of reason"[130] whose progress we have been following throughout the twelfth, thirteenth, and fourteenth centuries.

Marsilius of Inghen's commentary on the *Sentences* is divided into questions rather than distinctions. At the beginning of each question, however, the author announces the distinction or distinctions in connection with which the question is asked, for example: "About the second and third distinctions, in which the Master states the unity of essence and Trinity of persons, it is asked, fifthly, whether there is only one God."[131] As one can see, there is no one-to-one correspondence between distinctions and questions. Frequently, though certainly not always, several distinctions are grouped into one question. Distinction 32 of Book I is the only one to receive two questions; yet it is not rare for Marsilius to devote several questions to a particular group of distinctions—for instance, distinctions 2 and 3 of Book I are treated in questions 5, 6, and 7. Sometimes the questions attached to a particular group overlap; for example, question 6 in Book III is attached to distinctions 5 through 7, while question 7 concerns distinctions 7 and 8. These peculiarities show that Marsilius still respects the general structure of Peter Lombard's theology, but within this general framework creates foci of doctrinal interest according to contemporary concerns. There is a clear emphasis upon Books I and II, which are analyzed in 47 and 24 questions, respectively. Books III and IV, on the other hand, receive a much shorter treatment, in only 15 and 13 questions, respectively. Marsilius formulates no questions at all on distinctions 17 through 42 of Book IV; this may of course be due to the incomplete state in which his commentary has come down to us.[132]

The first questions of Books I, II, and III present the central portions of the *principia* that Marsilius had to deliver as bachelor at Heidelberg. It is an unusual phenomenon that Marsilius incorporated his opening lectures into his published commentary, but his decision enables us to catch a glimpse of the structure of the *principia* at Heidelberg in the late fourteenth century. Question 1 of Book I opens with the following words:

> Having thus by the mercy of God completed the first two [tasks], namely, the invocation of the divine name and the brief commendation of Sacred Scripture, I come to the third, namely, the statement of a question or doubt for discussion with the other fathers and my masters.[133]

The "brief commendation of Sacred Scripture" was a kind of sermon, to be delivered upon a passage of Scripture that was selected in function of the relevant book of the *Sentences*. Marsilius does not mention the fourth part of the *principia*, which consisted of a word of thanks to the audience.[134] The opening lecture on Book I is devoted to the question of "whether the diversity of perfections of entities produced in the created realm is derived from a diversity of the ideas that exist in the uncreated realm."[135] This Neoplatonically inspired question must have been of great topical interest.[136]

But now to the internal structure of the questions that constitute Marsilius's *Sentences* commentary. The old question-and-answer format still provides the frame within which each question unfolds, just as in the case of Gregory of Rimini. Thus, at the beginning of each question, after the formulation of the problem, Marsilius juxtaposes arguments pro and con, to which he returns at the very end. The "real action," however, takes place in the articles that make up the body of each question. What is notable is the manner in which Marsilius formulates and then unfolds individual questions. Question 2 of Book I, for instance, which is attached to the prologue of the *Sentences*, is presented thus: "Concerning the prologue of the first [book] of the *Sentences*, it is asked, in the first place, whether theology is one science about God as its subject."[137] Since the question compresses three issues into one phrase— namely, the issues of the scientific character of theology, of its unity, and of its subject—Marsilius needs to break it up into parts before it can

be answered with the necessary precision. He does so by identifying one main question (*quaesitum*) and one or several assumptions (*supposita*) implied in the question. In the case of question 2, one presupposition assumes that theology is a science, another presupposes that it is a unified science, while the *quaesitum* concerns the subject matter of theology. The arguments pro and con are correspondingly more complex than in the old-style questions, since we now find arguments in favor of and against each *suppositum* and *quaesitum*.

These arguments having been stated, Marsilius divides the question into articles—in the current case, five. Their topics are the origin and kinds of knowledge, the nature of theology as distinct from other habits of inquiry, the scientific character of theology, the unity of the theological science, and the subject of theology. There is no uniform structure that each of Marsilius's articles follows; rather, they are composed like a modern book chapter, in which an author freely combines various rhetorical elements in view of a particular theme and the manner in which he wants to treat it. Let us take article 2 as an example. It starts with a series of three *notabilia*, "points worth noting," which offer several distinctions of ways in which theology may be understood. Let us read the second one:

> Secondly, it should be noted that each of these kinds of knowledge is twofold, since one [of them] is discovered in the natural light [of reason], such as the assentient kinds of knowledge that are common to us and the gentiles [i.e., non-Christians]. Others are founded in revelation, such as the science of canon law, and theology with its parts. They are distinguished in the following manner: The science of canon law has as its subject the Catholic human being who can be directed to eternal life through the statutes of the Church; it is concerned with the truths that are expressed in the books of canon law and with those that are not embodied in them (*et extravagantibus eorum*). Sacred theology, however, has God as its subject insofar as he is the end of the wayfarer's life which can be attained through formed faith—or according to some other such specification following the opinion of others. It is handed down in the books of the Bible, either in itself or in its principles, about which more will be said later.[138]

Note how many of the central themes of Marsilius's theology are combined in this passage: the clear distinction between philosophy and theology, the significance of canon law, the nature of theology as *scientia pietatis*, but also Marsilius's lack of dogmatism on issues not clearly defined by the Church.

After the three *notabilia*, which have supplied clarifications essential for the following analysis, article 2 continues with a series of three doubtful issues, or *dubia*, regarding the nature of a theological proposition, the characteristics of theological discourse, and the sources of theological truth. Of these, the third *dubium* is structurally the most interesting, since it includes not only a distinction of four sources of theological truth, but also a corollary—that is to say, a conclusion immediately following from the distinctions—and two objections with responses.

Each of Marsilius's articles is composed of these elements and others: *notabilia*, *dubia*, expositions of the positions of other theologians and refutations, conclusions (that is to say, theses by Marsilius), corollaries, and so forth. As one can see, the dialogue-based literary form of the older *Sentences* commentaries has dissolved, making room for a much more versatile and individual structure that no longer forces the author to submit to a communally shared form of composition. The different parts of each article are no longer held together by the dynamics of an (even imagined) dialogue, but by the logic of linear discourse.[139]

Chapter Four: The Long Fifteenth Century
Back to the Sources

WAS THE transformation of *sacra pagina* into *scientia divina* in the thirteenth century a case of progress or of decline? The judgment appears to
depend upon the vantage point from which it is formulated. A Thomist
would argue that the rigorous application of ideals of scientific discourse
to theology in the thirteenth century, and especially in the thought of
Thomas Aquinas, yielded one of the most impressive Christian systems
ever conceived. Yet, as we have seen, this judgment was not shared by
the majority of theologians in the late thirteenth and fourteenth centuries. Duns Scotus, Ockham, and their followers labored to free God
from the metaphysical embrace of *scientia divina*, employing the distinction between *potentia absoluta* and *potentia ordinata* in order to bring about
what Heiko Oberman termed "the epochal shift from God-as-Being
to God-as-Person."[1] According to the logic of this shift, the structure
of the universe bears no necessary connection with the divine being,
such that one could read the cosmos as a vast text, whose words are
all "reverberations of the eternal *Logos*."[2] No, God can be approached
only through the historical covenant into which he has entered with
his people. God's freedom in establishing this covenant underscores the
radical contingency of the created order. Since the latter possesses no

metaphysical structures that could be traced back to the Creator, it is best analyzed at the level of the existing individual. To posit any reality beyond that of the individual creates unnecessary speculative baggage.

Again, one could ask whether such nominalism should be construed as an advance or rather as a dangerous aberration in the history of Christian thought. The previous chapter has shown that, on the one hand, nominalism became firmly ensconced in the *Sentences* commentaries of the fourteenth century, enjoying the support of all the major theologians of the day. On the other hand, many thinkers, especially toward the second half of the century—theologians such as Gregory of Rimini and Marsilius of Inghen—perceived a need to correct some of the less fortunate consequences of the nominalist revolution, in particular, the temptation to treat theology as a logical exercise in analyzing signifiers. Thus, they attempted a return to the tradition, a fact to which Gregory's profound Augustinian learning testifies just as much as Marsilius's long lists of acceptable theological opinions. However, Marsilius's inability to decide among these opinions or to synthesize them forced him to look elsewhere for certainty. Therefore, in his thought, *scientia divina* mutated into a science about the dogmatically defined teachings of the Church: the authority of the Church now functioned as the ultimate guarantor of theological knowledge.

It would appear, then, that in intellectual history, progress somehow *is* decline; or, to put it in less paradoxical terms, all progress is inseparably connected with an element of decline. If this thesis is correct—and the present context obviously does not lend itself to a detailed discussion of the philosophy of history—then the history of ideas could be conceived as an interplay of light and shadow: each period in the history of thought would highlight a particular aspect, or particular aspects, of reality, but only at the expense of other aspects that are forgotten and neglected. In articulating the foundations of the philosophy of history just sketched out, Martin Heidegger employed the terms of "concealment" (*Verborgenheit*) and "unconcealment" (*Unverborgenheit*). For Heidegger, the unconcealment of increasingly large segments of reality by means of science and technology cannot but lead to a progressively deeper concealment of the mystery of Being.[3] I think that one does not stretch Heidegger's insights too far by applying them to the history of Christian theology in the Middle Ages. Fourteenth-century nominalism could

thus be read as a reaction against the danger, inherent in *scientia divina*, of "forgetting" that the mystery of God and his creation cannot be captured in even the most sophisticated theological systems.[4] Nominalism itself, however, produced the paradoxical effect of obscuring this mystery even further, precisely in its attempt to safeguard it.

It is in the spirit outlined in the preceding paragraphs that we are now going to approach the "long" fifteenth century—the fifteenth century understood as leading up to the Reformation.[5] This century continued the task of rebuilding Christian thought in the wake of the mixed blessing of nominalism, but also in the face of the multiple social and cultural challenges that followed the Black Death. In the century after its first outbreak in 1347, recurrent visitations of the plague cut Europe's overall population to one third of its pre-plague levels. As many masters who did not succumb to the disease fled from the cities of Western Europe, the Black Death was one of the factors that caused the center of European intellectual activity to gravitate toward the East, from Oxford and Paris to places such as Prague, Krakow, Vienna, Leipzig, and Erfurt.[6]

It is not surprising that this period in European history was experienced as a time of crisis.[7] However, as Heiko Oberman noted, the fifteenth century was also "a time of remarkable recovery" as it formulated answers to the redoubtable challenges that it faced.[8] To some of the more philosophical and theological answers to these challenges we now turn.[9]

John Capreolus

At the turn of the fourteenth and fifteenth centuries, the University of Paris was deeply embroiled in battles between representatives of nominalism and of the older thirteenth-century theology, especially that of Thomas Aquinas. Aquinas, at that stage, had few followers outside the Dominican order, although he was canonized in 1323 and, two years later, the bishop of Paris, Stephen of Bourret, lifted the condemnation of 1277 insofar as it touched upon Thomistic theses. Yet the nominalists remained suspicious. The conflict came to a head in 1387, when a Dominican friar from Aragon, John of Montson (Juan de Monzon), defended a series of controversial theses in two disputations—called the *vesperiae* and the *resumptio*—that were required of newly appointed masters of theology.[10]

Fourteen of these theses were immediately condemned by the Parisian theology faculty. When the Dominican order subsequently appealed to Pope Clement VII at Avignon and the pope upheld the Parisian decision, the Dominican masters refused to accept the papal ruling. As a consequence, they were excluded from the university until 1403.[11]

The controversial theses were all related to the central issue of divine omnipotence.[12] Following his confrère Thomas Aquinas, John of Montson denied the immaculate conception of the Virgin Mary, the possibility of multiple worlds, and the existence of several angels belonging to the same species; by contrast, in consonance with Book II, chapter 30, of Thomas's *Summa contra gentiles*, John asserted the existence of absolute necessity within the created order. All these positions were poison in the eyes of the prevailing nominalist theology, jeopardizing as they did God's omnipotence and freedom from all necessity. To say the least, then, in the early fifteenth century the climate at the University of Paris was not favorable to Thomism.

Just four years after the return of the order to the university, in 1407, a young Dominican named John Capreolus (ca. 1380–1444) came to Paris to study theology and, of course, to lecture upon Peter Lombard's *Book of Sentences* as part of his career as a bachelor. It is during those years that John began the composition of a *Sentences* commentary, the first book of which he completed in 1409. In 1411, however, John was recalled from Paris to teach in his home province of Toulouse. He was to spend the rest of his life there, working first at the study house of the order in Toulouse and then at Rodez, a town a bit farther to the north, at the heart of the region called "Rouergue" where John Capreolus was born. He completed the remaining volumes of his commentary at Rodez, no doubt on the basis of notes taken already in preparation for his Parisian lectures: Book II in 1426, Book III in 1428, and Book IV in 1432.[13]

The *Sentences* commentary on which John embarked during his Parisian years and which was to become his life-project is, at first glance, nothing but a *lectura secundum alium*—a "reading according to another." We first encountered this approach in the fourteenth century, when theologians started contenting themselves with simple quotation or paraphrase of their predecessors' texts, due no doubt to a certain tiredness and disaffection with the theological enterprise. That, however, was not at all the motive behind John Capreolus's endeavor, about one third of

which consists of excerpts from the works of Aquinas. His intent was to mount a comprehensive defense of Thomas Aquinas's theology against the Angelic Doctor's critics. That is why his *Sentences* commentary is entitled *Defensiones theologiae divi Thomae Aquinatis*, "Arguments in Defense of the Theology of the holy Thomas Aquinas."[14] John summarizes the goal of his *Defensiones* on the very first page:

> However, before I come to the conclusions, I premise one [remark] that I wish to be taken as understood throughout the entire commentary: it is that I intend to introduce nothing of my own but, rather, to relate only opinions that seem to me to be in accordance with St. Thomas's ideas, and to adduce no proofs for the conclusions in addition to his own words, except rarely. On the other hand, I propose, in the appropriate places, to adduce the objections of Peter Auriol, Scotus, Durand, John of Ripa, Henry [of Ghent], Guido the Carmelite,[15] Garro [that is, William of Ware], Adam [Wodeham], and of other attackers of St. Thomas, and to solve them by what St. Thomas said.[16]

The Scope of the Defensiones

The extract just translated already provides an indication of the scope of John Capreolus's *Sentences* commentary. Despite the literary genre that John chose for his defense of Thomas Aquinas, Peter Lombard's teachings are of no interest to him. In fact, the Master is not even mentioned in our programmatic excerpt. Instead, it is Aquinas whose teachings stand at the center of the *Defensiones*. If John nonetheless opted for the form of the *Sentences* commentary, his choice is most easily explained by custom and tradition: at the beginning of the fifteenth century, the *Sentences* commentary was still unrivaled as the main vehicle of large-scale theological composition.[17] Moreover, since Aquinas's opponents typically offered their criticisms of the Angelic Doctor in commentaries on the *Sentences*, it was most convenient to assemble and refute these objections in the order in which they were made.[18] Furthermore, as Aquinas was himself the author of a *Sentences* commentary, it was often easy to correlate his arguments with those of his detractors. Such are the advantages of a standardized platform for academic debate.

The questions that John Capreolus raises in his *Defensiones* cover all four books of the *Sentences*, and again all the distinctions within the individual books—although some distinctions receive more questions than others and a few are joined. For example, at the end of Book I we find only a single question on distinctions 45 through 48. What is the source of the questions that John asks? If he had decided simply to copy the questions in Thomas's *Sentences* commentary, he would not have been able to develop an effective response to the challenges of the fourteenth century, whose new theological foci led to emphases that were notably different from those of Aquinas and his contemporaries. Therefore, we find many typically nominalist issues addressed at length in John's commentary—for instance, the important fourteenth-century discussion concerning God's knowledge of future contingents (Book I, dist. 38)—while he has shortened or jettisoned debates that were no longer pressing in his day. Thus, while Aquinas devoted four questions in seven articles to use and enjoyment (the classical topic from the opening of Book I of the *Sentences*), John has cut the issue down to three questions (moreover, his questions are the functional equivalent of a Thomistic article).

The Structure of the Defensiones

Our programmatic excerpt also explains the internal composition of John's questions. In each, he first introduces a series of "conclusions"—a term used to mean "theses" since the middle of the fourteenth century—that are supported by arguments quoted from the works of Aquinas. The conclusions are followed by objections, arranged conclusion by conclusion, which John has derived from the writings of Aquinas's most influential detractors. These critics are all identified by name, although precise references to their works are missing, the understanding being that their arguments occur in the same distinction of their *Sentences* commentaries.[19] In cases where this is not so, John does provide references.[20] It is interesting that the name John mentions first in the text which we are commenting upon—Peter Auriol—belongs to a thinker who is generally less known in our own day, especially by comparison with such towering figures as Duns Scotus and William of Ockham. But apparently the intellectual landscape looked quite different in the

early fifteenth century, when Aquinas's "principal adversary"[21] was perceived to be this Peter Auriol, who is in fact the authority quoted most frequently in the objections. Peter Auriol, a Franciscan, was a student of Scotus's, whose incipient nominalism he developed further in his own monumental *Sentences* commentaries, which contain sustained attacks against Thomistic doctrines. He died in 1322 as archbishop of Aix-en-Provence.

In our translated passage the list of adversaries serving as sources for objections is by no means complete. For example, there is no mention of Gregory of Rimini, who is cited almost as frequently as Peter Auriol; neither does Ockham's name occur, despite the fact that John is of course aware of the importance of the Venerable Inceptor's ideas and examines them in key places. Rather than presenting a long list of thinkers here, let us simply say that John Capreolus's reading was vast, and that in the *Defensiones* he digested "a massive amount of textual material."[22]

The third and final stage in each *quaestio* consists of a refutation of the anti-Thomistic arguments, a refutation "by means of what St. Thomas said." The latter phrase should not be understood too narrowly: while the responses to the objections often incorporate quotations from Aquinas, this is not always so. Frequently John formulates his own answers.

The literature on John Capreolus contains the misleading claim that each of his questions comprises three articles.[23] This general statement is not correct, as a look at even the very first question of the prologue reveals: "In this question there will be two articles. In the first of these, conclusions will be posited. In the second, objections will be advanced."[24] The refutation of the objections forms part of article two as well. It is true that there are some questions in Book I which contain three articles; however, each of the articles is devoted to a different topic (for instance, Book I, dist. 40, qu. 1). Again, question 3 of distinction 19 in Book I is an example of a question that involves only a single article. Thus, there is a certain variety in John's use of the article form—at least in Book I. For the secondary literature's statement concerning the three articles does hold true for Books II through IV, in which John consistently employs the following standard format for his articles: article 1—conclusions; article 2—objections; article 3—solutions. He must have discovered the convenience of this format in rethinking his *Defensiones* after his departure from Paris.[25]

In the previous chapter, in discussing the literary form of Gregory of Rimini's *Lectura* on the *Sentences*, we noted the way in which Gregory stretches the structure of the thirteenth-century commentary to its limits, by inserting the main body of his discussion in between corresponding sets of arguments and responses at the very beginning and end of each question (see Figure 10, p. 115). John Capreolus uses the same format in his questions. Lest this analysis become too abstract, let us read the introductory paragraphs of distinction 1, question 1 of Book I:

> Concerning the first distinction of the first [book] of the *Sentences*, I ask, first, whether enjoyment is an act of the will.
>
> And it is argued that it is not, because no act of the intellect is an act of the will. But enjoyment is an act of the intellect. Therefore. [The conclusion is not spelled out.] The major [premise] is obvious from itself. The minor [premise], however, is proven: Because beatitude is an act of the intellect, since it is an act of the most excellent power, which is the intellect, as it appears in [book] one of the *Ethics*. Enjoyment, however, is beatitude. Therefore etc.
>
> An argument for the opposite [position] is made thus. For according to the Master, in the letter [of the text], enjoyment is love. It is certain, however, according to everyone, that love is an act of the will.
>
> Now in this question, just as in the preceding ones, there will be two articles. In the first, the opinion of St. Thomas will be posited by means of conclusions. In the second doubts will be advanced.[26]

The two announced articles follow, the first offering a series of six Thomistic theses and the second a long series of arguments, and corresponding responses, concerning conclusions three to six. And then, at the end, where the attentive reader would expect a return to the initial set of arguments pro and con, there is ... nothing! John has either forgotten about them or found them too insignificant to pursue. In other questions, he occasionally does return to what he often calls the "foot" (*pes*) of the discussion (meaning the beginning of the question, that upon which it rests); yet he always does so in a perfunctory manner, with a remark such as this one from the end of question four of the prologue:

"With respect to the argument made at the foot of the question, [the so-lution] is obvious from what has already been said."[27] One may ask why John did not simply drop the superfluous "frame" around his articles, which is so evidently useless in the context of his own project. The an-swer no doubt lies in the force of an old custom, which took centuries to wither away.

The Discovery of Doctrinal Individuality and Development

In a continuation and culmination of trends originating in the four-teenth century, the debate with recent medieval authorities stands at the center of John Capreolus's questions, whereas the old "frame" of the questions has lost its significance—I mean the arguments from Scripture, Aristotle, Augustine, and other ancient authorities that were paramount in the twelfth and thirteenth centuries. It is logical, then, that recent or contemporary authors no longer appear simply as "some people" (*quidam*), but that the *Defensiones theologiae divi Thomae Aquinatis* identify the author of every recent argument by name. In this manner, there emerges a rich tableau of doctrinal options and currents that includes not only the major schools—nominalism versus realism, Scotism versus Thomism, etc.—but many nuances within them. Thus, there are nu-merous "minor" thinkers whose ideas John Capreolus examines, such as John of Ripa or Guido the Carmelite.[28] In John's *Defensiones*, therefore, we find an explicit acknowledgement of an unprecedented diversity of individual authors—despite the fact that John's goal, to be sure, is not simply to create an inventory of opinions, but rather to refute these posi-tions so as to demonstrate the superiority of the thought of St. Thomas Aquinas. The Thomistic school has recognized the latter part of John's achievement by giving him the honorific title of *princeps Thomistarum*, "prince of the Thomists."

The *Defensiones*, however, have more to offer than a Thomistically oriented doxography of philosophy and theology between 1274 (the year Thomas Aquinas died) and the early fifteenth century. John Capreolus also recognized that Thomas's own positions evolved; that is to say, he understood that the mere juxtaposition of quotations from different parts of Thomas's works would not succeed in the task of presenting a coherent Thomistic synthesis. Rather, it was necessary to grasp the

relationship among Thomas's writings and to adjudicate between sometimes conflicting views expressed therein. In this manner, John did for
Thomism what earlier generations of Christian thinkers—thinkers belonging to previous layers of our "onion"—accomplished for Scripture
and the Fathers, namely, to harmonize a diversity of authoritative teachings or "sentences." In the process, John helped bring about a shift of
emphasis, in discussions within the Thomistic school, from Thomas's
Sentences commentary to his more mature *Summa*.

This aspect of John Capreolus's project was not totally unprepared by
earlier developments. Since the early fourteenth century, there circulated concordances detailing "articles in which Thomas said something
different in the *Summa* than in the writings on the *Sentences*" (*articuli in quibus Thomas aliter dixit in Summa quam in Scriptis Sententiarum*).[29]
Furthermore, in the controversy surrounding John of Montson and the
place of Thomism at the University of Paris, one of the Dominicans'
main opponents, Pierre d'Ailly, had accused Aquinas of incoherence
and self-contradiction.[30] The *Defensiones* respond to this critique, first,
through comprehensive knowledge of the Thomistic corpus. To give
an example, in the famous distinction 17 of Book I, on charity, John
does not rely primarily upon Thomas's *Sentences* commentary in order to
explain the Thomistic position on the subject; rather, he quotes from or
refers to different parts of the *Summa theologiae*, of the *Disputed Questions
on the Virtues*, the *Sentences* commentary, the *Disputed Questions on Truth*,
and the *Summa contra gentiles*. Here is how he documents a simple terminological point:

> Grace itself, however, given this multiplicity of effects, is called
> "prevenient" and "subsequent," "operating" and "cooperating":
> [it is called] "operating" by reason of its first effect, "cooperat-
> ing" with respect to the second; "prevenient" with respect to the
> first [effect], "subsequent" with respect to the second. For grace,
> understood according to its earlier effect, can always be called
> "prevenient"; and understood according to its later effect, it can be
> called "subsequent." But on this, see [*Summa theologiae*] 1^a2^{ae}, qu.
> III, art. 3; 2 *Sentences*, dist. 26, qu. 1, art. 5; and *On Truth*, qu. 27,
> art. 5.[31]

But what if tensions obtain between or among different places where Aquinas pronounces himself on a particular subject? Then the divergent loci need to be weighed up in light of hermeneutic principles that John enunciates explicitly:[32]

1. The first principle calls for an attempt to scrutinize the texts in question more profoundly, as John believes that tensions and contradictions in Thomas's works are often merely apparent and can be resolved easily if the texts are only examined more closely.[33]

2. Sometimes, however, contradictions are real. Then, the first question one has to ask oneself is whether the texts adduced are authentic; for if they are not by St. Thomas, the evidence they provide is spurious. The treatise *On the Nature of Matter* (*De natura materiae*) is a case in point: John expresses doubts concerning Thomas's authorship that are justified, as we now know.[34]

3. Furthermore, we should make a distinction between, on the one hand, statements that Aquinas made in passing, or in contexts in which the issue under consideration was not the focus of his attention and, on the other hand, passages in which the same matter is treated formally and directly. In cases of doubt, the latter should be given greater weight.[35]

4. When a statement found in one of Aquinas's writing puzzles us, due to its divergence from his usual teachings, we must reckon with the possibility of a scribal error, a *vitium scriptorum*.[36]

5. On occasion, we may have to admit that the saintly doctor made a remark inadvertently, without being aware of the fact that he was contradicting a statement made earlier on. Such lapses will easily be forgiven in light of the length of many of Aquinas's works, such as his *Sentences* commentary.[37]

6. Chronology furnishes John Capreolus with a more substantial criterion to decide between contradictory teachings. John's assumption is that Aquinas's thought evolved and matured over

time, so that one should hold the doctrine that he developed last (*tenendum est quod ultimo dicit*).[38]

7. The chronological principle finds its most important application in the primacy that John accords Aquinas's teachings in the *Summa theologiae*, which he acknowledges as containing the Angelic Doctor's final, most considered doctrinal pronunciations. He summarizes this hermeneutic principle as follows: "What I have said about concordance with or discordance from the *Summa* must be the rule and guiding principle in such matters."[39] John likens the *Summa* to Augustine's *Retractations*, a work in which the Bishop of Hippo looked back upon his literary production and corrected himself on many issues.[40]

In conclusion, we may say that there is a certain dynamism, if not in John Capreolus's doxography of later medieval thought, then certainly in his understanding of Thomism. John realizes that Thomas's thought, rather than being a static monolith, underwent internal development—in a word, that it has a history.

Denys the Carthusian

The movement back to Aquinas that we have witnessed in John Capreolus has its roots deep in the fourteenth century, when theologians felt a need to counterbalance the more egregious consequences of nominalism with a return to older approaches presumed to be sounder. In Marsilius of Inghen, a certain preference for the thought of Thomas Aquinas already emerged, although Marsilius was not ready to mount a defense of Thomism comparable in scope and ambition to the project of the *princeps Thomistarum*. In the *Sentences* commentary of Denys the Carthusian (1402/03–71), this "spirit of 'back-to-the-sources'"[41] finds another, different expression. While Denys's massive work acknowledges the preeminence of Thomas Aquinas as an authority in scholastic theology, it goes beyond John Capreolus in attempting to do for the fifteenth century what Peter Lombard accomplished for the twelfth: to create a synthesis of all preceding Christian thought.

A Second Peter Lombard

Denys views himself, quite explicitly, as a second Peter Lombard. In the prologue to his *Sentences* commentary, he writes:

> Yet, although the deficiency, smallness, and paucity of the wisdom of the way [that is, of this life] are enormous by comparison with the wisdom of the Fatherland, nonetheless the wisdom revealed at the time of the evangelical law is very splendid and great. [This wisdom was revealed] first by Christ, then by the mission and inspiration of the Holy Spirit, next by the glorious apostles and evangelists, then by the holy Fathers, and finally by the Catholic and scholastic doctors, excellently learned not only in the divine Scriptures but also in all philosophy. [This wisdom] powerfully exceeds that of the philosophers, but also of the theologians of the Old Testament and of the natural law. For—as Gregory testifies— just as wisdom grew in the course of time before the coming of the Savior, so it also does in the meantime [since his coming]. And most of all from the time when Master Peter Lombard, bishop of Paris, collected his *Book of Sentences*, wisdom appears to have received much and great elucidation, growth, and abundant increase. Which Isaiah once foresaw, saying, *the earth is filled with the knowledge of the Lord, as the covering waters of the sea* [Is. 11:9], that is to say, very abundantly. And those things that were hidden have been brought forth into the light; the difficulties of the Scriptures have been unknotted; and points that can be objected to the Christian faith, and have been objected by the faithless, have been solved outstandingly. Indeed, the aforesaid Master and illustrious learned scholastics who have written famously on the *Book of Sentences*, have subtly discussed, magisterially made clear, and Catholically treated not only the more difficult places of Scripture, but also the words and writings of the holy Fathers, who have written much that is difficult and obscure in their expositions of the Scriptures and other treatises.
>
> Since it is known, however, that almost innumerable people have already written upon this *Book of Sentences*, and that moreover even today some are writing [on it]—perhaps even more than is

useful, as due to some less illustrious writings of recent people, the more illustrious writings of the older ones are less attended to, read, and investigated—hence it is my intention in this work to prepare a kind of collection of extracts (*quamdam facere extractionem et collectionem*) from the commentaries and writings of the most authoritative, famous, and excellent doctors, and to bring the reflection of these doctors back into one volume. For just as the very text of the *Book of Sentences* is gathered from the words and testimonies of the holy Fathers, so this work too is put together (*adunetur*) from the doctrines and writings of the aforesaid writers upon the *Book of Sentences*.[42]

One is tempted to call Denys's eloquently articulated theology of history "modern," given both his clear understanding of his own place within intellectual history and his emphasis upon progress in the unfolding of Christian thought. Denys's grasp of historical process certainly goes beyond that of John Capreolus, who discovered the dynamism animating the Thomistic oeuvre but presented a static doxography of later medieval thought. Upon closer inspection, however, the application of the "modern" label to Denys turns out to be slightly misleading. First, Denys does not believe that history necessarily produces progress; there can be decline as well, as his remark on the "less illustrious writings" of some more recent *Sentences* commentators shows: these less valuable writings have even come to overshadow the older, more precious *Sentences* literature. (As we shall discover, by these "less illustrious writings of recent people" Denys means the nominalist literature of the fourteenth century, especially post-Scotus.) Secondly, the theology of history that this passage encapsulates is Neoplatonic in inspiration. Wisdom, Denys argues, unfolds in the course of salvation history, spreading as though in concentric circles from a center that is the Incarnation itself. But then, a movement of folding-back occurs, lest the multiplicity of insights be lost in dispersal (as has perhaps happened in the "less illustrious writings"). The first stage of this movement of return was none other than Peter Lombard's *Book of Sentences*. The *Sentences* subsequently served as the center of a second unfolding, which is now reduced to unity by Denys the Carthusian himself.

Note the words that Denys employs to describe his intention in composing the *Sentences* commentary: he will strive to bring the tradition

"back into *one* volume" (*in unum volumen redigere*), a volume "put together" (*adunetur*) from the teachings of the greatest commentators on Peter Lombard. *Adunare* literally means "to make one." We are dealing here with a dialectical movement of an unfolding of unity into multiplicity that is followed by a folding-back into a more differentiated unity—the kind of movement that I described in the Introduction (summarized in Figure 2, p. 18). According to Neoplatonic thought, such is the rhythm not only of commentary traditions but of reality as a whole: God, the One, overflows into an abundance of particular manifestations (also called "theophanies"), all of which are marked by a desire to return to their Source. The Christian Neoplatonist and mystic (Pseudo-)Dionysius the Areopagite, who wrote in the fifth century, is one of the most important inspirations for Denys's thought—and, appropriately, the first non-scriptural authority invoked in the prologue to the *Sentences* commentary: "the most perfect knowledge that we have of the most high God in this world is by denial and taking away [of attributes] from him, in the manner that the second chapter of the *Mystical Theology* of the divine Dionysius also explains...."[43]

The Place of Scholastic Theology in the Quest for Wisdom

Denys the Carthusian's *Sentences* commentary is not a product of scholasticism as ordinarily understood. Denys pursued university studies only briefly, in the arts faculty of the University of Cologne during the years 1421–24. At Cologne he became acquainted with the *via Thomae*, as he terms it himself, "the way of Thomas," which was favored by the local masters.[44] In 1424 or 1425, however, Denys realized his longtime dream of becoming a Carthusian. He entered the Charterhouse at Roermond (in the Netherlands), which he did not leave until his death in 1471— with the exception of a journey that he took with Nicholas of Cusa in 1451–52 and the years between 1466 and 1469, when he functioned as rector of a newly founded Carthusian monastery. In other words, for Denys the study of Peter Lombard and his commentators was part of a monastic—and not a scholastic—life. Indeed, the reading and compilation of books formed part of the Carthusian vocation. Guigo, the influential fifth prior of the Grande Chartreuse, included composition, especially of preaching material, in his rule, the *Consuetudines* (1127/28). Study became an even more important part of Carthusian life in the later

Middle Ages, when the order attracted intellectuals who were dissatisfied with the state of theological studies at the universities. Scholarship
within the Carthusian order now developed into more than an aspect
in the "reformation" of the individual monk's soul. It became part of a
larger desire to contribute to a *reformatio* of the Church as a whole.[45]

Obviously, the Carthusian order was not alone in assigning study an
important place in its rule, and Denys was not the first religious to compose a *Sentences* commentary. However, many of the authors—including
religious authors—whose *Sentences* commentaries originated in the
university milieu failed to integrate theological speculation with piety
and devotion: that, after all, was one of the foremost complaints against
nominalism. Denys, on the other hand, ponders frequently upon the
place of study within the life of the monk, and his huge *Sentences* commentary is only one part of an immense corpus that is "hierarchically
ordered" to reflect the order of wisdom itself.[46] Thus, the first treatise
Denys composed after entering the Charterhouse was devoted to the
Carthusian life. This was followed by reflections on the gifts of the Holy
Spirit. Denys's next priority was to complete commentaries upon all
the books of Scripture, which he did between 1434 and 1457. Denys's
literary activity radiated, as it were, from a clearly identified spiritual
center, to embrace, in the end, almost every aspect of human thought
and culture. His ultimate goal was, Neoplatonically speaking, to reduce
the multiplicity of manifestations in which God's wisdom is scattered to
the unity of the divine Wisdom itself. With this goal in mind, Denys
even authored a collection of 900 sermons, both for religious and for
laypeople.[47]

The prologue to his *Sentences* commentary is one of several passages
in his oeuvre where Denys outlines the order of wisdom and indicates
how scholastic theology fits into this hierarchy. First, he explains, there
exists a wisdom that is uncreated. It is identical with the "super-wis-
est God himself" (*ipsemet supersapientissimus Deus*).[48] Uncreated wisdom
is followed by created wisdom, which can again be divided into two
kinds. Infused wisdom represents one of the seven gifts of the Holy
Spirit; inseparably connected with charity, it is a grace that saves the one
on whom it is bestowed. Caused wisdom, on the other hand, pertains to
the order of *gratia gratis data*, "grace gratuitously given"; in other words,
it is a grace that is not salvific and not necessarily infused by God. In

fact, caused wisdom can be acquired through study. If the study pertains to the created world (as in philosophy), we are dealing with natural caused wisdom. Even if it is acquired naturally, however, caused wisdom can also have a supernatural source, as in the case of knowledge of Sacred Scripture:

> This is the kind [of wisdom] that we are talking about [in the *Sentences* commentary]. Just as this [wisdom] is superior to acquired natural philosophic wisdom, so it is inferior not only to uncreated Wisdom, but also to that [wisdom] which is the gift of the Holy Spirit. Accordingly, this wisdom, which consists in the understanding of the Scriptures, is rightly called a gift of grace gratuitously given: for it is common to good and bad people, indeed to good and bad angels; and its growth is ordered to others, since through it a person is rendered capable of defending the faith, of arguing and explaining it, and of edifying his neighbors.[49]

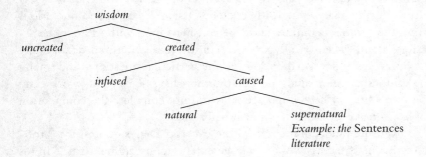

Figure 12: The order of wisdom according to Denys the Carthusian

Denys is of course right in claiming that the study of theology is not necessarily salvific. Today, it is not rare to have atheist or agnostic scholars conducting fine research on Scripture and other religious topics. Thus, even the "bad" person—to use Denys's terminology—is capable of contributing to an understanding of the faith. This situation is analogous to that of a priest who, although not in a state of grace himself, is still able to dispense the sacraments validly.

Even if Denys acknowledges the difference (and possibly distance) between the enterprise of scholarly, scholastic theology and the personal piety of the theologian, his hierarchy of kinds of wisdom makes it clear

that such theology, properly understood, can only be a stepping-stone in an ascent to higher forms of wisdom. Further on in his prologue, he emphasizes that "science without virtues lacks proper form" (*scientia quippe sine virtutibus est informis*). The scrutiny, he adds, "of the most high, incomprehensible divine matters" needs to be "characterized by modesty and reverence, together with a recognition of the weakness of one's own mind, and proceed from a zeal for truth and from piety ...."[50]

The Composition of Denys's Sentences Commentary

Denys's commentary on Peter Lombard fills seven volumes in the 42-volume modern edition of the works of the "Ecstatic Doctor." It therefore represents a major part of his literary achievement and was the fruit of the labors of a lifetime. The scope of the work is vast, as Denys provides detailed commentary on each distinction of each of the four books of the *Sentences*. Following the intention outlined in the prologue, this commentary does not simply add Denys's opinion to the chorus of existing theological views. Rather, Denys assembles extended quotations from the *Sentences* commentators he considers most authoritative, he arranges them systematically so as to constitute a structured doxography or overview of doctrinal options on the particular questions, and finally he synthesizes and adjudicates. Denys must have started this work early on in his literary career and probably did not complete the compilation of his *Sentences* commentary much before 1464.[51]

Given the range and length of the excerpts Denys quotes, it is probable that he based his work to a large extent upon original texts.[52] In his *Sentences* prologue, Denys himself says, "I have procured with considerable effort (*grandi labore*) the writings of those whom I will quote more frequently in this work."[53] But how did he obtain these writings, living as he did in the isolation of his Roermond cell? The answer lies in his "reportedly enormous correspondence,"[54] through which he maintained something like a private interlibrary loan system, requesting books from friends and colleagues, to whom he would return them after he had finished consulting and excerpting from them. In this correspondence, Denys also liberally gave away writings of his own without retaining copies.[55] According to Neoplatonic principles, the source of an emanation never diminishes as it gives of itself to others.

In light of the effort that Denys put into the compilation of his *Sentences* commentary, it is remarkable that no copies were made of it in the Middle Ages. But then again, Denys composed his works at the dawn of the modern age, when the printing press finally superseded the long tradition of transmitting texts in handwritten copies. There is a single manuscript, now preserved in the Vatican Library, that contains excerpts.[56] Thus, the work remained largely a private enterprise until it appeared in print, namely, in the edition of Denys's works that Dirk Loër and other Carthusians from the Charterhouse at Cologne prepared in the 1530s. The autograph was probably destroyed as the edition was typeset, so there is no possibility of going beyond this first printed text—which is not unproblematic, as Denys's handwriting was difficult to decipher and the Cologne editors sometimes took "fairly large liberties" with the text.[57]

Even if the *Sentences* commentary by Denys the Carthusian had no medieval readers, it played a crucial part in his own literary activity. Kent Emery considers that the *Sentences* commentary functioned as a kind of "memory system" or "storehouse" upon which Denys was able to draw in composing other works, such as treatises or sermons.[58] By memorizing the order of distinctions in the *Sentences*, Denys was able to retrieve, quickly and conveniently, authoritative quotations on theological matters that he had previously "stored" in his *Sentences* commentary; these quotations he would then weave together in fresh combinations to generate new texts.

The Structure of Denys's Sentences Commentary

Denys's own *prooemium* or prologue, the principal points of which we have already considered, is followed by an interesting section in which the author, after the manner of an anthology, presents excerpts from the *Sentences* prologues of four scholastic commentators: Peter of Tarantaise, Thomas Aquinas, Bonaventure, and Richard of Middleton. The selection appears programmatic: these authors all represent an older, pre-nominalist approach to theology. Peter of Tarantaise, whom we encountered briefly in Chapter Two, attempted to synthesize the positions of Bonaventure and Thomas, in addition to enjoying particular authority due to his accession to the papacy (as Innocent V). Similarly,

Richard of Middleton was a thirteenth-century Franciscan whose works draw principally upon Bonavanture, Thomas, and Henry of Ghent. Denys's selections are not quotations in the modern sense of the term, according to which scholarly accuracy requires faithfulness to the letter of the original. His paraphrases, however, remain close to the originals. Where they do not—as in the case of the passage from Bonaventure, which is heavily abridged—Denys warns his reader, "Thus in a nutshell Bonaventure" (*Haec sententialiter Bonaventura*).

Peter Lombard's own text forms an integral part of the commentary by the Ecstatic Doctor, rather than being dropped, as was the wont of the fourteenth-century commentators. Initially, it must have been Denys's intention to furnish the Master's prologue and each distinction with a detailed "exposition of the text" (*expositio textus*). The reader of these careful literal expositions feels transported back into a twelfth-century gloss as Denys explicates Peter Lombard's text word for word, frequently incorporating questions into the commentary. It is, however, difficult to take all these questions seriously. Some appear contrived and pedantic. Thus, on Peter Lombard's opening words, "Longing to cast something of our want and poverty along with the little poor woman into the treasury of the Lord …," Denys raises the following "difficulty":

> But against this one could object as follows. For although the Master placed the proem at the beginning of this book, nonetheless (as appears from the tenor of this prologue) he composed the prologue after completing the book. Since, then, this book is a big thing, a splendid gift, an opulent offering, it does not seem that in producing this book, he cast something modest along with the little poor woman into the treasury of the Lord ….[59]

Denys must quickly have come to the conclusion that such painstaking discussion of Peter Lombard's twelfth-century text was no longer appropriate in the middle of the fifteenth; or that, at least, it detracted from his task of synthesizing the teaching of the Master's commentators. For, in fact, the expositions break off rather abruptly in the middle of the one devoted to distinction three, where Denys suddenly declares:

> The second part of this distinction follows [in Peter Lombard's text]. In it, the Master shows from words of Augustine how a

vestige of the super-worthiest Trinity is reflected in creatures. And what occurs about this [topic] in the text, will become clear in the questions.... The third part of this distinction, however, begins here: "But now we come to this consideration." [This is] where he shows how the super-blessed Trinity is reflected in a higher way in the rational creature, after the manner of an image. And the letter will be evident in the questions.[60]

At the beginning of the next distinction, Denys's excuse is much shorter: "This is distinction four, the letter of which does not require exposition."[61] From this point onward, Denys contents himself with brief summaries—often in a few lines—of Peter Lombard's own teaching. The focus of the commentary therefore is not Peter Lombard but his commentators.

Essentially, the Ecstatic Doctor's *Sentences* commentary consists of series of questions upon the individual distinctions (all of which are covered). There are no articles. In the selection of questions, he lets himself be guided by the commentaries of the thirteenth, not of the fourteenth century, as he does not appear to consider nominalism to be part of the tradition that he wishes to unify. Only Scotus is often quoted at length, as a borderline fourteenth-century authority—a theologian espousing the key nominalist distinction between *potentia ordinata* and *potentia absoluta*, practicing "subtlety," but stopping short of the Ockhamist denial of the existence of universals outside the mind. Yet even for Scotus the Ecstatic Doctor sometimes expresses disdain. For instance, in his discussion of distinction 17 he writes:

Finally, Scotus introduces many difficulties about this question—[difficulties that are] as it appears, superfluous [and] characterized by curiosity. To dwell upon them seems to be a racking of one's brains (*fractio capitis*) and an impediment to devotion, rather than a fruitful occupation.[62]

Perhaps it was not possible to bring nominalism into the mix, as it were, of the synthesis that Denys intended—after all, every synthesis requires a common doctrinal denominator. Nevertheless, the absence of nominalism as a positive ingredient in Denys's thought means that the latter is not fully representative of the state of late medieval philosophy and theology.

Finally, how does Denys resolve the tensions among the authorities whose positions he strategically juxtaposes in his commentary? Let us take his commentary on distinction 17 of Book I as an example. In the first question, Denys asks, "Is charity, by which the rational or intellectual creature loves God and the other things that should be loved out of charity, a created virtue that inheres formally [in the soul], or is it the Holy Spirit itself?"[63] The commentary starts by arguing for the second alternative, citing Peter Lombard and seven additional arguments. Then the discussion turns to the opposite position: "Against this, there stands the common teaching of the doctors."[64] Denys first adduces 1 Cor. 13:13, "And now there remain faith, hope, and charity, these three," a verse that he interprets as proving that faith, hope, and charity "belong to the same order." Since faith and hope are agreed to be created virtues, the same follows for charity.

The scriptural argument is supported by two long extracts from Thomas Aquinas, the first from the *Sentences* commentary, the second from the *Summa*. There follow further passages from Peter of Tarantaise, Richard of Middleton, and Bonaventure, all of whose arguments Denys endorses, though he adds a minor clarification to Peter's position. Albert the Great, he then adds in a brief summary, "does not write about these matters anything different from the doctors quoted above."[65] Matters become more interesting as we move on to the next author, Giles of Rome, an Austin Friar and independent-minded Thomist who lectured at Paris in the late thirteenth century:

Although he concludes that charity is an inherent created virtue, [Giles] nonetheless endeavors to prove that the arguments which Thomas adduces in order to prove this are not suitable, insofar as [Thomas claims that] an act proceeds only through a form or inherent habit. [The arguments are not suitable] because the blessed in the Fatherland contemplate the divine essence not through a created species that informs them, but through the fact that the divine essence is joined to their intellect[s] in lieu of an intelligible form. Thus, the created will is also capable of proceeding to the act of loving through the fact that the Holy Spirit is joined to it in lieu of habitual charity.[66]

This argument occasions a rare concession on Denys's part to the fundamental nominalist distinction between *potentia ordinata* and *potentia absoluta*. Yes, it is possible for the omnipotent God to show himself supernaturally, that is to say, without an intelligible species or form inhering in the created soul; and therefore, by analogy, we must also admit that the Holy Spirit can immediately—without mediation—cause us to love God and neighbor: "We do not deny that, through God's omnipotence, something can, in an utterly supernatural manner, occur differently, namely, in the manner in which the Master imagines it. Therefore, the arguments of the holy doctor [that is, Aquinas] come to the right conclusion according to the common law, the natural way, and the more suitable way. [These arguments], however (as has been touched upon), do not detract from God's omnipotence, such that he could act differently."[67] Despite the terminology invoked in this remarkable passage—omnipotence over against "common law"—Denys's concession should not be attributed to any kind of sympathy for nominalism. It should rather be interpreted as an expression of his immersion in Neoplatonically inspired mysticism and, indeed, of his own mystical experience: Denys believed in the possibility of a vision of God face-to-face in this life.[68] Throughout his writings, Denys is prepared to depart from Thomas when the latter is at odds with his mystical experience or with his greatest authority, the "divine Dionysius." A perfect example is Denys's reaction to Thomas's innovation whereby the Angelic Doctor declared Being to be God's first and most proper name, rather than Goodness. In the *Elementatio theologica*, a condensation of important points of doctrine from the *Sentences* commentary, Denys first appears to agree with the Thomist position, but then he adds: "Therefore this noun, *good*, applies to God most properly, insofar as he is the principle of emanation both to the inside [of the Trinity] and to the outside."[69]

But back to the discussion of charity in the commentary on the *Sentences*. Giles of Rome raises another argument against Thomas. Even if we consider charity according to the common law—that is to say, admitting that a created habit is necessary to elicit an act of charity—this does not necessarily mean that this habit has to be charity itself. Instead, Giles suggests, justifying grace (*gratia gratum faciens*) fulfills this function. This, Giles maintains, is the reason why Peter Lombard saw no need to posit a special habit of charity: justifying grace alone suffices. Denys,

however, disagrees, siding with what he regards to be the consensus of the doctors and offering several arguments to support his position.

Scotus reinterpreted Peter Lombard's denial of the status of charity as a created virtue along similar lines as Giles of Rome. The Subtle Doctor therefore is the authority whom Denys examines next: "It seems to me," he paraphrases Scotus, "that the Master taught something different on this matter than what is commonly attributed to him .... Hence I say that charity and grace are *one* habit, which is taken for granted in the current context: and the Master [too] wanted this, although he did not say so explicitly."[70] Denys, predictably after his refutation of Giles of Rome, refuses to go along with Scotus's reading of the Lombard. He believes that there is no textual support for such an interpretation: "if the Master had been of the opinion that [charity and grace] are in reality identical, he would not have denied clearly that there is a habit of charity in the soul, just as he did not deny that there is a habit of grace. Thus, Scotus's solution does not proceed according to the intention of the Master."[71] Moreover, the identification of charity with saving grace produces not only textual, but theological difficulties as well: one of the several which Denys mentions consists in the consequence that grace would exist in the will.

Denys finds confirmation of his rejection of Giles's (and also Scotus's) understanding of charity in Durand of St. Pourçain. Durand was a kind of dissident Dominican whose *Sentences* commentary, authored in the first decade of the fourteenth century, challenged many Thomistic positions. After quoting Durand at some length and adding a minor correction, Denys finally returns to the initial seven arguments in favor of the Master's teaching, refuting them one by one.

In distinction 17, whose structure is typical of Denys's approach in his commentary on the *Sentences*, Denys aims at a synthesis of the principal authorities of the thirteenth century. The teaching of Thomas Aquinas occupies a central position in this endeavor, serving as it does as the focus of the consensus that the Ecstatic Doctor is searching. Denys is reluctant to depart from this "common teaching of the doctors" (*communis doctrina doctorum*), but he will do so if the tradition of Dionysian mysticism requires it. In distinction 17, therefore, he is one of the few medieval thinkers to admit that Peter Lombard's identification of charity with the Holy Spirit represents a tenable position, given some caveats.

Denys likes to quote authors such as Giles of Rome and Durand of St. Pourçain, who worked in the orbit of Thomas Aquinas yet modified his thought in certain respects. This strategy enables him to generate controversial discussion within the broad parameters of the thirteenth-century "consensus." Against this background, it makes sense that Denys adduces almost no representatives of fourteenth-century nominalism, with the exception of Scotus—whose use of the distinction between *potentia ordinata* and *potentia absoluta* prepared the ground for the full-blown nominalism of Ockham and his followers. The Subtle Doctor, however, serves largely a negative function: rather than incorporating Scotus's positions into the synthesis, Denys cites them to illustrate censurable departures from the "common teaching of the doctors."

Gabriel Biel

Both John Capreolus and Denys the Carthusian battled against nominalism, regarding it—as did many of their contemporaries—as jeopardizing piety and sound theology. Yet the followers of the *via moderna*—the "modern way," as nominalism was often called to distinguish it from the *via antiqua*, the "old way" of the thirteenth century (including Scotus)—continued to reign strong at many universities of the fifteenth century. One of them was Erfurt, in eastern Germany, where Gabriel Biel (ca. 1425–95) taught in the arts faculty in the 1440s and received part of his theological education in the 1450s, thereby becoming acquainted with the Ockhamist approach to philosophy and theology. His years at Erfurt undeniably left an enduring impression upon the orientation of Biel's thought; nevertheless, he was more than a simple adherent of Ockham. We know that from 1453, Biel was enrolled for several years at the University of Cologne, which was firmly committed to the "old way" of Albert the Great and Thomas Aquinas.[72] Moreover, like Denys the Carthusian, Biel placed great emphasis upon a healthy balance between scholarship and piety. In the middle years of his life, between 1457 and 1484, he completely interrupted his university career, instead devoting himself to pastoral aspects of the life of the Church. Thus, in the late 1450s and early 1460s, he served as a cathedral preacher and vicar at Mainz. At this time, he also joined the Brethren of the Common Life, a powerful movement of spiritual renewal that also influenced Denys the

Carthusian. In due course, Biel assumed increasingly important functions among the Brethren: in 1470 he became provost of the Brethren House of St. Mark's at Butzbach, and in 1477 he helped found a new community at Urach (all in the Upper Rhine region of Germany). Biel must have been around 70 years old when, in 1484, he received his first appointment as master of theology at the new University of Tübingen. During his years there, from 1484 until his retirement around 1490, he completed the first three books of a comprehensive commentary upon Peter Lombard's *Sentences*. It is controversial whether he started this commentary from scratch after his appointment or whether, by contrast, the work was the fruit of his many years of teaching at schools of the Brethren of the Common Life.[73] It is undisputed, on the other hand, that Book IV of the commentary was composed after Biel's retirement from Tübingen, at the Brethren House of St. Peter's at Schönbuch. It breaks off after distinction 22.

Shortly after Biel's death in 1495, his pupil Wendelin Steinbach readied the four books of his *Sentences* commentary for publication; they were printed at Tübingen in 1501 after an autograph that is now lost.[74]

Biel's Program in his Sentences *Commentary*

Not surprisingly against the background of Gabriel Biel's intellectual and spiritual career, his nominalism is of a complex kind. Like Denys the Carthusian's Thomism, Biel's Ockhamism is tempered by his desire to synthesize—not simply to defend and perpetuate the teaching of a particular school, but to move beyond it toward a *summa* of the tradition. Let us read a significant excerpt from Biel's preface:

> Our purpose and intention is to apply ourselves to theological study, through which (by the inspiration of divine grace) we may arrive at wise knowledge of our Lord God. [This knowledge] is true wisdom and wise science to the extent that, as knowledge of God grows in us, so does the fervor of divine charity, which alone (like a "bond of perfection" [Col. 3:14]) renders us pleasing to God, perfects us, and unites us.[75]

Note Biel's reference, from the outset, to the necessary link between knowledge and charity. True wisdom exists only to the extent that it is

accompanied by charity. Biel continues:

> Since Scripture, by which we are led to know God, is extremely broad, it is indeed detrimental, difficult, and almost useless to send especially beginners and children who are firstborn in sacred theology into such a large and spacious ocean. This is why, for the glory of the Catholic faith and the profit of its students, Master Peter Lombard, bishop of Paris, like a bee collecting arguments (*velut apis argumentosa*), composed a useful work from the beehives of the holy Fathers—namely, the books of the *Sentences*, in which, in an order both carefully considered and excellent, he gathered together and brought back to unity the theological teachings, along with the texts testifying to them. [He did this] "so that it might not be necessary for someone searching to go through a large number of books, [someone] to whom the anthology offers without labor what he seeks."[76]

After this apposite and eloquent characterization of Peter Lombard's goal in the *Book of Sentences*, Biel moves on to situate his own project within the history of commentaries. He writes:

> The later lovers of the holy letters and masters, most acute searchers for truth, adhered to, and in our times still adhere to, the teaching ordered in this fashion and the appropriate order of teaching, and they lean upon them, arguing both theological questions, and frequently others, in the scholastic manner about the issues that the Master assembled in his marvelous work.[77]

The emphasis here is on the order of the material gathered together in the *Book of Sentences*; it is this arrangement—Biel quite correctly observes—that has remained most authoritative in Peter Lombard's work, rather than the Master's own positions:

> Nevertheless, as they employ various ways and means (even sometimes contrary ones), although they aim at and strive to reach the same goal, it is necessary and experience teaches the one wishing to advance that it is most useful to choose *one* of these ways; [this is so] lest it happen to the trembling and ignorant wayfarer

wandering hither and thither that he be made strong in nothing and err, rather than attaining the mete[78] of truth. Therefore, we have for now chosen the teaching of one [authority] that is more familiar to us, and we shall follow it principally and for the most part, nonetheless adducing the "sentences" of others when it will appear fitting. God, to whom the whole heart lies open, is our witness when we say that we make light of no one who writes in a sound and Catholic manner. May such temerity be far from us! We venerate, praise, and honor the teachings of everyone, and we ever give thanks and immortal praise to those usefully laboring, as it were, in the vineyard of the Lord. The tenor of our collection and abbreviation will prove that I am speaking the truth.[79]

Biel presents the need to choose a particular "way" (*via*) over against others in a manner that is very humble; one could almost say "subjective." Rather than arguing for the superiority of his preferred school, he suggests that the reasons for his choice are contingent: they lie in his greater familiarity with the approach in question and in the need to align oneself consistently with a particular school in order to avoid erring about in doctrinal confusion. Furthermore, Biel intimates that his choice is of a provisional nature: "for now" (*pro nunc*) he has opted to go along with one of the particular *viae*, pending (presumably) the possibility of arriving at a more comprehensive, more adequate grasp of the truth. Biel also promises us that he has already attempted to hint, at least, at such a synthesis by including ideas by representatives of other schools in his commentary. The spirit of Biel's work is clearly one of synthesis and broad catholicity, of a return to the tradition as a whole.

We have not yet learned from Biel himself who the authority is that he has elected to follow. He announces his choice a few lines after the previously quoted paragraph:

Since it is our goal to abridge the teachings and writings of the Venerable Inceptor, William of Ockham the Englishman, most zealous searcher for the truth, concerning the four books of the *Sentences*, we shall endeavor, led by divine assistance, to raise scholastic questions concerning the prologue and the individual distinctions. Moreover, where the aforesaid doctor writes more

prolifically, [we shall endeavor] to shorten his "sentence" and his words—and especially in the first [book], in which he raises and resolves questions regarding the individual distinctions more deeply and broadly than in the remaining writings. In the other [books], however, where he writes little or nothing, [we shall endeavor] to bring together into one—to the extent that I shall be able to—sentences of other doctors that do not depart from the principles of the said doctor, [collected from] the beehives of the most famous men. This is why it seemed proper to call our work "collection" (*collectorium*) as well as "epitome." Furthermore (as is the wont of the scholastic school), occasionally we shall relate and say some things that indubitably can be said upon the basis of his principles, although the doctor himself may seem to hold the opposite. In all this, the theological asseveration often repeated by me is presupposed: through this, I absolutely subject both myself and my collection here, and anything else that I shall teach or say, to the correction of the holy Mother Church and to the judgment of any orthodox person who has a better grasp. "The just man shall correct me in mercy" and in fraternal charity; "but let not the oil of the sinner fatten my head" [Ps. 140:5]![80]

Biel's references to the "scholastic" questions that he is going to raise, and to the customs of the "scholastic" school, indicate a certain distance precisely from the scholastic method. It is only because he is no longer completely steeped in the scholastic approach, being capable of conceiving of other methods (such as more pastoral genres of composition), that Biel sees a need to be specific about his procedure.

We learn that Biel's intention is to produce a *Sentences* commentary based upon nominalist principles, and indeed upon Ockham's own *Ordinatio*, which he promises us to condense and abridge. The problem, however, is that Ockham left us an *ordinatio*—that is to say, a fully developed commentary—only upon Book I. For the remaining books, all we have are students' lecture notes (*reportationes*). As a consequence, it will become necessary to extrapolate in applying his principles to the topics covered in Books II through IV. Biel believes that he will be able to accomplish this task by drawing upon the work of other commentators, to the extent that their thought is compatible with nominalism.

Thus, Biel's *Sentences* commentary assumes the character of both a "collection" and an "epitome"—a collection insofar as it brings together a broad range of texts chosen from a variety of authors, and an epitome inasmuch as it presents a summary of the *Ordinatio* and other writings by Ockham. *Collectorium* is the title that Wendelin Steinbach used for the 1501 printing. I think that this term hearkens back to Peter Lombard's own prologue, in which the Master spoke of his intention to "compile" (*compegimus*) a volume from the most authoritative witnesses to the faith. Also note Biel's description of his project as "bringing together into one" (*in unum comportare*) the teachings of various authorities; the idea of synthesis is clearly on his mind.

The Sources of the Collectorium

In Biel's *Sentences* commentary, the transition from *epitome* to *collectorium* really occurs between Books II and III. In other words, Books I and II are largely based upon quotations and paraphrases from the writings of both Ockham and other representatives of nominalism, such as Gregory of Rimini and Pierre d'Ailly. Scotus is invoked frequently as well. In Books III and IV, however, the balance of Biel's sources appears stunningly different, as there is a clear preponderance of representatives of the "old way": Alexander of Hales, Bonaventure, and (in particular) Thomas Aquinas.[81] John L. Farthing counted, and analyzed, 421 passages in which Biel examines Thomistic teachings in the *Collectorium*.[82] This number makes Aquinas the authority ranking fourth in the quantity of Biel's references and quotations, after Augustine, Ockham, and Scotus.[83] What is more, according to Farthing "in more than 95 percent of the citations" Biel ends up embracing Thomistic positions in one form or another, so as to allow the Angelic Doctor's views to become part of his synthesis.[84] Frequently, when he does feel compelled to disagree, such conflicts of opinion are due less to differences in substance than to Biel's Ockhamist conviction according to which theology rests upon the authority of Scripture and of the Church, therefore not admitting of scientific proof. For example, in Book I, dist. 35, art. 2, on God's knowledge of everything other than himself, Biel remarks, "And although this conclusion [that God knows all] is true and believed by faith, nonetheless it cannot be proven evidently by means of natural reason that it

cannot be refuted—even though many [authorities] adduce various reasons, such as St. Thomas in Part I, qu. 14, art. 5 and elsewhere, [reasons] some of which the doctor cites in the text."[85]

It is not easy to determine exactly how successful Biel was in carrying out his ambitious project of incorporating large parts of the "old way" into a theology of essentially nominalist inspiration. Does the result amount to no more than a hodgepodge of irreconcilable views or is it, indeed, a genuine synthesis? Only a detailed examination of the doctrinal contents of the entire *Collectorium*—a work of over three thousand pages in its modern critical edition—would be able to answer this question. Let me only say here that, in some places at least, Biel's attempted synthesis is reminiscent of Marsilius of Inghen's "anything goes" approach. Thus, in a question in Book III that addresses a difficult Christological issue, Biel leaves it up to his readers whether they wish to embrace the views of the *via antiqua* or rather those of the *via moderna*:

> Concerning the matter of this question, there are two contrary opinions, neither of which can be disproven in a demonstrative manner. One is that of Scotus, Ockham, and generally of the moderns.... The other opinion is that of Henry of Ghent (in *Quodlibet* XIII, qu. 2), to which—as Giovanni Pico della Mirandola records in his *Apology*, qu. 4—he tended in his old age as to the more probable opinion, having dismissed the first one. It also seems to some people that it is the opinion of Alexander of Hales.... I want to pursue both [opinions] only in the manner of a report (*recitative*), without any assertion, leaving it to the judgment of the reader which should be judged more probable. And according to this [procedure], there will be two articles in the question, to which a third will be added about the solution of some doubts.[86]

The Structure of the Collectorium

Biel does not break with the habit, dominant since the fourteenth century, of affording very little attention to Peter Lombard himself. The text upon which he comments, at least in the first two books, consists in the writings of William of Ockham. Occasionally, he explicitly refers to the *Ordinatio* as "the text" being considered.[87] Nonetheless, at the begin-

ning of each book and of each distinction, Biel devotes a few lines to a summary of the gist and basic structure of Peter Lombard's argument. In these summaries, the word "text" designates the *Book of Sentences* itself. Biel likes to boil the Master's main points down to a short series of theses or "conclusions."

Questions are the main vehicle that Biel employs to address the theological matters arising in connection with each distinction. Many distinctions receive only one question, but there can be up to ten when the difficulty of the subject matter—or, rather, Ockham's exhaustive treatment—calls for such a detailed approach. Thus, in Book I we find ten questions on distinction 3 and eight on distinction 17. There is some variety in the structure of the questions; we have already seen one in Book III that consists of three articles, the first of which explains one opinion, the second another, while the third addresses *dubia*. Right at the beginning of the commentary on the prologue, question 1 is divided into four articles: "In this question, the author [that is, William of Ockham] first clarifies his terms; then he asks whether knowledge regarding God can be had by the created intellect; thirdly, he responds to a question; fourthly, he raises doubts and resolves them."[88] However, the prevailing format of Biel's questions has them falling into three articles: one clarifying the terms of the debate, another positing a series of *conclusiones*, and a third addressing further doubts. To illustrate the workings of this tripartite article-structure, and gain further insight into Biel's synthetic method, let us examine a particularly interesting question in Book III: "Whether the redemption of the human race was necessarily accomplished through the Passion of Christ qua man."[89]

Article 1 opens with a long discussion that the first edition identifies as a *notabile* in the margin of the page: a point "to be noted." The first article of each question typically consists of one or more such *notabilia*, which set the terms of the debate. In this particular "notable point," we are introduced to Anselm's argument in the treatise *Cur Deus homo* (*Why God Became Man*), an argument according to which Christ's death was indeed necessary, as the only way in which God could redeem the human being, created to enjoy the beatific vision, from the debt incurred in the Fall. After presenting this argument in four logical steps, and documenting it carefully with references to *Cur Deus homo*, Biel comments, "Although these arguments of the blessed Anselm are pious and clear,

nonetheless they prove nothing unless they proceed from the presupposition of the divine ordinance."[90] We have here the typical nominalist
move: Anselm's argument—Biel objects—illegitimately subjects God to
necessity, being oblivious of the fact that the logic of salvation is contingent upon an order freely created by God himself. A long refutation of
Anselm's demonstration now follows, based upon this principle. In article 2, then, we move on to two "conclusions," again identified as such
in the margins.

Conclusion 1 is that, "just as the redemption of the human race was
not necessary, so neither was this particular mode of redemption." Yet
conclusion 2 concedes, "The mode of redemption through the Passion
of the only-born was the most fitting of all the modes through which
the human race could be redeemed."[91] In nominalist terms, "fitting"
(congruens) designates arguments that are not necessary and logically de-
monstrative—they cannot be, given God's radical freedom—yet that
capture something of the divinely ordained structure of reality. Each
conclusion is accompanied by a concise proof. At the end of the second, Biel refers the reader to the "fitting" treatment of the subject in
Peter Lombard, Thomas Aquinas, Bonaventure, and Alexander of
Hales. Again, we see evidence of Biel's general approach: attempting
to incorporate the tradition into a framework that is broadly nominalist in inspiration, he rejects only arguments that blatantly contradict the
"modern way." Finally, article 3 is devoted to the discussion of two *dubia*, or points for further debate. The first specifies the manner of our
redemption through Christ's suffering and death, citing a text from
Scotus. The second asks whether this particular mode of redemption
was really the most fitting one, given the fact that God could also have
saved us by other means.

I have already touched upon the structuring elements that appear in
the margins of the first edition of 1501: the articles of each question, as
well as the elements within the articles (mainly *notabilia*, *conclusiones*, and
dubia), are clearly marked. There is no way to ascertain whether Gabriel
Biel himself wished for his text to be published in this manner, but it is
likely, given the long-standing development of the genre toward ease
and efficiency of consultation. The 1501 edition also contains detailed
tables of contents at the end of each volume; upon the basis of these,
Wendelin Steinbach compiled a general alphabetical table of contents

(*inventarium generale*), which was printed on the first pages of volume one.[92] In a brief foreword, Steinbach explains the rationale behind his work. It is, he writes, that the tables of contents of the individual books are not arranged in alphabetical order, which makes it difficult to find particular subjects for those "who have not committed to memory the commonly known topics of the *Book of Sentences*."[93] This is an interesting remark, hinting as it does at the fact that the structure of the *Sentences* may, at the beginning of the sixteenth century, no longer have been commonly accepted as the lodestar of theological inquiry, that is to say, as providing the general systematic framework in which reflection on particular theological topics had to situate itself. Be that as it may, Steinbach's table of contents proffers the reader an index that combines alphabetical with topical principles of organization. Thus, for instance, the entry for *caritas*, "charity," also covers the closely related terms of *amor* and *dilectio* (that is, types of love).

On the Eve of the Reformation

From our consideration of three of the most influential *Sentences* commentators of the fifteenth century, there emerges a provisional, but fairly clear, picture of the state of the genre on the eve of the Reformation. John Capreolus, Denys the Carthusian, and Gabriel Biel represent radically different theological options: Capreolus is a committed Thomist, Denys a Dionysian adherent of the "old way," and Gabriel Biel a moderate, synthesizing nominalist. Yet the *Sentences* commentaries of all three thinkers share a common feature, and that is the desire to reduce the tradition once again to unity—that is to say, in a way, to repeat the project of Peter Lombard himself. In Denys's prologue, the parallel with the Lombard is rendered explicit. The strategies, however, that these theologians employ to achieve their goal vary considerably: John, intent on refuting the "modern way," only allows it to play a negative role in the *Defensiones*. His focus is completely on Thomas Aquinas. Denys appears more open to genuine synthesis, but even for him, nominalism is out of bounds. Gabriel Biel is perhaps the thinker most seriously committed to synthesis, as he uses nominalism as an umbrella for a broad range of positions that belong both to the *via antiqua* and the *via moderna*. In terms of our "onion" model of the development of traditions, the fifteenth cen-

tury clearly marks a stage of contraction or "folding-back," that is to say, an attempt to prevent the tradition's expansion from dissipating its core.

There seems to be another common trend in the fifteenth century. The attempt to overcome the doctrinal differences of the past involves a return to the sources, but not a return to the *Book of Sentences* itself. In fact, we remember Denys the Carthusian's ambitious literal expositions of the text of the *Sentences*: they break off abruptly, and tellingly, in distinction three. What does remain authoritative about the *Sentences*, however, is the structure of the work, which continues to guide large-scale theological composition. What is more, such comprehensive theological composition is still considered worthwhile. In other words, we appear to have returned to the pre-fourteenth-century ideal of systematic coverage of the main points of the Christian faith.

We found a remarkable awareness of historical development and process in Denys the Carthusian, an awareness made possible by Denys's Neoplatonic background. Neoplatonism, after all, is a philosophy that views all of reality as fundamentally dynamic. John Capreolus too understands the importance of development in relation to thought, viewing as he does Aquinas's writings as undergoing a process of maturation and evolution. Chronological considerations are central in John's presentation of a harmonious synthesis of Aquinas's thought. In this regard, Gabriel Biel seems to have the least to offer. He juxtaposes and combines ideas in the old scholastic manner, like pieces in a large intellectual (but timeless) puzzle. Odd, one might say, for a nominalist, who so strongly believes that God is not bound by metaphysical necessity but is best understood through his self-revelation in history. By contrast, Biel joins Denys in emphasizing the need to conduct theoretical inquiry in a climate of devotion and piety.

Now let us explore to what extent Martin Luther's work on the *Sentences* can meaningfully be read against the backdrop of these fifteenth-century trends.

Martin Luther

Martin Luther (1483–1546), an Austin Friar, was educated at the universities of Erfurt and Wittenberg, in an intellectual climate that was nominalist in orientation. John Duns Scotus, William of Ockham,

Gregory of Rimini, Marsilius of Inghen, Pierre d'Ailly, and Gabriel Biel were the central authorities whose writings Luther's teachers drew upon in their books and lectures. We know from a later remark by the Reformer that he prepared himself for his ordination to the priesthood (in 1507) by eagerly studying Biel's commentary on the Mass: "When I read in it, my heart was bleeding."[94] Alongside nominalism, a growing humanist movement flourished in Luther's intellectual environment. This "Erfurt humanism," as it has come to be called, manifested itself in a variety of ways, from an interest in music to the publication of textbooks for the study of ancient languages; it included, as well, an emphasis on the need to read the Scriptures. The humanist program led to some criticism, initially very limited, of scholastic theological methods.[95] These ideas did not fail to leave their impression on the young Luther.[96]

Luther lectured on the *Sentences* at the University of Erfurt between 1509 and 1511. His lectures took place three times a week over a period of two years.[97] Luther based his classes on an edition of Peter Lombard's work that was printed by Nikolaus Keßler of Basel in 1489; this text came complete with summaries (*conclusiones*) of the book's principal theses by one Henry of Gorkum (ca. 1386–1431) and the old Parisian list of positions commonly rejected by the schools; we first encountered the latter in Bonaventure. Luther never developed his lectures into a commentary comparable in scope to the scholastic works that we have been examining so far. This is a significant observation in itself: Luther knew the scholastic exercise and literary genre of the *Sentences* commentary, but he left it behind very quickly. Yet his glosses, jotted in the margins of the printed text, have survived (see Figure 13).[98] They testify to the fact that, even before his theological education was complete, Luther was ready to challenge some of the fundamental methodological assumptions of scholastic theology. He did so by means of a paradoxical move—namely, by returning to the thought of Master Peter Lombard himself. Luther undermined scholastic theology by taking its founder seriously.

Figure 13: Luther's glosses on the *Sentences* in Nikolaus Keßler's 1489 edition: Book I, distinction 17, beginning (Zwickau, Ratsschulbibliothek, 19.5.7).

habitu minor. i. in forma serui quam accepit. His autoritatibus ostenditur aperte filius secundum formam serui minor patre: et seipso et spiritusancto.

Hylarius aliter dicit. scilicet quod pater sit maior nec filius tamen minor. e

Hylarius autem dicere videtur: quod pater sit maior filio. nec tamen filius minor patre. Pater enim dicitur maior propter autoritatem. quia in eo est autoritas generationis: secundum quam dicitur. Pater maior me est. Et apostolus. Donauit ei nomen quod est super omne nomen. Cum ergo ait. Pater maior me est. hoc est ac si diceret. donauit mihi nomen. Si ergo (inquit Hylarius in .ix. lib. de tri.) donantis autoritate pater maior est. nunquid per doni confessionem filius minor est. Maior itaque donans est. sed minor iam non est: cui vnum esse donatur. Ait enim. Ego et pater vnum sumus. Si non hoc donatur iesu vt confitendus sit in gloria dei patris: minor patre est. Si autem in ea gloria dei donatur esse qua pater est. habes et in donantis autoritate. quia maior est. et in donatis confessione. quia vnum sunt. Maior itaque pater filio est. et plane maior. Cui tantum donat esse quantus est ipse. cui innascibilitatis esse imaginem sacro natiuitatis impartit. quam ex se in forma sua generat. Audisti lector quid super hoc dicat Hylarius. cuius verba vbicunque occurrerint. diligenter nota. pieque intellige.

Ista est distinctio sedecia. In qua magister postquam egit de processione spiritussancti temporali. incipit agere de missione eius visibili. Et circa hoc tria facit. Nam primo ostendit spiritumsanctum esse visibiliter missum. Secundo subdit qualiter visibiles missiones filii et spiritussancti se habeant ad inuicem. Tertio subiungit qualiter filius et spiritussanctus secundum istas missiones se habeant ad patrem. Primum facit a principio distinctionis vsque ibi. Sed prius querendum est. Secundum ab inde vsque ibi. Hylarius aut dicere videtur. Tertium vero ab inde vsque ad finem distinctionis. In speciali vero sententia magistri stat in tribus propositionibus. quarum prima est hec. Spiritussanctus ad modum filii est missus dupliciter. scilicet visibiliter et inuisibiliter. Et probatur sic. Spiritussancti temporalis missio est creature sanctificatio. sed creature sanctificatio dupliciter fit. aliquando cum apparentia alicuius visibilis signi. quandoque vero effectu solum interiori sine visibili signo. igitur missio spiritussancti est duplex. scilicet visibilis et inuisibilis. Istam rationem intendit magister in textu. vnde proponit primo. Sicut filius dupliciter est missus. scilicet in carnem visibiliter. et in castas mentes inuisibiliter. Sic spiritussanctus visibiliter apparuit in die penthecostes in specie linguarum ignearum. aliisque vicibus in specie columbe. et quotidie illabitur mentibus fidelium inuisibiliter. Et subdit postea: quod illa visibilis spiritussancti missio non fuit nisi quedam signus apparentia vel manifestatio in corporali creatura: tamen in signo manifestationis prout magister inducit in textu ex autoritate beati Augusti.

Secunda propositio est hec. Spiritussanctus non dicitur minor realiter tota trinitate propter suam visibilem missionem. sicut filius propter suam. Hanc propositionem magister insinuans querit. Quare spiritussanctus ratione sue visibilis missionis non dicitur minor patre. sicut filius ratione sue incarnationis seu visibilis missionis dicitur minor tota trinitate. Et respondet quod spiritussanctus non assumpsit columbam vt esset columba. sed vt in ea appareret. et vt per eam designaret inuisibilem missionem. filius autem assumpsit humanam naturam non solum vt in ea appareret. sed etiam vt esset homo. Et ideo filius secundum illam suam visibilem missionem dicitur minor non solum patre sed etiam seipso et angelis. vt patet ibi. Paulominus minuisti eum paulominus ab angelis et cetera. Ad quod magister adducit multas autoritates. vt patet in textu. Tertia propositio est hec. Pater autoritate donandi est maior filio sibi essentialiter equali. Hanc propositionem probat magister autoritate Hilarii .ix. de trini. dicentis. Donantis autoritate pater est maior. nunquid per doni confessionem filius est minor. Maior itaque donans est. sed minor iam non est. cui vnum esse donatur. Igitur patet hanc propositionem esse veram.

De missione spiritussancti qua inuisibiliter mittitur. a

Iam nunc accedamus ad assignandam missionem spiritussancti qua inuisibiliter mittitur in corda fidelium. Nam ipse spiritussanctus qui deus est: ac tertia in trinitate persona. (vt supra ostensum est) a patre et filio ac seipso temporaliter procedit. id est mittitur ac donatur fidelibus. sed que sit ista missio siue donatio: vel quomodo fiat considerandum est.

Premittitur quiddam ad hanc ostensionem necessarium. scilicet quod spiritussanctus est charitas qua diligimus deum et proximum. b

Hoc autem vt intelligibilius doceri: ac plenius percipi valeat premittendum est quiddam ad hoc valde necessarium. Dictum quidem est supra: et sacris autoritatibus ostensum. quod spiritussanctus amor est patris et filii quo se inuicem amant et nos. His autem addendum est: quod ipse idem spiritussanctus est amor siue charitas: qua nos diligimus deum et proximum quando caritas ita est in nobis vt nos faciat diligere deum et proximum. tunc spiritussanctus dicitur mitti vel dari nobis. et qui diligit ipsam dilectionem qua diligit proximum. in eo ipso deum diligit. quia ipsa dilectio deus est. i. spiritussanctus d

Luther's Prologue

The Keßler edition of the *Book of Sentences* in which Luther added his glosses also contains an extended note written on the inside of the book's front cover (see Figure 14). Luther's authorship of this note, which acts as a kind of prologue to the whole, was disputed by some Reformation scholars—Heiko Oberman among them.[99] Today, however, its authenticity can be considered to be firmly established, in particular through graphological analyses.[100] Here is what Luther has to say:

> Although I have held that the spoils of philosophy are not to be utterly rejected insofar as they are suitable to the sacred matters of theology (*ad Sacra theologiae accommodam*), nevertheless the prudent restraint and unsullied purity of the Master of the *Sentences* seem extremely proper, in that in every respect he so relies upon the lights of the Church, and especially upon Augustine (the brightest light, whose praise is never sufficient), that he seems to hold in suspicion, as it were, whatever is anxiously explored but not yet known by the philosophers. And certainly, to occupy oneself devotedly with these thorn bushes, weeds, and what is close to sheer jokes—what else does this amount to, I ask, but to build oneself labyrinths from which there is no return, to dig under the sand, and, to put it more pointedly, to push the rock of Sisyphus and to turn the wheel of Ixion? What will be the end of opinions and most pugnacious sects? The world is full of Chrysippuses, yes even Chimeras and Hydras! The poets could fashion nothing more expressive and humorous to ridicule the quarrels, battles, and sects of the philosophers, than such monsters as these: laughable indeed, yet also appropriate and most acute in their witty pungency. Therefore, love sound, faithful, and pure authors, or at least (if necessarily it must be so) join them to you in secular familiarity (*populari fac sint tibi familiaritate conjuncti*), the philosophers I mean, that is to say, the doubters full of opinions.[101]

Considered against the background of the fifteenth-century *Sentences* commentaries that we have studied, Luther's prologue exhibits elements of both continuity and discontinuity. The desire to overcome

Figure 14: Luther's prologue to the *Sentences* on the front cover of Nikolaus Keßler's 1489 edition (Zwickau, Ratsschulbibliothek, 19.5.7).

Sententiarum veritas, in sanctis libris Eccle-
siastici inuestiganda est. Aug. lib. et doctrina
Christiana cap. 31.

sectarian divisions is common amongst the authors of the long fifteenth century. John Capreolus, Denys the Carthusian, and Gabriel Biel all endeavored to achieve this goal, albeit in different ways. What is new in Luther, however, is that he puts the blame for these divisions squarely upon philosophy. Theology—so the future Reformer insinuates—has lost its integrity not due to internal divisions, but as a result of relying excessively upon philosophical methods. Note that Luther's rejection of philosophy is not absolute, recognizing as he does that there may be some legitimate theological use to "the spoils of philosophy." The latter expression alludes to Augustine, who in his treatise *De doctrina christiana* (*On Christian Teaching*) recommended that Christians avail themselves of pagan philosophy just as the Israelites took Egyptian treasures with them in their exodus.[102]

Now, if philosophy is characterized by dangerous and futile sectarianism, the solution to philosophical (and theological) confusion cannot lie in any synthesis of such inherently flawed intellectual constructions. Consequently, the responsible theologian must return to a period when the influence of philosophy upon theology was limited—and Luther identifies this period in his prefatory note: it includes Augustine and Peter Lombard, who perhaps stand for the Church Fathers and pre-Aristotelian scholasticism. Of course, Augustine and Peter Lombard do not enjoy equal status; rather, the latter appears reliable to Luther precisely because of his fidelity to the Augustinian heritage. Augustine, in turn, is authoritative as a "light of the Church."

Reservations concerning the role of philosophical reasoning within theology were a recurrent theme of nominalism—from Ockham's denial of the scientific status of theology to Marsilius of Inghen's reliance upon canon law in the elaboration of theological doctrine. Moreover, as we discovered, critics of nominalism took offense at the use of sophistical riddles and similar excesses of logical subtlety. Perhaps such *sophismata* are what Luther has in mind when he speaks of philosophical ideas that border on sheer jokes. No nominalist or anti-nominalist, however, went so far as to associate philosophy—as Luther does—with mere opinion.

The final sentence of the passage has puzzled interpreters. Murphy surmised that it could have been "hastily written."[103] For why would Luther, after inveighing at length against the dangers of philosophy, urge his students to familiarize themselves with the ideas of these "doubters full of opinions"? Admittedly, Luther adds the caveat, "if necessarily

it must be so" (*si ita fieri sit necesse*), that is to say, "if you have to study philosophy." Perhaps the expression "secular familiarity" (*popularis familiaritas*) further clarifies his position: the theologian does not have to shun philosophy altogether, but must remain aware of its ultimately secular nature. Thus, he needs to embrace it with great caution.[104]

We must, finally, advert to the strong humanist overtones of Luther's prologue. Luther indulges in imagery from classical literature—somewhat paradoxically, one might add, because if Peter Lombard is the example of theological method that he proposes to follow, Luther's prologue should surely be replete with biblical references! That this is not the case shows us that a renaissance, a return to the sources, is never an identical repetition of the old; it is a creative and imaginative use of the past in view of present questions and needs.

The Implementation of Luther's Program in his Glosses on the Sentences

Luther's glosses on the *Sentences* cover Books I through III; in the margins of Book IV, there is nothing except half a dozen references to Augustine. Luther himself does not explain the absence of commentary on the sacramental and eschatological parts of the *Sentences*. Did he run out of time before being able to complete "reading" the Master's work with his students? It is possible, but we do not know for sure.

The content of Luther's glosses falls into four groups:[105]

(1) Many marginal notes draw attention to the structure of Peter Lombard's text. Interestingly, Luther consistently divides each distinction into three parts, independently of the number of chapters. This tripartite division is indicated in the margins: *2ᵃ pars, 3ᵃ pars* (the first part naturally coincides with the beginning of each distinction). Occasionally, Luther adds a brief summary: "second part, in which he sets forth the testimonies of the Old Testament," "third part, where he adduces the authorities of the New Law";[106] or, "second part of the distinction, with one question," "third part of the distinction, with three questions."[107] On distinction 1 of Book I, we find the following diagram:[108]

The Master	{	sets forth (*proponit*) what the material is about
		lays out in order (*disponit*) the difference of things
		sets them over against each other (*opponit*) by three ... [illegible]

(2) Numerous glosses furnish literal commentary on individual words and phrases. For example, in Peter Lombard's prologue Luther elucidates words such as *penuria*, "penury" (for which he offers the synonym *paupertas*, "poverty"), or *munire*, "to fortify" (Luther offers *roborare*, "to strengthen"). His intention is to assist his students' understanding of the text by providing synonymous terms for words that they may not readily recognize or by paraphrasing difficult and obscure expressions.

(3) The largest number of glosses, however, consists of references to Peter Lombard's sources. In his prologue—no doubt due to the more literary, less scholastic character of this text—the Master identified none of his scriptural and patristic quotations. Luther, however, is careful to note that "this prologue is for the most part Hilary, Book X, and Augustine, Book III, of *On the Trinity*."[109] He also points out in the margin where Peter Lombard has woven scriptural passages into his preface. In the main body of the *Sentences*, where the Master did of course provide references, Luther renders them more precise, especially when they concern Scripture and Augustine. Thus, for instance, in distinction 2, chapter 2 of Book I, Peter Lombard cites the Bishop of Hippo on the order in which the doctrine of the Trinity should be treated: "as Augustine teaches in Book I of *On the Trinity*." Luther adds: "chapter 2."[110] Again, in distinction 35 of Book I, in a place where the *Book of Sentences* quotes "the prophet Isaiah," the glosses specify: "chapter 64 and 1 Cor. 2."[111] These are just two examples of a procedure that is in evidence, very consistently, throughout Luther's glosses.[112]

The young bachelor frequently comments on the original texts. To use an example from the opening pages of the glosses, in the margin facing a quotation from Book XIII of *On the Trinity*, Luther has written: "Read this chapter! The discussion on the blessed life, which cannot be related briefly here, is golden as well as outstanding."[113] To be able to offer such observations, and to complete Peter Lombard's references, Luther must have had the text of *On the Trinity* in front of him as he was preparing his glosses—together with (at least) several other Augustinian texts and a copy of the Bible.[114] In a note on distinction 2, chapter 4, of Book I we encounter a reference to a popular Hebrew dictionary—proof of the glossator's seriousness in taking theology back to its biblical foundations.[115] On the other hand, it is striking that only seven references to post-twelfth-century authors occur in the margins of Luther's copy of the *Sentences*.[116] Luther's intention, then, is clear: it is to lead his

students back, beyond the "sectarianism" of high scholasticism, to Peter Lombard—and, through him, to the biblical and patristic sources of his theology.

(4) This interpretation is confirmed by the fourth kind of marginal remarks, namely, theological reflections that are occasioned by the subjects treated in the *Book of Sentences*. Right at the beginning of the work, Luther echoes Peter Lombard's own frequently voiced sentiment on the inadequacy of all human efforts to talk about God. Quoting Hilary of Poitiers, he writes:

Nothing has been given [to us] for human utterance about the things of God, other than the word of God. All else is narrow, limited, encumbered, and obscure. If someone wishes to show a point by means of words other than those by which it was said by God, either he does not understand or he gives the readers nothing to understand." Thus [Hilary]. In what way do our own people, more subtle than distinguished, give credence to this?[117]

Evidently a rhetorical question! Luther's "subtle" contemporaries fail to pay sufficient respect to Scripture, instead engaging in a form of speculative theology that is far too dependent upon philosophical terminology, especially upon "the stinking rules of the logicians"[118] and "Aristotle, the stinking philosopher."[119] Peter Lombard, by contrast, appears in Luther's glosses as someone who answers questions well, with the appropriate restraint: "The Master responds—and very well too—that…."[120] In a context in Book II (dist. 30, chap. 15) where the transmission of original sin is at issue, Luther follows the Master against Gabriel Biel, since the Lombard's argument, Luther feels, stays closer to the biblical evidence: "Gabriel, along with others, denies what the Master says here on the multiplication of nature. See him, in Book 3, dist. 4, qu. 1, last doubt. I agree with the Master, renouncing the ghosts of the philosophers, since the Master comes closer to the Gospel, concerning the multiplication of breads."[121]

We are far from having exhausted the gamut of theological reflections in Luther's glosses. Some are quite long, so that scholars have been able to use them to reconstruct the young Austin Friar's views on specific theological topics, such as Trinitarian theology.[122] We will examine Luther's stance on a different issue, one with whose history we are already familiar: Peter Lombard's identification of charity with the Holy Spirit.

"The Master appears not to be speaking utterly absurdly": Luther on Distinction 17

Luther's commentary on distinction 17 at first appears to be completely in tune with the scholastic consensus. The following excerpt from the *Book of Sentences* represents one of the central passages in Peter Lombard's argument for the identification of charity with the Holy Spirit. In this text, I have indicated the placement of Luther's marginal glosses by means of lower-case letters (a, b, c ...). The excerpt itself will immediately be followed by an explanation of the content of Luther's marginalia.

> **He establishes through authorities that this is so.** Lest, however, we be viewed as insinuating something of ourselves into such an important matter, we shall corroborate through sacred authorities what has been said.—On this [matter] Augustine says in book VIII of *On the Trinity*:[a] "He who loves his neighbor, as a consequence loves love[b] itself principally. *God*, however,[c] *is love* [1 Jn. 4:8 and 4:16]; it follows, therefore, that he loves God principally."[123] Again, in the same [book]: "*God is love*, as John the Apostle says. Why, then, do we go and run to the heights of the heavens and the depths of the earth, searching Him who is with us, if we want to be with Him? Let no one say: I do not know what I should love. Let him love his brother, and let him love the very love.[d] Indeed, he knows the love with which he loves[e] more than the brother whom he loves. Now, see, God can become better known to him than his brother, plainly better known[f] because more present, because more interior, because more certain. [He can] embrace love[g] [who is] God (*amplectere dilectionem Deum*), and through love[h] embrace God. This is the love that unites all the good angels and all the servants of God[i] in a bond of holiness.[j] We are the more holy, therefore, [and] the more void of the swelling of pride, the fuller we are of love; and he who is full of love, of whom is he full if not of God?"[124k] Through these words, Augustine sufficiently shows that the very love with which we love God and neighbor *is* God.[125]

In his first marginal note, *a*, Luther merely specifies Peter Lombard's reference, adding, "in chapter 8, and in the penultimate [chapter]." In

note *b*, he clarifies, "even uncreated," to show that Augustine means that someone who loves his neighbor, through this created love, is brought into communion with a greater, uncreated love. Why is this the case? Because, as Luther explains in note *c* ("this is the reason"), God himself is love. But how do the created and uncreated loves relate to each other? Luther throws light upon this question in note *d*, where he writes, "efficient [love]." In other words, the person who loves his or her brother, in so doing also loves the love that is the efficient cause of such created charity—and this efficient cause is God himself. Luther further adds to note *d*: "It is impossible to love the same love itself, since the object and act of love would be identical." So, in loving my neighbor, I do not love my own act of love, but rather the uncreated love that, as efficient cause, makes me love the neighbor.

We now approach a crucial point in Luther's exegesis, namely, the question as to whether God, who causes human charity, can be *identified with* that charity. In note *e*, Luther unambiguously rejects such an identification, since he notes, "not formally but finally or efficiently." God is not formally "the love with which" (*dilectionem qua*) someone loves his or her neighbor, but only that love's efficient or final cause. Thus, God "is" my charity only to the extent that my charity is aimed at God and caused by him.

Note *f* is of no doctrinal consequence: "he explains himself," Luther writes. And notes *g* and *h* emphasize once again that if we embrace God as the cause of our love, we do so "efficiently" (note *g*), while our own act of love is "formal" (note *h*), that is to say, possesses its own form, different from God. Luther further comments on the love that "unites all the good angels and all the servants of God": "namely, [there is] one spirit in them and one charity" (note *i*). In what sense? Note *j* gives the answer: "Here I ask, What do you mean by 'bond'? There is no other response than, 'formal love.'" This sentence most likely means that the angels and servants of God all share the ability to love each other, and their Creator, in an act of charity that is formally their own. Note *k* is the last one on our extract, and it reads, "since he is always with love"— in other words, someone who is full of love can be said to be full of God since God, in particular in the person of the Holy Spirit, always accompanies the human act of charity.[126]

Luther's glosses continue along the same lines, until he finally sums up his position in the following lengthy note:

For guidance to solve the authorities of Augustine.

First, it needs to be known that charity (whatever the case may be [in the realm] of the possible) is *de facto* always given with the Holy Spirit, and the Holy Spirit with it and in it.

Secondly, when Augustine says that love is God, this should not be understood with precision or exclusively, that is to say, as though love were only God. Rather, it must be admitted that love is God; but not only. Rather, there is also a created love. Just as, "Christ is our faith, justice, grace, and satisfaction." And the Master appears not to be speaking utterly absurdly in saying that the habit is the Holy Spirit. For that comment on the habits has its reputation (*habet opinionem*) from the words of Aristotle, the stinking philosopher. Otherwise one could well say that the Holy Spirit is charity, who through itself joins with the will to produce the act of loving—if there were no decision of the Church to the contrary.[127]

This passage has provoked much commentary, even an entire book.[128] Only one commentator, however, has drawn attention to the fundamental difficulty that arises as one attempts to understand Luther's meaning: the fact that, in the extract that we just read, Luther is contradicting what he said in his earlier glosses on distinction 17.[129] Let us analyze the extract step by step.

As he is offering his students "guidance" on how to interpret the passages from Augustine that stand at the center of the discussion over charity, Luther's first point is that, whatever the situation may be *de potentia absoluta*, in fact—given the way God has arranged his creation—charity is always closely associated with the Holy Spirit. Secondly, Luther continues, it would be mistaken to identify all love with God or, more specifically, with the Holy Spirit. Not all love is of such high dignity; thus, in addition to the uncreated love that is identical with God, there also exists a created one. This crucial distinction is missing in the *Book of Sentences*. Now comes the decisive sentence: "the Master appears not to be speaking utterly absurdly in saying that the habit is the Holy Spirit"[130]—that is to say (I understand Luther as holding), Peter Lombard is right in maintaining that an uncreated charity is at work in certain kinds of human love, and that this uncreated charity, rather than being a habit, should be identified with the Holy Spirit itself. Furthermore,

Peter Lombard's conception is preferable to the later scholastic consensus precisely because the latter depends upon the Aristotelian ethical notion of "habit."

Luther knew exactly what a habit is according to the "stinking philosopher": in 1508–09 he lectured on the *Nicomachean Ethics* at the University of Wittenberg. A habit is an ethical disposition that is formed through the repeated performance of a particular kind of action: thus, repeated cowardly acts will lead to cowardice, a vice; by contrast, consistent courageous acts will establish the habit of courage, a virtue. Habits, then, are the result of human action; there is no room in Aristotle's ethics for grace in the formation of virtue. Christian thinkers adapted Aristotle's notion of habit by postulating that some habits were divinely infused rather than autonomously acquired; in scholastic theology, subsequent to the critique of Peter Lombard's identification of charity with the Holy Spirit, charity became the primary instance of such an "infused virtue."

What is at stake in this debate is the very being of the Christian. Love or charity is the heart of the Christian life: "For all the law is fulfilled in one word: *Thou shalt love thy neighbor as thyself*" (Gal. 5:14). The ontological status of charity therefore decides the ontological status of the Christian. If the love of neighbor *is* God, a wholly uncreated reality, then the person who loves has his being outside himself, as it were.[131] Love takes the Christian beyond himself. This is the meaning of Peter Lombard's conception in the *Book of Sentences*. If, on the other hand, charity is a habit created in us by God, or (which is the same thing) a virtue infused in us by God, then we somehow *possess* our being as Christians; it resides within ourselves, even though not absolutely so. Luther objects to the latter view, and therefore has to reject the use of the concept of habit in the theory of charity.[132]

Or, rather, Luther hints at the possibility of returning to Peter Lombard's identification of charity with the Holy Spirit, intimating that he considers the Lombard's position to be very attractive—but then he recoils since he believes that the Church has pronounced herself authoritatively on this matter.[133] In 1509–11, Luther is not yet the Reformer.

Conclusion: Understanding Tradition with Denys the Carthusian

TWO PRINCIPAL questions have guided the argument of the preceding chapters. First, what was the structure of the tradition of the *Book of Sentences* in its development between 1158, when Peter Lombard released the final redaction of the work, and 1511, when Martin Luther completed his term as *baccaleureus Sententiarum*? In what layers and stages did this tradition unfold and, in particular, what transformations did the *Sentences* commentary undergo as a literary genre? Secondly, since the history of *Sentences* commentaries includes the crucial period of transition from the later Middle Ages to the early modern era, our introduction expressed the expectation that an analysis of certain methodological and formal features of the *Sentences* literature might provide insights into the nature of this transition. In the following pages, I will attempt to summarize the principal findings of this book, and in doing so formulate some tentative answers to these two questions.

At the beginning of the tradition of the *Sentences*, in the twelfth century, we discovered two complementary tendencies in the development of the genre: on the one hand, a trend toward abbreviation and simplification of the work, mainly for the purposes of basic instruction, and on the other hand, a desire to elaborate upon Peter Lombard's text through the addition of marginal glosses. Master Bandinus's abridgment

of the *Sentences* illustrates the first of these tendencies, while the Pseudo-Poitiers gloss provides an important example of the second. Originating in the margins of the Lombard's work, certain sets of glosses quickly mutate into keyword glosses (such as the Pseudo-Poitiers gloss); these compositions already possess a certain degree of internal coherence and thus independence from the original text. It is not possible, however, to read a keyword gloss without consulting the *Book of Sentences* itself. By the beginning of the thirteenth century, the genre of the keyword gloss transforms into that of the *Sentences* commentary, whose argument is situated at a further remove from the original text.

In the course of the thirteenth, fourteenth, and fifteenth centuries, the *Sentences* commentaries would become the new centers of theological discourse, displacing the text in the margins of which they originated.

It is necessary to add a word here about the conception of the theological project that we encountered in the earliest strata of the *Sentences* literature. *Sacra* or *divina pagina*, as envisaged by a thinker such as the author(s) of the Pseudo-Poitiers gloss, is a project consisting in the clarification of "things to be believed and things to be done," with an emphasis upon the former, that is to say, upon matters of what we would call dogmatic theology. It is practiced, in the words of the gloss itself, by "eager doctors who apply themselves tenaciously to the thorough examination of Sacred Scripture." Thus, all theology is viewed as being centered upon the study of Scripture. In fact, strictly speaking theology does not yet exist; it is still *sacra pagina*, "sacred page." Consequently, those practicing *sacra pagina* speak a language that is suffused with biblical images. Textbooks, by contrast, are considered remedial tools for the use of those not capable of reading Scripture itself, or not willing to do so. Moreover, the "eager doctors" see themselves as following in the footsteps of the great authorities of the past, lest they "cross the limits that [the] Fathers have set."

In their method of interpretation, the doctors make a fundamental assumption, namely, that the universe is a cosmos—an ordered whole whose parts harmonize with each other and, ultimately, refer to the Creator. In the words of the Pseudo-Poitiers gloss,

There is some difference between the signs (*signa*) of theology and the signifiers (*significantia*) of the liberal arts; for in the latter

utterances are called "signifiers," in the former things [are called] "signs." In fact, in the sacred page any thing is called "sign" by which something is signified in it, but any thing whatsoever can have as many significations as it has internal or external properties, or harmonies (*convenientias*) with another thing.

In the thirteenth century, *sacra pagina* becomes *scientia divina*, "divine science." *Scientia divina* no longer speaks the metaphorical language of Scripture, but the univocal conceptual language of Aristotle and of the liberal arts. Where Pseudo-Peter of Poitiers has recourse to the Genesis account of Moses' ascent of Mount Sinai to elucidate the nature of the theological project, his thirteenth-century colleagues prefer much more sober definitions. Thomas Aquinas, for example, will say that "the divine being knowable through inspiration is the subject matter of this science," specifying in a few words that theology is a science (*scientia*) with its particular mode of knowledge (*cognitio*) and a subject matter that is best approached in terms of being, or metaphysically (*ens divinum*). In order to transform the metaphorical language of Scripture into "doctrine," *scientia divina* proceeds "according to the order of the discipline" (*secundum ordinem disciplinae*), as Thomas declares in his prologue to the *Summa*. This means that theological knowledge is methodically generated according to the intrinsic requirements of scientific reasoning. No wonder, then, that Thomas is dissatisfied with the arrangement of the *Book of Sentences*, so that he feels compelled to compose his *Summa theologiae* in order to remedy the methodical and pedagogical shortcomings of the *Sentences* commentaries.

It would be mistaken, however, to imagine that thirteenth-century theology was out of touch with its sources (that is to say, principally Scripture, the *Book of Sentences*, the Fathers of the Church, and Aristotle). Yet these sources were restructured according to the needs of theologians now actively *writing* doctrine, rather than merely attempting to *read* the text of the cosmos. Thus, Stephen Langton devises a new chapter division for the verses of Scripture, one not accentuating the narrative flow of the "stories" of the Bible but rather the logic of its "arguments." Alexander of Hales's distinctions and systematic derivations of the contents of the individual books of the *Sentences*—his *divisiones textus*—make available a rigorously structured skeleton for the study of

theology. His decision to lecture on the *Sentences* "ordinarily" marks a milestone in the move from *sacra pagina* to *scientia divina*: from now on, the *Book of Sentences* would stand beside Scripture as the basis for theological study. Robert Kilwardby, one of the greatest tabulators and indexers of the century, goes so far as to divide the *Book of Sentences* into new chapters, arrived at through logical derivation of the contents of the work. Thomas Aquinas compiles an alphabetical index of Aristotle's ethics. One point is clear, then: the theologians of the thirteenth century are not content to subject themselves to texts—Scripture, the *Book of Sentences*, or others—they become authors, in the modern sense of the term, manipulating ideas that are inserted into new conceptual frameworks. Not surprisingly, then, the treatment of Peter Lombard's own text comes to be secondary in their commentaries. No straight line, however, connects the methodological developments of the thirteenth century, which so clearly foreshadow modern conceptions of subjectivity, with the dawn of the modern age at the time of the Reformation.

This is because the condemnation of 1277 throws into question the very thrust of thirteenth-century theology. It alerts subsequent generations of thinkers to some of the dangers that accompany the transformation of *sacra pagina* into *scientia divina* or *sacra doctrina*. Does the rigorous Aristotelian conception of science, incorporated into the new theology, not suggest that God can be captured in the structures of human reasoning? To avoid this consequence, the nominalist current of thought that emerges in the first half of the fourteenth century insists that the insights of which "our theology" is capable depend upon God's *potentia ordinata*, that is to say, upon a free decision on the Creator's part to enter into a covenantal relationship with his people, and to honor that covenant. In principle, however—outside this covenantal relationship, that is—God could have ordered his relationship with creation in ways completely different from those that we have come to know and understand. Having secured God's freedom in this manner, the nominalist theologians feel authorized to unleash the logical tools of the liberal arts without restraint. If there obtains no necessary, metaphysical connection between the Creator and creation—if the connection is historical, covenantal, and hence contingent—then creation needs to be analyzed in itself, without recourse to a foundation in meta-realities such as God or universal, abstract natures that sustain it. For this reason, the nominalist

project is no longer aimed at understanding the cosmos through the analysis of signs, but rather at understanding the signifiers that we employ in speaking about the world. The signs are bent back onto themselves, as it were. Nominalism subsequently produces logical insights at which analytic philosophers of the twentieth and twenty-first centuries continue to marvel. (Recently, for example, the Canadian philosopher Claude Panaccio spurred an interesting debate by arguing that contemporary analytic philosophy still has much to learn from William of Ockham.[1])

These methodological trends are mirrored in the evolution of the *Sentences* commentary as a literary genre. As the cosmos—the ordered whole of the world depending upon its Creator—breaks down, so does systematic theology, the elaboration of which was so central to the twelfth and especially the thirteenth centuries. The *Sentences* commentaries, therefore, begin to emphasize individual points of doctrine, which are often developed at great length by means of logical tools, at the expense of the integrity of the field of theology as a whole. Peter Lombard's text, which had endeavored to present a coherent theoretical vision of the entire Christian faith, fades utterly into the background. We do not know exactly how the *Book of Sentences* was read in the classrooms of the universities of Paris or Oxford; it is clear, however, that it is no longer commented upon, in any proper sense of the term, in Scotus's or Ockham's *Ordinatio*, or in Gregory of Rimini's *Lectura*.

As the commentaries of the great nominalists become longer and longer, their discussions more and more sophisticated and loaded with technical detail, as the metaphorical language of Scripture is completely replaced by the precise tools of linguistic analysis, and as daring *sophismata* raise the specter of blasphemy, a disquieting possibility appears on the horizon: that of a "theologian" without faith. We are now so far removed from the center of the Christian tradition that its expansion has reached the limits of its possibility. Faced with this situation, nominalism itself tries to reverse course. In a thinker such as Gregory of Rimini, we therefore witness a first attempt to return to the sources of Christian theology: Gregory's *Sentences* commentary, although steeped in nominalism and equipped with the most advanced research tools of the day, displays detailed first-hand knowledge of Augustine. But this is not enough to stop the mounting unease with the direction of fourteenth-century theology. Marsilius of Inghen, at the very end of the

century, can be seen as pulling the emergency brake.

In Marsilius's *Sentences* commentary, theological reflection still takes place at a large distance from Peter Lombard and, indeed, from Scripture itself. Yet, troubled by his century's obsession with the subtle analysis of theological signifiers and the concomitant evacuation of spirituality from theology, Marsilius of Inghen attempts to reestablish a core of sound and edifying doctrine by renouncing originality in favor of respect for recognized authorities. These range from Bonaventure and Thomas Aquinas to Ockham and Gregory of Rimini. Unfortunately, Marsilius lacks either the intellectual acumen or the conceptual tools necessary to synthesize his authorities in a meaningful way. Thus, he contents himself with enumerating their divergent positions. Theology, in this manner, becomes a matter of pious choice. Only where the Church has pronounced herself dogmatically on particular issues, through councils or papal decrees that have entered into the body of canon law, is there theological certainty for Marsilius. By the end of the fourteenth century, then, *sacra pagina*, theoretical reflection upon Scripture, has mutated into a science concerning the dogmatic teachings of the Church, whose authority alone is now capable of guaranteeing certainty.

In the long fifteenth century, a gradual return to the core of the Christian tradition occurs. Like Marsilius of Inghen, the authors of this century deliberately renounce further expansion of the tradition, instead endeavoring to hold it together through a movement in reverse. Although their strategies to accomplish this contraction are diverse, they all attempt large-scale syntheses: John Capreolus offers a synthetic reading of the entire Thomistic corpus, coupled with the intention to refute those parts of the tradition that he considers incompatible with Thomism—nominalism, in particular. Denys the Carthusian sets out to combine the "old way" with elements of Dionysian mysticism. Gabriel Biel's *Collectorium* represents a similar attempt to accomplish a synthetic reading of the scholastic tradition, but from a nominalist perspective. To take stock of the tradition in this manner requires all three authors to develop doxographies, that is to say, ordered accounts of the relationship of the systems of thought preceding them. Some of the fifteenth-century authors that we considered display a vivid sense of history in elaborating these doxographies. Indeed, Denys the Carthusian's prologue to his *Sentences* commentary contains a fully worked-out theology of history:

the Christian theological tradition, according to Denys, radiated out from its scriptural center; was for a first time synthesized in the *Book of Sentences*; expanded once again from this new, richer center, only to call for another movement of contraction in a second Peter Lombard—Denys the Carthusian himself.

Denys is more radical in his movement back to the sources than either John Capreolus or Gabriel Biel. He envisages the possibility of a return to the *Book of Sentences* itself: after all, we have seen him attempt a twelfth-century-style literal commentary—a keyword gloss, in fact—on the *Book of Sentences*. Somehow, the time was not yet ripe for such a radical renaissance of the Master, so that Denys felt forced to give up this project. But he was an accomplished biblical scholar, and like Gabriel Biel he strongly emphasized the need for theology to take place within the context of a spiritual journey.

What is perhaps most striking about the *Sentences* commentators of the fifteenth century is their ability to step back, in a certain sense, outside the tradition preceding them, in order to consider and assess it as a whole. This element of fifteenth-century thought, more than any other, indicates the dawn of a new age. John Capreolus, Denys the Carthusian, and Gabriel Biel sensed that they were at the end of a certain stage of the tradition, that it was time to sum up.

And Luther? It would be silly, at the end of this modest book, to offer anything but the most tentative assessment of Luther's role in the transition from the late Middle Ages to modernity. The literature on the topic is vast and controversial. Nevertheless, the following thesis appears warranted on the basis of our study: at least as a *Sentences* commentator, Luther broke with the tradition only by being faithful to it. Luther radicalized the movement back to the sources that was already characteristic of the fifteenth century, by penetrating through the layer of scholastic commentators of Peter Lombard to the work of the Master himself. Furthermore, not content with that, the future Reformer reduced the *Book of Sentences* to its own sources: Scripture and Augustine. (Gabriel Biel, who completed his *Collectorium* little more than a decade before Luther lectured on the *Sentences*, still considered Scripture a vast ocean too dangerous for students to enter.) Perhaps what we witness in Luther, then, is only the contraction of the Christian tradition that had to follow its enormous development and expansion in the patristic and scholastic

periods. One could also describe this movement as the reinscription, into the center of the tradition, of its scriptural core, marginalized in centuries of elucidation and commentary.

★ ★ ★

The theory of the tradition that this study appears to confirm is not new. It is Denys the Carthusian's. We already encountered it in the following text, cited in Chapter Four:

> [T]he wisdom revealed at the time of the evangelical law is very splendid and great. [This wisdom was revealed] first by Christ, then by the mission and inspiration of the Holy Spirit, next by the glorious apostles and evangelists, then by the holy Fathers, and finally by the Catholic and scholastic doctors, excellently learned not only in the divine Scriptures but also in all philosophy.... just as wisdom grew in the course of time before the coming of the Savior, so it also does in the meantime [since his coming]. And most of all from the time when Master Peter Lombard, bishop of Paris, collected his *Book of Sentences*, wisdom appears to have received much and great elucidation, growth, and abundant increase.... And those things that were hidden have been brought forth into the light; the difficulties of the Scriptures have been unknotted; and points that can be objected to the Christian faith, and have been objected by the faithless, have been solved outstandingly. Indeed, the aforesaid Master and illustrious learned scholastics who have written famously on the *Book of Sentences*, have subtly discussed, magisterially made clear, and Catholically treated not only the more difficult places of Scripture, but also the words and writings of the holy Fathers, who have written much that is difficult and obscure in their expositions of the Scriptures and other treatises.
>
> Since it is known, however, that almost innumerable people have already written upon this *Book of Sentences*, and that moreover even today some are writing [on it]—perhaps even more than is useful, as due to some less illustrious writings of recent people, the more illustrious writings of the older ones are less attended to, read, and investigated—hence it is my intention in this work to

prepare a kind of collection of extracts from the commentaries and writings of the most authoritative, famous, and excellent doctors, and to bring the reflection of these doctors back into one volume. For just as the very text of the *Book of Sentences* is gathered from the words and testimonies of the holy Fathers, so this work too is put together from the doctrines and writings of the aforesaid writers upon the *Book of Sentences*.

In this passage, Denys describes the Christian tradition as a movement of expansion and contraction involving several phases. First, there is the outpouring of God's wisdom from within the Trinity itself, through the Incarnation and the mission of the Holy Spirit. This wisdom is then explained and elaborated upon by the apostles and evangelists—we are essentially talking about the composition of the New Testament here, in which the personal wisdom revealed in the Son and the Spirit is preserved, remembered, and represented as text. The New Testament, in its turn, is elucidated by the Church Fathers, who are followed by the scholastics. In Peter Lombard, there occurs a collection of the tradition as unfolded up to that moment in history. Denys regards the *Book of Sentences* as the starting point of a further explication of the wisdom of Scripture, but he has certain reservations about this stage: perhaps this expansion has gone too far. What is needed, therefore, is a robust gathering together of the tradition of *Sentences* commentaries, just as the *Book of Sentences* itself brought together the manifold manifestations of wisdom preceding it. In the mystical bent of his writings, though not in this particular passage, Denys furthermore reminds us of the personal core of the tradition: all those "wise" texts ultimately serve no other purpose than to lead us to Wisdom, that is to say, to the Spirit and the Son and the Father. The expansion of the tradition would be devoid of meaning without this crucial moment of return.

Denys the Carthusian's theory of the Christian tradition bears some resemblance to the one that we found earlier in the Pseudo-Poitiers gloss. The latter adds one insight that is, in fact, completely in tune with Denys's own theology, and with which Denys would have agreed entirely: the center of the tradition, Wisdom, is itself inaccessible except in moments of vision and ecstasy. Only Moses was allowed to ascend the mountain and encounter God. The Christian tradition, therefore, is an

attempt to put into words the inexpressible mystery of God and, indeed, of human existence itself. Because of this mystery, Scripture expresses itself metaphorically; it is not a scientific, univocal text. To assume that it is constitutes a fundamental misunderstanding, apart from being deeply out of tune with the Christian tradition. Curious and insecure as we are as human beings, however, we long for certitude, attempting to shed as much light as we can upon those strange metaphors and stories. The result is theology in its various forms. Yet if theology becomes too scientific, it must ultimately fail. This, I take it, is the lesson of the thirteenth and fourteenth centuries.

Finally, are all traditions not a bit like the Christian tradition? Have not all the great texts of human history—those that have become the centers of traditions—spoken to the great questions of human existence? And is it not also characteristic of a great text not to have merely one meaning, but to remain forever obscure and elusive? After more than two millennia of interpretation, do we know what Plato's *Republic* means? Is there a final interpretation of Shakespeare's *Hamlet*? Of the Koran? No; we continue to center our lives around these texts, to let our lives be structured by them, to immerse ourselves in traditions of interpretation, only to return to the texts themselves, again and again.

Further Reading and Research

Introduction

The following book is recommended as the classic study on the intellectual history that forms the background of the "theological movement" of the twelfth century, and on Peter Lombard's place in it. Although dated in places, de Ghellinck's scholarship remains exemplary:

Joseph de Ghellinck, S.J., *Le mouvement théologique du XII*e *siècle. Sa préparation lointaine avant et autour de Pierre Lombard, ses rapports avec les initiatives des canonistes. Études, recherches et documents*, Museum Lessianum, Section historique 10 (Bruges: Éditions "De Tempel"; Brussels: L'édition universelle; Paris: Desclée-de Brouwer, 1948).

The most comprehensive treatment of Peter Lombard's theology is

Marcia L. Colish, *Peter Lombard*, 2 vols., Brill's Studies in Intellectual History 41 (Leiden/New York/Cologne: Brill, 1994).

The focus of Colish's study is the superiority of the *Book of Sentences* by comparison with theological syntheses by other contemporary masters. For a more concise introduction to the theology of the *Book of Sentences*, which disputes

some of Colish's interpretations, see

Philipp W. Rosemann, *Peter Lombard*, Great Medieval Thinkers (New York: Oxford University Press, 2004).

Rémi Brague has written a stimulating attempt to capture the essence of the Western tradition in the mechanisms it devised for the reception of texts and ideas:

Rémi Brague, *Eccentric Culture: A Theory of Western Civilization*, trans. Samuel Lester (Notre Dame, IN: St. Augustine's Press, 2002).

Chapter One

On the earliest glosses and abbreviations of the *Book of Sentences*, the work of an older generation of scholars—especially Joseph de Ghellinck, Artur Michael Landgraf, Odon Lottin, and Raymond Martin—continues to be indispensable. Landgraf's detailed manuscript studies have perhaps made the most important contribution to an understanding of the development of the *Sentences* literature in the twelfth century. Landgraf summarized the most important results of his work in sections of

Artur Michael Landgraf, *Einführung in die Geschichte der theologischen Literatur der Frühscholastik unter dem Gesichtspunkte der Schulenbildung* (Regensburg: Gregorius-Verlag, 1948), esp. 93–109.

The book consists largely of references to manuscripts and secondary literature. Although it has not been translated into English, there exists an updated French edition:

Artur Michael Landgraf, *Introduction à l'histoire de la littérature théologique de la scolastique naissante*, ed. Albert-M. Landry, O.P., trans. Louis-B. Geiger, O.P. (Montreal: Institut d'études médiévales, 1973).

Since Landgraf's work continues to be a necessary starting point for anyone wishing to conduct research on the *Sentences* literature of the twelfth and early thirteenth centuries, the following more complete list of his publications on the subject might be useful:

"Notes de critique textuelle sur les *Sentences* de Pierre Lombard," *RTAM* 2 (1930): 80–99.

"Problèmes relatifs aux premières Gloses des *Sentences*," *RTAM* 3 (1931): 140–57.

"Recherches sur les écrits de Pierre le Mangeur," *RTAM* 3 (1931): 292–306 and 341–72.

"Zwei Gelehrte aus der Umgebung des Petrus Lombardus," *Divus Thomas* 11 (1933): 157–82.

"Mitteilungen zum Sentenzenkommentar Hugos a S. Charo," *Zeitschrift für katholische Theologie* 58 (1934): 391–400.

"Die Stellungnahme der Frühscholastik zur wissenschaftlichen Methode des Petrus Lombardus," *Collectanea franciscana* 4 (1934): 513–21.

"Die Sentenzen des 'magister ignotus,'" in *Aus der Geisteswelt des Mittelalters. Studien und Texte Martin Grabmann zur Vollendung des 60. Lebensjahres von Freunden und Schülern gewidmet*, ed. Albert Lang, Joseph Lechner, and Michael Schmaus, Beiträge zur Geschichte der Philosophie und Theologie des Mittelalters, Supplementband III/1 (Münster: Aschendorff, 1935), 332–59.

"Drei Zweige der Pseudo-Poitiers-Glosse zu den Sentenzen des Lombarden," *RTAM* 9 (1937): 167–204.

"Sentenzenglossen des beginnenden 13. Jahrhunderts," *RTAM* 10 (1938): 36–55.

"The First *Sentence* Commentary of Early Scholasticism," *The New Scholasticism* 13 (1939): 101–32.

"Bearbeitungen von Werken des Petrus Lombardus," *Collectanea franciscana* 10 (1940): 321–37.

"Abaelard und die Sentenzen des 'magister ignotus,'" *Divus Thomas* 19 (1941): 75–80.

"Frühscholastische Abkürzungen der Sentenzen des Lombarden," in *Studia mediaevalia in honorem admodum Reverendi Patris Raymundi Josephi Martin* (Bruges: De Tempel, 1948), 171–99.

Der Sentenzenkommentar des Kardinals Stephan Langton, Beiträge zur Geschichte der Philosophie und Theologie des Mittelalters 37/1 (Münster: Aschendorff, 1952).

Chapter Two

Two axes of research on the thirteenth-century *Sentences* commentaries appear particularly promising. On the one hand, we need to know more about individual commentators and their works. Even more so than the preceding one, this chapter was only able to scratch the surface of material that requires closer scrutiny. For this research, an excellent starting point is the following article by Russell Friedman, which offers a brief description of the major *Sentences* commentaries of the second half of the thirteenth century; Friedman's footnotes provide an up-to-date list of relevant literature:

Russell L. Friedman, "The *Sentences* Commentary, 1250–1320: General Trends, the Impact of the Religious Orders, and the Test Case of Predestination," in *Mediaeval Commentaries on the* Sentences *of Peter Lombard: Current Research*, vol. 1, ed. G.R. Evans (Leiden/Boston/Cologne: Brill, 2002), 41–128.

On the other hand, a point of considerable consequence in the history of the Western intellectual tradition concerns what I have called the "Copernican turn" that occurred in the thirteenth century: the increasing emphasis placed on the signifier over against the sign; the transformation of *sacra pagina* into theological "science," largely constituted by the internal coherence of its method; and the rise of the human author as an individual bestowing order upon a universe of signifiers. Did these developments prepare the ground for the modern turn toward the subject? The thesis is tempting but requires closer examination, both on the level of detailed historical study of the available evidence and from a more synthetic point of view, that of a large-scale theory of the unfolding of the Western tradition. The following literature is arranged from more historical to more speculative approaches:

Mary A. Rouse and Richard H. Rouse, *Authentic Witnesses: Approaches to Medieval Texts and Manuscripts* (Notre Dame, IN: University of Notre Dame Press, 1991).

A.J. Minnis, *Medieval Theory of Authorship: Scholastic Literary Attitudes in the Later Middle Ages*, 2nd ed. (Aldershot, England: Wildwood House, 1988).

Ivan Illich, *In the Vineyard of the Text: A Commentary to Hugh's "Didascalicon"* (Chicago and London: University of Chicago Press, 1993).

Walter J. Ong, S.J., *Ramus, Method, and the Decay of Dialogue: From the Art of*

Discourse to the Art of Reason (Cambridge, MA: Harvard University Press, 1958; reprinted, Chicago and London: University of Chicago Press, 2004).

Walter J. Ong, S.J., *Orality and Literacy: The Technologizing of the Word*, New Accents (London and New York: Methuen, 1982).

Catherine Pickstock, *After Writing: On the Liturgical Consummation of Philosophy*, Challenges in Contemporary Theology (Oxford: Blackwell, 1998).

Chapter Three

The work of William J. Courtenay provides indispensable background on the intellectual history of the fourteenth century. Perhaps Courtenay's principal contribution consists in having identified the distinction between *potentia ordinata* and *potentia absoluta* as the pivotal point of the English reaction to the theological crisis of the late thirteenth century:

Schools & Scholars in Fourteenth-Century England (Princeton, NJ: Princeton University Press, 1987).

Covenant and Causality in Medieval Thought: Studies in Philosophy, Theology, and Economic Practice, Variorum Reprint CS206 (London: Variorum Reprints, 1984).

The following volume contains several contributions treating the development of *Sentences* commentaries in the fourteenth century:

Mediaeval Commentaries on the Sentences *of Peter Lombard: Current Research*, vol. 1, ed. G.R. Evans (Leiden/Boston/Cologne: Brill, 2002).

Particularly helpful is the synthetic piece by Paul J.J.M. Bakker and Chris Schabel on "*Sentences* Commentaries of the Later Fourteenth Century" (425–64).

An important question not addressed in Chapter Three concerns the dramatically different assessments that exist about the overall meaning and value of the intellectual life of the fourteenth century. Philosophers of the analytic tradition generally view the shift toward nominalism—that is to say, toward theology as the logico-semantic analysis of signifiers—with the greatest sympathy, given the fact that such nominalism is in accord with their own conception of lan-

guage as the irreducible medium of human knowledge. The analytic tradition consequently emphasizes late medieval advances in logic, which it tends to dissociate, however, from their theological context. Although no longer quite up to date, the *Cambridge History of Later Medieval Philosophy* offers a significant overview of the fruits of the analytic approach:

Cambridge History of Later Medieval Philosophy, ed. Norman Kretzmann, Anthony Kenny, and Jan Pinborg (Cambridge: Cambridge University Press, 1982).

On the other hand, it is tempting to regard the fourteenth century as a period of intellectual decline, in particular by comparison with the great theological syntheses of the thirteenth century. Yet such a view is oblivious of the fact that it is the thirteenth century which gave rise to the fourteenth; or, less simplistically put, that the thought of the fourteenth century responded to deep unease about the influence of extraneous elements upon Christian theology: Was God's freedom compromised by the Aristotelian emphasis upon the lawfulness and (limited) autonomy of the natural order? Was the specificity of theological inquiry (and of the Christian message) compromised by the uncritical adoption of Aristotelian paradigms of scientific method? Admittedly, the fourteenth-century attempts to rectify the perceived problems of their predecessors did not fail to produce some unforeseen and perhaps unfortunate consequences: Marsilius of Inghen's increasing reliance upon canon law as a source of theological truth can be seen as troubling. It reflects a situation where confidence in truth—formerly regarded as the result of painstaking reflections upon the tradition and efforts to reconcile discordant voices—is so enfeebled that the only way to guarantee it appears to come "from above," through legislation.

For some current reflections on the evaluation of the intellectual life of the fourteenth century, one may consult the following collective volume:

"Herbst des Mittelalters?" Fragen zur Bewertung des 14. und 15. Jahrhunderts, ed. Jan A. Aertsen and Martin Pickavé, Miscellanea Mediaevalia 31 (Berlin and New York: de Gruyter, 2004).

Chapter Four

Luther is a particularly central and fascinating figure for anyone attempting to understand the transition from late medieval to modern thought: for—to some extent at least—this transition occurred through Luther himself as he challenged the late medieval heritage in his own theology and life. The literature on Luther's medieval roots is vast; the following list begins with some of the works by the late Heiko Oberman, who was the leading authority on the "medieval Luther" in the second half of the twentieth century:

Heiko A. Oberman, *Forerunners of the Reformation: The Shape of Late Medieval Thought Illustrated by Key Documents* (Cambridge: Clarke, 2003)—an anthology of late medieval texts with commentaries, first published in 1966.

Heiko A. Oberman, *The Dawn of the Reformation: Essays in Late Medieval and Early Reformation Thought* (Grand Rapids, MI: Eerdmans, 1986)—contains some of Oberman's most influential essays.

Heiko A. Oberman, *Luther: Man between God and the Devil* (New Haven, CT: Yale University Press, 1989)—an intellectual biography of the Reformer.

The Work of Heiko A. Oberman: Papers from the Symposium on His Seventieth Birthday, ed. Thomas A. Brady, Jr., et al., Kerkhistorische Bijdragen 20 (Leiden/Boston/Cologne: Brill, 2003).

Continuity and Change: The Harvest of Late Medieval and Reformation History. Essays Presented to Heiko A. Oberman on His Seventieth Birthday, ed. Robert J. Bast and Andrew C. Gow (Leiden/Boston/Cologne: Brill, 2000).

Steven Ozment, *The Age of Reform, 1250–1550: An Intellectual and Religious History of Late Medieval and Reformation Europe* (New Haven and London: Yale University Press, 1980).

Leif Grane, *Contra Gabrielem: Luthers Auseinandersetzung mit Gabriel Biel in der Disputatio Contra Scholasticam Theologiam 1517*, Acta theologica danica 4 (Aarhus: Gyldendal, 1962)—a more narrowly focused study, devoted to Luther's critique of Gabriel Biel in his famous "Disputation against Scholastic Theology" from 1517.

Conclusion

Denys the Carthusian's theory of the development of the Christian tradition in a "breathing" movement of expansion and contraction is part of a larger meta-

physics. According to the principles of Neoplatonic thought to which Denys is committed, all of reality is animated by a similar dynamism: as the cosmos emanates from God, the "One," in an ordered hierarchy, this created multiplicity of beings longs to return to the unity of its Source. While this Neoplatonic metaphysics influenced the thought of many medieval theologians, ranging from Augustine to Thomas Aquinas, in some authors, such as Denys the Carthusian, it becomes a leitmotiv.

Some of the best work on Neoplatonism, considered not simply as a historical phenomenon but as a viable system of thought, has been done by the German philosopher Werner Beierwaltes:

Identität und Differenz, Philosophische Abhandlungen 49 (Frankfurt am Main: Klostermann, 1980).
Denken des Einen. Studien zur neuplatonischen Philosophie und ihrer Wirkungsgeschichte (Frankfurt am Main: Klostermann, 1985).
Platonismus im Christentum, 2nd ed., Philosophische Abhandlungen 73 (Frankfurt am Main: Klostermann, 2001).
Platonismus und Idealismus, 2nd ed. (Frankfurt am Main: Klostermann, 2004).

In North America, important venues for the study of Neoplatonism are the *Journal of Neoplatonic Studies* and the series "Studies in Neoplatonism, Ancient and Modern," which is edited by R. Baine Harris and published by the State University of New York Press.

Glossary

article: Since the thirteenth century, the article (*articulus*) is usually the smallest subdivision in *Sentences* commentaries, which are divided into books, **distinctions**, **questions**, and articles. It is important to note, however, that not every author follows this schema. See **dialectical method**.

baccaleureus Sententiarum: Literally, "bachelor of the *Sentences*." Graduate student of theology charged with the task of delivering lectures on the *Book of Sentences*. This task is part of the requirements that the bachelor must meet in order to become **master**.

Christological nihilianism: A teaching often attributed to Peter Lombard according to which Christ, as human, is "nothing" (*nihil*). Christological nihilianism does not deny the Incarnation, but is an attempt to avoid certain problems arising from the Christian belief that Christ was both God and a human being. It was condemned in 1170 and again in 1177. There is some evidence that Peter Lombard may have defended Christological nihilianism in his oral teaching, but he does not subscribe to it in the *Book of Sentences*.

common law (*lex communis*): A technical term used in **nominalism**, "common law" designates the laws or structures of creation to which God has freely subjected his actions and which therefore define his ordered power (*potentia ordinata*).

conclusion (*conclusio*): Since the fourteenth century, "conclusion" can denote any thesis, and not necessarily a judgment reached through syllogistic reasoning.

dialectical method: Dialectical thought typically proceeds in three steps: a position is first affirmed, then it is cast into doubt through counterarguments, and finally a synthesis or reconciliation of the opposing viewpoints is sought. **Scholastic** thought is dialectical in its method, drawing the content of the arguments that it weighs up and synthesizes from the Christian tradition. The literary form of the *Sentences* commentaries reflects the dialectical approach of **scholasticism**, for example in the structure of the typical thirteenth-century **articles**: question, arguments for one side, arguments for the opposite position, solution, return to the initial arguments.

distinction (*distinctio*): (1) Division introduced into the *Book of Sentences* by Alexander of Hales at the level between Peter Lombard's books and chapters. (2) Discernment of different senses of a word or phrase, or of complementary aspects of reality (for example, things vs. signs, nature vs. grace, ***potentia absoluta*** vs. ***potentia ordinata***).

divina pagina*:** See ***sacra pagina.

divisio textus*:** Literally, "division of the text." Part of a *Sentences* commentary in which the author explains the structure of a particular portion of Peter Lombard's text so as to identify the main steps of the argument. A feature mainly of *Sentences* commentaries of the thirteenth century. Compare ***expositio textus.

doxography: From the Greek *doxa*, "opinion," and *graphein*, "to write." A catalog or inventory of positions held by various thinkers.

***dubia circa litteram*:** "Doubts concerning the letter" of the text of the *Sentences*, that is to say, close discussion of questions arising directly from Peter Lombard's argument. The *dubia circa litteram* are a feature of thirteenth-century commentaries.

efficient cause: A term used in the Latin tradition of Aristotelian metaphys-

ics, "efficient cause" designates the external agent that brings about a particular change. For example, fire is the efficient cause that changes wood into ashes.

epistemology: Branch of philosophy that analyzes the nature of knowledge (Greek *epistēmē*) and the conditions under which it is possible.

eschatology: From Greek *eschatos*, "last." Part of theology that explores the events believed to occur at the end of time, after the Second Coming of Christ.

exemplary cause: A thing or event that serves as the exemplar or model of another, such that it comes to be shaped after the former. For example, according to Alexander of Hales, God's perfect love is the exemplary cause of human charity.

expositio textus: Literally, "exposition of the text." Close literal commentary.

final cause: The end or goal (Latin, *finis*) that prompts the **efficient cause** to act. For instance, the final cause of my composing this glossary is the clarification of central terms that I have used in this book.

formal cause: The inner form, shape or structure of a thing.

gloss: (1) Word, phrase or short note added in the margins of a text (marginal gloss) or between its lines (interlinear gloss) for explanation and commentary. Marginal and interlinear glosses that are separated from the main text and arranged continuously form keyword glosses. (2) *Glossa ordinaria* ("standard Gloss"): a compilation of excerpts from the Church Fathers and medieval authorities that were placed in the margins or between the lines of the text of Scripture to serve as commentary. Standardized in the twelfth century in the school of Anselm of Laon.

lemma (pl. lemmata): In keyword **glosses** and commentaries, words or phrases quoted from the main text to indicate the material being discussed.

master: From the Latin *magister* ("teacher"), this term designates the fully

qualified teacher at a school or university. "The Master" became a phrase respectfully used to describe Peter Lombard.

material cause: The matter or stuff from which a thing is made. For instance, the material cause of a book is paper—except in the case of e-books, of course, whose material cause is bits.

negative theology: Aspect of theology that emphasizes what we cannot know about God, due to his transcendence. According to negative theology, all concepts are problematic in their application to God, since they are incapable of conveying God's infinite nature. Thus, negative theology "negates" divine attributes such as goodness, beauty, and truth. The writings of Pseudo-Dionysius the Areopagite (5th c.) were the most influential source of negative theology in the Christian tradition.

nominalism: Nominalism is usually defined as the theory according to which universal concepts are mere "names" (*nomina*) without any reality outside the human mind. For example, a nominalist would claim that there is nothing in reality that corresponds to the concept of "dog," for all that exists is individual dogs. No one has ever seen just "dog," only Labradors, collies, German shepherds, etc. (Indeed, no one has ever met just "Labrador," but only individual representatives of the species such as Fido.) Realists, by contrast, maintain that all individual dogs really have something in common: an essence of dogness that has reality within the individual dogs. Nominalism cannot be properly understood without its roots in the distinction between *potentia absoluta* and *potentia ordinata*.

ordinatio: Latin term that literally means "ordering." The **masters** of the fourteenth century, who often lectured on the *Book of Sentences* several times during their careers, sometimes prepared "ordered" versions from the notes that they had taken for these lectures, or even from student notes (see *reportatio*). *Ordinatio* is the title for a *Sentences* commentary revised in this fashion.

phenomenology: A current in twentieth-century philosophy that attempts to leave behind the **epistemological** preoccupations of modern thought and instead endeavors to return to the "things themselves." Phenomenology thus

brackets questions about the reality of the world that we perceive, or the correspondence of our knowledge with reality. Rather, it proceeds by describing minutely what is actually given to human consciousness.

potentia absoluta: God's "absolute power," which is not accessible to human understanding. In other words, from the perspective of *potentia absoluta*, there are no laws intelligible to the human being that could constrain God's will or help predict his actions. A key term in **nominalism**. Compare *potentia ordinata*.

potentia ordinata: God's "ordered power" designates the way in which God has freely subjected his absolute power to a covenant with his people. Since God has historically "ordered" his will in accordance with what we know about him from Scripture and from creation, his actions now follow humanly intelligible structures. Compare *potentia absoluta*.

principium (**pl.** *principia*): Solemn opening lecture that the *baccalaureus Sententiarum* had to deliver at the beginning of his commentary on each of the four books of the *Sentences*.

question (*quaestio*): The **distinctions** in *Sentences* commentaries are usually further divided into questions.

reportatio: A set of student notes. *Reportatio*, "report," is often used as the title of *Sentences* commentaries that we know only from such notes.

sacra doctrina: "Sacred doctrine." See *scientia divina*.

sacra pagina: "Sacred page" refers both to the text of Scripture and to theology insofar as the latter is conceived strictly as an elucidation of the Word of God, that is to say, as arising in the margins of the biblical text (literally or metaphorically). See **gloss**. Theology in this sense contrasts with *scientia divina* and **systematic theology**.

saturated phenomenon: In the thought of Jean-Luc Marion, the saturated phenomenon is an element of experience that challenges the boundaries of

human thought, forcing its structures to reconstitute themselves around this extraordinary thing or event. Revelation, for example, is a saturated phenomenon. Marion employs this concept to overcome the limitations of traditional **phenomenology**, which holds that the possibilities of experience are circumscribed by "horizons." The notion of saturated phenomenon is of considerable theological consequence: if the divine can be understood as a saturated phenomenon, it is not necessarily reduced to the capacities of human thought but rather shapes the latter. This alternative is at stake in the tension between *sacra pagina* and **systematic theology**.

scientia divina: Literally, "divine science." See **systematic theology.**

scholastic, scholasticism: Scholasticism has been defined in different ways, for example through the **dialectical method** that scholastic authors characteristically employ to treat philosophical and theological issues. Understood in this way, scholasticism is almost as old as the Christian tradition itself. In this book, however, the word is used in a narrower sense: it designates the Christian thought that, from the twelfth century onward, flourishes most prolifically in the institutional setting of professional schools (in Latin, "school" is *schola*) and universities.

semiotics: A recent field in the humanities that understands all things as signs. The fundamental characteristic of all things, according to semiotics, is to signify.

sentence (Lat. *sententia*): An authoritative statement of doctrine. Thus, Peter Lombard's *Book of Sentences* is a collection of such authoritative statements.

sophisma (pl. *sophismata*): A tool of instruction typical of fourteenth-century **nominalism**, *sophismata* are "sophisms" that present shocking conclusions based upon false premises or flawed syllogistic reasoning. The point was to sharpen the audience's ability to detect logical errors, but in doing so the *sophismata* sometimes offended religious sentiments. "Christ is present in the sacrament of the Eucharist not differently than in ordinary bread, in wood, or in a stone" is such a *sophisma*.

systematic theology: The principal characteristics of systematic theology are two. (1) It presents its reflections upon the faith in an order that is not based on the narrative flow of Scripture (unlike the **gloss**). Instead, systematic theology seeks to arrange the contents of the faith in a "logical" or "rational" order. For example, whereas the Bible presupposes the existence of a Creator-God and opens with the Genesis accounts of creation, systematic theology begins with a discussion of the existence and nature of God, the inner-Trinitarian relationships, etc. (2) Systematic theology aims not only at a logically ordered but also at a comprehensive account of the faith: every piece of Christian teaching must find its appropriate place in the whole. Systematic theology contrasts with *sacra pagina*, which it replaces from the twelfth century onward. The medieval term for systematic theology is *scientia divina*.

Wirkungsgeschichte: A German word that designates the reception—literally, the "history of the effect"—of a work or idea.

Notes

Notes to the Acknowledgements

1 Marcia L. Colish, *Peter Lombard*, Brill's Studies in Intellectual History 41 (Leiden: Brill, 1994), 1.
2 Ibid., 2.

Notes to the Introduction

1 I owe this distinction to Henri Cloes, "La systématisation théologique pendant la première moitié du XIIe siècle," *Ephemerides theologicae lovanienses* 34 (1958): 277–329.
2 For this idea of renaissance, see Rémi Brague, *Eccentric Culture: A Theory of Western Civilization*, trans. Samuel Lester (Notre Dame, IN: St. Augustine's Press, 2002).
3 On the origins and development of the term "sentence," *sententia*, see Mariken Teeuwen, *The Vocabulary of Intellectual Life in the Middle Ages*, CIVICIMA: Études sur le vocabulaire intellectuel du moyen âge 10 (Turnhout: Brepols, 2003), 336–39.
4 Marcia L. Colish, "Systematic Theology and Theological Renewal in the Twelfth Century," *Journal of Medieval and Renaissance Studies* 18 (1988): 135–56, at 138.
5 It should be clear, however, that the unity of Scripture is extremely complex, since the Bible is composed of the two Testaments, each of which falls into books with different "authors."
6 Joseph de Ghellinck, S.J., *Le mouvement théologique du XIIe siècle*, Museum Lessianum, Section historique 10 (Bruges: Éditions "De Tempel"; Brussels: L'édition universelle; Paris: Desclée-de Brouwer, 1948), 2.

7 The precise dates of when the *Book of Sentences* ceased being a tool of theo-logical instruction vary from institution to institution. At the University of Louvain, for example, a royal chair devoted to the *Sentences* existed as late as 1568, and Thomas Aquinas's *Summa theologiae* was officially introduced by royal edict only in 1596. See Victor Brants, "La création de la chaire de théolo-gie scolastique et la nomination de Malderus à l'université en 1596," *Analectes pour servir à l'histoire ecclésiastique de la Belgique* 34 (1908): 46–54; H. De Jongh, "Deux letttres se rapportant à la substitution de la Somme de saint Thomas aux Sentences de Pierre Lombard dans l'enseignment de la théologie à Louvain en 1596," ibid. 35 (1909): 370–76; and Raymond-M. Martin, O.P., "L'introduction officielle de la 'Somme' de saint Thomas à l'ancienne Université de Louvain," *Revue thomiste* 18 (1910): 230–39.

Notes to Chapter One

1 On the role of canon law in the rise of systematic theology, see Joseph de Ghellinck, S.J., *Le mouvement théologique du XIIᵉ siècle*, Museum Lessianum, Section historique 10 (Bruges: Éditions "De Tempel"; Brussels: L'édition uni-verselle; Paris: Desclée-de Brouwer, 1948), 416–510. De Ghellinck's view has been challenged by Nikolaus M. Häring, "The Interaction between Canon Law and Sacramental Theology in the Twelfth Century," in *Proceedings of the Fourth International Congress of Medieval Canon Law*, ed. Stephan Kuttner, Monumenta Iuris Canonici, Series C, 5 (Vatican City: Biblioteca Apostolica Vaticana, 1976), 483–93.

2 A good introduction to the intellectual climate of the twelfth century is R.N. Swanson, *The Twelfth-Century Renaissance* (Manchester and New York: Manchester University Press, 1999).

3 R.W. Southern, "The Scholastic Metropolis of Northern Europe," in his *Scholastic Humanism and the Unification of Europe*, vol. 1: *Foundations* (Oxford: Blackwell, 1995), 198–233.

4 For the state of research on the *Glossa ordinaria*, see the excellent summary in Titus Lenherr, "Die 'Glossa Ordinaria' zur Bibel als Quelle von Gratians Dekret," *Bulletin of Medieval Canon Law* 24 (2000): 97–121, at 97–101.

5 The virtues possess a similarly ambiguous status.

6 See the historical overview in Pierre Petitmengin, "*Capitula* païens et chré-tiens," in *Titres et articulations du texte dans les œuvres antiques. Actes du Colloque international de Chantilly, 13–15 décembre 1994*, ed. Jean-Claude Fredouille and Simone Deléani, Études augustiniennes 152 (Paris: Institut d'études augusti-niennes, 1997), 491–507. I thank Michael Gorman for this reference, and for a long letter on the early history of lists of chapter headings.

7 *Œuvres de Robert de Melun*, t. III: *Sententiae*, vol. 1, ed. Raymond M. Martin, O.P., Spicilegium sacrum lovaniense 21 (Louvain: Spicilegium sacrum lovani-ense, 1947), p. 49, l. 26–p. 50, l. 1.

8 Peter Lombard, *Sentences*, Prologue (p. 4).

9   On this topic, one may consult the stimulating study by Ivan Illich, *In the Vineyard of the Text: A Commentary to Hugh's "Didascalicon"* (Chicago and London: University of Chicago Press, 1993).

10 The modern notion of authorship is brilliantly analyzed and questioned by Michel Foucault in his essay, "What Is an Author?" (trans. Josué V. Harari), in *Essential Works of Foucault*, ed. Paul Rabinow, vol. 2: *Aesthetics, Method, and Epistemology* (New York: The New Press, 1998), 205–22.

11 Peter Lombard, *Sentences*, Prologue, 3.

12 Ibid., 4.

13 See Raymond M. Martin, O.P., "*Filia Magistri*: un abrégé des *Sentences* de Pierre Lombard. Notes sur un manuscrit conservé à la bibliothèque John Rylands à Manchester," *Bulletin of the John Rylands Library* 2 (1915): 370–79, at 373f. The following list is an adaptation of Martin's.

14 For a provisional list of surviving manuscripts, see Stegmüller, *Repertorium*, 1: 6–8 (nos. 11–22).

15 Thus, MS. Cambridge, Pembroke College, 101, fols. 41–46, offers *Exceptiones libri sententiarum*.

16 One example of this case is MS. Oxford, New College, 145, fols. 13–50, which further condenses the abbreviation contained in MS. Oxford, Bodleian Library, Laud. Misc. 397, fols. 7–106.

17 Examples are MS. Dublin, Trinity College, 275, fols. 119–29, MS. Oxford, Balliol College, 230, fols. 159–165, and MS. Cambridge, Corpus Christi College, 459, fols. 114–24. These are copies of a lexicon attributed to Roger of Salisbury.

18 The manuscript tradition is documented in Stegmüller, *Repertorium*, 1: 48f. (no. 94). The claim that the work was authored by a certain Hildegundis was examined, and rejected, by Paul Lehmann, "Hildegundis oder Bandinus," *Historische Vierteljahrschrift* 29 (1934): 177–9. Lehmann concluded that Hildegundis, whose name appears in one of the manuscripts, must have been a scribe.

19 See Frid. Guil. Rettberg, *Comparatio inter Magistri Bandini libellum et Petri Lombardi sententiarum libros quattuor* (Göttingen: Dieterich, 1834). The fullest account of the literary history of Bandinus's abbreviation is the one by Ed. Dhanis, art. "Bandinus," in *Dictionnaire d'histoire et de géographie ecclésiastiques*, vol. 6 (Paris: Letouzey et Ané, 1932), 488f.

20 Magister Bandinus, *Sententiarum libri quatuor*, Book I, dist. 1 (PL 192: 971).

21 On the origins and development of the term *sacra pagina*, see the important article by Joseph de Ghellinck, S.J., "*Pagina* et *sacra pagina*. Histoire d'un mot et transformation de l'objet primitivement désigné," in *Mélanges Auguste Pelzer. Études d'histoire littéraire et doctrinale de la scolastique médiévale offertes à Monseigneur Auguste Pelzer à l'occasion de son soixante-dixième anniversaire*, Recueil de travaux d'histoire et de philologie, 3rd series, fasc. 26 (Louvain: Bibliothèque de l'université and Éditions de l'Institut supérieur de philosophie, 1947), 23–59.

22 I have examined the Lombard's teaching on charity in my article, "*Fraterna dilectio est Deus*: Peter Lombard's Thesis on Charity as the Holy Spirit," in *Amor*

amicitiae—On the Love that is Friendship: Essays in Medieval Thought and Beyond in Honor of the Rev. Professor James McEvoy, ed. Thomas A.F. Kelly and Philipp W. Rosemann, Recherches de théologie et philosophie médiévales, Bibliotheca 6 (Louvain: Peeters, 2004), 409–36. The article contains a complete translation of chapters 60 to 65.

23   Magister Bandinus, *Sententiarum libri quatuor*, Book I, dist. 17 (PL 192: 993f.).

24   Ibid., 996.

25   See Cicero, *Pro Caecina*, § 61: *frigida ieiunaque calumnia.*

26   Rosemann, *Peter Lombard*, 127.

27   Peter Lombard, *Sentences*, Book III, dist. 7, chap. 3, no. 3 (p. 66). A remark by Marcia Colish is helpful to understand this spirit of the sentence collections: "… the sentence collection is the antithesis of the theological textbooks, even systematic ones, geared to the needs of lay audiences or designed to inspire monastic contemplation. For, instead of seeking to settle questions with an authoritative *ipse dixit*, their goal is to raise questions and to promote theological speculation" (Marcia L. Colish, "From the Sentence Collection to the *Sentence* Commentary and the *Summa*: Parisian Scholastic Theology, 1130–1215," in *Manuels, programmes de cours et techniques d'enseignement dans les universités médiévales*, ed. Jacqueline Hamesse, Publications de l'Institut d'études médiévales—Textes, études, congrès 16 [Louvain-la-Neuve: Institut d'études médiévales, 1994], 9–29, at 12f.).

28   Magister Bandinus, *Sententiarum libri quatuor*, Book III, dist. 6 (PL 192: 1075).

29   See Rosemann, *Peter Lombard*, 130.

30   Rettberg, *Comparatio*, 10, was the first to notice this distortion, although he confounded the *habitus* theory with Christological nihilianism.

31   See Martin, "*Filia Magistri*," esp. 376–79. Further discussion of the work is contained in Artur Landgraf, "Mitteilungen aus dem Sentenzenkommentar Hugos a S. Charo," *Zeitschrift für katholische Theologie* 58 (1934): 391–400, at 391–93.

32   The dependence of *Filia Magistri* upon the *Summa aurea* was demonstrated by H. Weisweiler, S.J., "Théologiens de l'entourage d'Hugues de Saint-Cher," *RTAM* 8 (1936): 389–407.

33   The manuscripts are listed in Stegmüller, *Repertorium*, 1: 175f. (no. 373).

34   See Martin, "*Filia Magistri*." I am grateful to Mr. John Hodgson, Keeper of Manuscripts, and his staff at the John Rylands University Library of Manchester for invaluable assistance in identifying the manuscript, which had not yet been assigned a call number when Martin described it. The correct identification is MS. Manchester, John Rylands University Library, Latin 203. *Filia Magistri* occurs on fols. 75r–256r.

35   MS. Manchester, John Rylands University Library, Latin 203, fol. 75r–v (edited in Martin, "*Filia Magistri*," 376). For my translation, I have checked Martin's transcription against the manuscript.

36   Martin, "*Filia Magistri*," calls the work "un résumé des Sentences *up to date*" (375).

37 MS. Manchester, John Rylands University Library, Latin 203, fol. 75v.

38 The best account of Peter Lombard's "flying glosses" on the *Sentences* is provided in the article by Artur Landgraf, "Notes de critique textuelle sur les *Sentences* de Pierre Lombard," *RTAM* 2 (1930): 80–99. For details concerning the composition of the *Sentences*, see Peter Lombard, *Sentences*, vol. 1, 122*–29* (prolegomena by Ignatius Brady).

39 This example, along with the following ones, is taken from Joseph de Ghellinck, S.J., "Les notes marginales du *Liber sententiarum*," *Revue d'histoire ecclésiastique* 14 (1913): 511–36 and 705–19.

40 The relationship between marginal and keyword glosses is aptly summarized in H. Weisweiler, S.J., "Eine neue frühe Glosse zum vierten Buch der Sentenzen des Petrus Lombardus," in *Aus der Geisteswelt des Mittelalters*, ed. Albert Lang, Joseph Lechner, and Michael Schmaus, Beiträge zur Geschichte der Philosophie und Theologie des Mittelalters, Suppl. 3 (Münster: Aschendorff, 1935), 1:360–400, at 388f.

41 This excerpt is from the Pseudo-Poitiers gloss, as partially edited by Ludwig Hödl, "Die Sentenzen des Petrus Lombardus in der Diskussion seiner Schule," in *Mediaeval Commentaries*, 25–40, at 37 (in MS. Naples, Biblioteca nazionale, VII C 14, the passage occurs on fol. 15v).

42 This misattribution was first corrected in a letter from Odon Lottin, O.S.B., to Artur Landgraf; Landgraf reproduced Dom Lottin's note in his article, "Notes de critique textuelle" (see n. 38), 81f. Lottin reprinted this note, together with a later article on the Pseudo-Poitiers gloss, in his *Psychologie et morale aux XIIe et XIIIe siècles*, vol. 6: *Problèmes d'histoire littéraire de 1160 à 1300* (Gembloux, Belgium: Duculot, 1960), 119–24.

43 See Philip S. Moore, *The Works of Peter of Poitiers, Master in Theology and Chancellor of Paris (1193–1205)* (Washington, DC: The Catholic University of America, 1936), 151–53.

44 For the manuscripts of the Pseudo-Poitiers gloss, see Stegmüller, *Repertorium*, 1: 10 (no. 28). Artur Landgraf attempted to disentangle some of the branches of the Pseudo-Poitiers gloss in his article, "Drei Zweige der Pseudo-Poitiers-Glosse zu den Sentenzen des Lombarden," *RTAM* 9 (1937): 167–204.

45 On the use of the *accessus* in medieval literature, see Edwin A. Quain, S.J., *The Medieval Accessus ad Auctores* (New York: Fordham University Press, 1986); this is a reprint in book form of a classic article that first appeared in *Traditio* 3 (1945): 215–64.

46 The metaphor of the stronger nail driving out weaker ones stems from Cicero's *Tusculan Disputations*, 4.35.75.

47 The prologue translated here was edited, in two parts and from two different manuscripts, by Raymond-M. Martin, O.P., "Notes sur l'œuvre littéraire de Pierre le Mangeur," *RTAM* 3 (1931): 54–66, and Odon Lottin, O.S.B., "Le prologue des Gloses sur les Sentences attribuées à Pierre de Poitiers," *RTAM* 7 (1935): 70–3. (The latter article was reprinted in Lottin's *Psychologie et morale aux XIIe et XIIIe siècles*, vol. 6, 119–24.) My translation is based upon my

own transcription from the first known manuscript of the gloss, MS. Naples, Biblioteca nazionale, VII C 14, fol. 2r.

48 The term "intertextuality" was coined by Julia Kristeva, who defined it as follows: "... any text is constructed as a mosaic of quotations; any text is the absorption and transformation of another." See Kristeva, "Word, Dialogue, and Novel," in her *Desire in Language: A Semiotic Approach to Literature and Art*, ed. Leon S. Roudiez, trans. Thomas Gora et al. (New York: Columbia University Press, 1980), 64–91, at 66.

49 Peter Comestor's influence on the prologue of the Pseudo-Poitiers gloss was established by Martin, "Notes sur l'œuvre littéraire de Pierre le Mangeur."

50 See Moore, *The Works of Peter of Poitiers*, 163.

51 The interest of this theological use of the Exodus narrative was first noted by Martin Grabmann, *Die Geschichte der scholastischen Methode*, vol. 2: *Die scholastische Methode im 12. und beginnenden 13. Jahrhundert* (Freiburg im Breisgau: Herder, 1911; reprinted, Berlin: Akademie-Verlag, 1988), 504–6. Grabmann was followed by Ludwig Hödl, "Die Sentenzen des Petrus Lombardus," 26f.

52 Ludwig Hödl has commented on the use of the term *facultas*, "faculty," in this text that was written before the official foundation of the University of Paris, in 1200. See Hödl, "Die Sentenzen des Petrus Lombardus," 27.

53 See MS. Naples, Biblioteca nazionale, VII C 14, fols. 12v–13r.

Notes to Chapter Two

1 One of the most lucid interpretations of the *Symposium* is the psychoanalytic one offered by Jacques Lacan in his Seminar VIII: Jacques Lacan, *Le séminaire*, ed. Jacques-Alain Miller, vol. 8: *Le transfert*, 2nd ed. (Paris: Seuil, 2001), 11–199.

2 Walter J. Ong, S.J., *Ramus, Method, and the Decay of Dialogue: From the Art of Discourse to the Art of Reason* (Cambridge, Mass.: Harvard University Press, 1958; reprinted, Chicago and London: University of Chicago Press, 2004), 152.

3 See Laura Light, "Versions et révisions du texte biblique," in *Le moyen âge et la Bible*, ed. Pierre Riché and Guy Lobrichon (Paris: Beauchesne, 1984), 55–93.

4 See Amaury d'Esneval, "La division de la Vulgate latine en chapitres dans l'édition parisienne du XIIIᵉ siècle," *Revue des sciences philosophiques et théologiques* 62 (1978): 559–68, esp. 563 and 566. See also Artur Landgraf, "Die Schriftzitate in der Scholastik um die Wende des 12. zum 13. Jahrhundert," *Biblica* 18 (1937): 74–94.

5 For an outline of Langton's life, see *Dictionary of National Biography*, ed. Leslie Stephen and Sidney Lee (Oxford: Oxford University Press, 1949–50), 11: 563–69, and, more recently, Klaus Reinhardt, art. "Langton, Stephan," in *Biographisch-Bibliographisches Kirchenlexikon*, ed. Friedrich-Wilhelm Bautz and Traugott Bautz, vol. 4 (Herzberg: Bautz, 1992), 1127–30. The classic volume by Sir Maurice Powicke remains the only general introduction to Langton's life and works: F.M. Powicke, *Stephen Langton* (Oxford: Clarendon Press, 1928).

6 It is MS. Naples, Biblioteca nazionale, VII C 14, which we already came across
   in our discussion of the Pseudo-Poitiers gloss in the previous chapter.

7 See Artur Landgraf, *Der Sentenzenkommentar des Kardinals Stephan Langton*,
   Beiträge zur Geschichte der Philosophie und Theologie des Mittelalters 37/1
   (Münster: Aschendorff, 1952), xviii.

8 See Artur Landgraf, "The First Sentence Commentary of Early Scholasticism,"
   The New Scholasticism 13 (1939): 101–32. More recently, Marcia Colish has
   followed Landgraf's opinion; see Marcia L. Colish, "From the Sentence
   Collection to the *Sentence* Commentary and the *Summa*: Parisian Scholastic
   Theology, 1130–1215," in *Manuels, programmes de cours et techniques d'enseignement
   dans les universités médiévales*, ed. Jacqueline Hamesse, Publications de l'Institut
   d'études médiévales—Textes, études, congrès 16 (Louvain-la-Neuve: Institut
   d'études médiévales, 1994), 9–29, esp. 24f.

9 Landgraf, *Der Sentenzenkommentar des Kardinals Stephan Langton*, 3 (fol. 86r, col. a).
   I have added the italics in order to highlight the logical structure of the passage.

10 See Rosemann, *Peter Lombard*, 146.

11 Ong, *Ramus, Method, and the Decay of Dialogue*, 132f.

12 MS. Naples, Biblioteca nazionale, VII C 14, fol. 3r, col. a: "non nulla tamen
   est differentia inter theologie signa et liberalium artium significantia. In illis
   enim uoces significantia, in hac res signa dicuntur. In sacra enim pagina signum dicitur omnis res per quam in ea aliquid significatur. Res autem quelibet
   tot significationes habere potest, quot habet proprietates intrinsecas uel extrin-
   secas uel cum alia re conuenientias." Both Martin Grabmann, *Die Geschichte
   der scholastischen Methode*, vol. 2: *Die scholastische Methode im 12. und beginnenden
   13. Jahrhundert* (Freiburg im Breisgau: Herder, 1911; reprint, Berlin: Akademie-
   Verlag, 1988), 507, and Ludwig Hödl, "Die Sentenzen des Petrus Lombardus
   in der Diskussion seiner Schule," in *Mediaeval Commentaries*, 25–40, at 28f.,
   have commented on the significance of this passage.

13 See study 4, "The Prose of the World," in my book, *Understanding Scholastic
   Thought with Foucault*, The New Middle Ages (New York: St. Martin's Press,
   1999), 103–32.

14 The difference between the sign and the signifier, as the Pseudo-Poitiers gloss
   understands them, exhibits numerous parallels with the distinction that Walter
   Ong established between oral and written language. For the former, words are
   "occurrences, events" the meaning of which depends on context, "whereas
   writing concentrates meaning in language itself" (Walter J. Ong, S.J., *Orality
   and Literacy: The Technologizing of the Word*, New Accents [London and New
   York: Methuen, 1982], 31, 106).

15 See Peter Lombard, *Sentences* I, dist. 46, chap. 7, nos. 3 and 4 (pp. 320f.).

16 Landgraf, *Der Sentenzenkommentar des Kardinals Stephan Langton*, 67 (fol. 92r,
   col. a).

17 Augustine already distinguishes object language and meta-language in his dialogue, *De magistro* (*On the Teacher*). I have examined Augustine's distinction
   in a book co-authored with the late linguist Werner Welte: *Alltagssprachliche
   Metakommunikation im Englischen und Deutschen* (Frankfurt: Lang, 1990), 13–17.

18 See Landgraf, *Der Sentenzenkommentar des Kardinals Stephan Langton*, 67 (fol. 92r, col. b).

19 Landgraf, "The First Sentence Commentary of Early Scholasticism," 120–5, contains a list of such disagreements. It is not comprehensive, however.

20 Landgraf, *Der Sentenzenkommentar des Kardinals Stephan Langton*, 18 (fol. 87r, col. b).

21 For a list of such references "outside" (*extra*), see Landgraf, *Der Sentenzenkommentar des Kardinals Stephan Langton*, xix–xxviii.

22 See ibid., 146f. (fol. 99r, col. b).

23 The classic work on the medieval system of higher education is Hastings Rashdall, *The Universities of Europe in the Middle Ages*, new ed. by F.M. Powicke and A.B. Emden, 3 vols. (Oxford: Oxford University Press, 1936; many reprints). On the distinction between ordinary and cursory lectures, see 1: 433–35. For the arrangements in the theology faculty at Paris in the thirteenth century, there is the more recent piece by Palémon Glorieux, "L'enseignement au moyen âge. Techniques et méthodes en usage à la Faculté de Théologie de Paris, au XIIIe siècle," *Archives d'histoire doctrinale et littéraire du moyen âge* 35 (1968): 65–186.

24 On Alexander's biography, see Magistri Aexandri de Hales *Glossa in quatuor libros Sententiarum Petri Lombardi*, 4 vols., Bibliotheca franciscana scholastica 12–15 (Quaracchi: Typographia Collegii S. Bonaventurae, 1951–57), 1: 56*– 75*. A briefer, more recent account is Christopher M. Cullen, "Alexander of Hales," in *A Companion to Philosophy in the Middle Ages*, ed. Jorge J.E. Gracia and Timothy B. Noone, Blackwell Companions to Philosophy 24 (Oxford: Blackwell, 2003), 104–08.

25 *Enchiridion symbolorum definitionum et declarationum de rebus fidei et morum*, ed. Heinrich Denzinger and Adolf Schönmetzer, S.J., 34th ed. (Barcelona, etc.: Herder, 1967), no. 804.

26 See ibid., nos. 749 and 750. For further discussion of Peter Lombard's Christology, see Rosemann, *Peter Lombard*, 118–33. The *Book of Sentences* does not actually teach Christological nihilianism, but Peter Lombard may have done so orally.

27 Bishop Grosseteste wrote: "But the time most appropriate for placing and fitting in at the foundation the stones we have mentioned (for there is a time for laying foundations, as there is a time for building [Eccl. 3:3]) is the morning hour of your ordinary lectures. All of your lectures, especially these early ones, should be drawn from the books of the New Testament and the Old. ... no intermediary, not even the edifices built by the Fathers upon the teaching of Scripture, can be substituted for the study of the foundations; some other time can be more fittingly set aside for such reading" (from *Epistola* 123, trans. in James McEvoy, *Robert Grosseteste*, Great Medieval Thinkers [New York: Oxford University Press, 2000], 163f.). For further analysis of Letter 123, see James R. Ginther, "Theological Education at the Oxford Studium in the Thirteenth Century: A Reassessment of Robert Grosseteste's Letter to the

Oxford Theologians," *Franciscan Studies* 55 (1998): 83–104. Ginther argues that Grosseteste's main purpose in this letter was "to bring Oxford into line with the standards set by the University of Paris" (104), where by the time when Grosseteste wrote his letter—that is, in the mid-1240s—the *Sentences* formed the object of lectures by the bachelors, not the masters of theology.

28 See Glorieux, "L'enseignement au moyen âge," 111–18 (on the bachelors' lectures on the *Sentences*) and 138–41 (on the *principia* in particular). A more detailed treatment of the *principia* is to be found in Franz (Cardinal) Ehrle, S.J., *Der Sentenzenkommentar Peters von Candia, des Pisaner Papstes Alexanders V. Ein Beitrag zur Scheidung der Schulen in der Scholastik des vierzehnten Jahrhunderts und zur Geschichte des Wegestreites,* Franziskanische Studien, Beiheft 9 (Münster: Aschendorff, 1925), 39–56; and, more recently, Venício Marcelino, "Der Augustinertheologe an der Universität Paris," in *Gregor von Rimini: Werk und Wirkung bis zur Reformation,* ed. Heiko A. Oberman, Spätmittelalter und Reformation 20 (Berlin and New York: de Gruyter, 1981), 127–94, at 174–83.

29 Peter Lombard, *Sentences* I, dist. 17, chap. 1, nos. 1 and 2 (141f.) and chap. 6, no. 9 (152). The English translation is from my article, "*Fraterna dilectio est Deus*: Peter Lombard's Thesis on Charity as the Holy Spirit," in *Amor amicitiae—On the Love that is Friendship: Essays in Medieval Thought and Beyond in Honor of the Rev. Professor James McEvoy,* ed. Thomas A.F. Kelly and Philipp W. Rosemann, Recherches de théologie et philosophie médiévales, Bibliotheca 6 (Louvain: Peeters, 2004), 409–36.

30 See Ignatius Brady, O.F.M., "The Distinctions of Lombard's *Book of Sentences* and Alexander of Hales," *Franciscan Studies* 25 (1965): 90–116.

31 Magistri Alexandri de Hales *Glossa* III, Divisio libri tertii (3: 1).

32 I mean this in the sense in which Heidegger defines science in his essay, "The Age of the World Picture": "Science becomes research through the projected plan and through the securing of that plan in the rigor of procedure. Projection and rigor, however, only develop into what they are in methodology" (in M. Heidegger, *The Question Concerning Technology and Other Essays,* trans. William Lovitt [New York: Harper Torchbooks, 1977], 115–54, at 120, trans. amended). Heidegger's representation of medieval thought in this essay is unsatisfactory, however.

33 Note that the division of biblical chapters into verses became current only in the sixteenth century. The editors of Alexander's text have inserted the verse numbers for the facility of the reader.

34 Magistri Alexandri de Hales *Glossa* I, Introitus (1: 1f.).

35 On the poor state of the tradition of the text, see the editors' remarks ibid., 1: 116*–26*.

36 See ibid., 1: 110*–16*.

37 For the editors' justification, see ibid., 1: 107*–10*.

38 Ibid., I, dist. 1, no. 2 (1: 7f.).

39 See ibid., I, dist. 17, esp. nos. 1–4 (1: 168f.).

40 Rashdall, *The Universities of Europe in the Middle Ages,* 1: 347.

41 An account of this monumental work is found in Fidelis a Fanna, O.F.M., *Ratio novae collectionis operum omnium S. Bonaventurae sive editorum sive anecdotorum* (Turin: Marietti, 1874).

42 See Edward A. Synan, "A Bonaventurian Enigma: 'praelocutio' or 'epilogus'? A Third Hypothesis," in *Bonaventuriana. Miscellanea in onore di Jacques Guy Bougerol OFM*, ed. F. Chavero Blanco, Bibliotheca Pontificii Athenei Antoniani 27 (Rome: Edizioni Antonianum, 1988), 2: 493–505.

43 *Commentaria in IV libros Sententiarum Magistri Petri Lombardi*, in *S. Bonaventurae opera theologica selecta* (editio minor), vols. 1–4 (Quaracchi: Typographia Collegii S. Bonaventurae, 1934–59), II, praelocutio (2: 1). The text of the *praelocutio* that is printed in the manual edition is superior to the one found in the older "official" edition of 1882–1902.

44 Ibid., 2: 2.

45 On the components of the *principium*, see Rashdall, *The Universities of Europe in the Middle Ages*, 1: 474–75, fn. 3; on the *protestatio* in particular, see Venício Marcolino, "Der Augustinertheologe an der Universität Paris," esp. 177. I owe the suggestion that the text at the beginning of Bonaventure's commentary on Book II of the *Sentences* might represent a *protestatio* to Stephen Dumont.

46 See Jacques Guy Bougerol, O.F.M., *Introduction à saint Bonaventure*, À la recherche de la vérité (Paris: Vrin, 1988), 188f.

47 As Edward Synan conjectured in the article cited in note 42 above.

48 Bonaventure, *Commentaria in IV libros Sententiarum*, I, 1: 1.

49 See Alasdair MacIntyre, *Whose Justice? Which Rationality?* (London: Duckworth, 1988), esp. chap. 19 ("Tradition and Translation").

50 As André Ménart puts it in his excellent interpretation of the prologue; see his article, "Une leçon inaugurale de Bonaventure. Le Prooemium du Livre des Sentences," *Études franciscaines* 21 (1971): 273–98, at 278.

51 Bonaventure, *Commentaria in IV libros Sententiarum*, I, quaestiones prooemii (1: 6).

52 On Aquinas as *baccalaureus Sententiarum*, see Jean-Pierre Torrell, O.P., *Saint Thomas Aquinas*, vol. 1: *The Person and His Work*, trans. Robert Royal (Washington, DC: Catholic University of America Press, 1996), 39–45.

53 See S. Thomae Aquinatis *Scriptum super libros Sententiarum*, ed. Pierre Mandonnet, O.P. and Marie-Fabien Moos, O.P., 4 vols. (Paris: Lethielleux, 1929–47), I, prologus, quaestio (1: 6–19).

54 The edition reads *physicas disciplinas* (ibid., 6), but the context shows this to be an erroneous transcription from the manuscripts. I thank Stephen Dumont for pointing this error out to me.

55 Ibid., art. 1, resp. (10).

56 Ibid., art. 4, resp. (16).

57 The following discussion draws on objection 4 of question 2.

58 For an excellent account of the problems of subalternation, especially as the theory was received in the Middle Ages, see Steven J. Livesey, *Theology and Science in the Fourteenth Century: Three Questions on the Unity and Subalternation*

of the Sciences from John of Reading's Commentary on the Sentences, Studien und Texte zur Geistesgeschichte des Mittelalters 25 (Leiden: Brill, 1989), chap. 2 (20–53).

59 S. Thomae Aquinatis *Sriptum super libros Sententiarum*, I, prologus, quaestio, art. 3, sol. 1 (12).

60 Robert Kilwardby, *Quaestiones in librum primum Sententiarum*, ed. Johannes Schneider, Bayerische Akademie der Wissenschaften—Veröffentlichungen der Kommission für die Herausgabe ungedrucker Texte aus der mittelalterlichen Geisteswelt 13 (Munich: Verlag der Bayerischen Akademie der Wissenschaften, 1986), qu. 1, 3.

61 I have commented in more detail on Bonaventure's question concerning the authorship of the *Sentences* in my article, "What Is an Author? Bonaventure and Foucault on the Meaning of Authorship," *Fealsúnacht: A Journal of the Dialectical Tradition* 2 (2001–02): 23–45.

62 There are a few exceptions, most notably distinction 27 of Book II, whose beginning Bonaventure suggests should be moved back to chapter 8 of the preceding distinction, in order to avoid a break between a question Peter Lombard formulates and the answer that it subsequently receives. See Bonaventure, *Commentaria in IV libros Sententiarum*, II, dist. 27, divisio textus (2: 671).

63 See Palémon Glorieux, art. "Sentences (commentaires sur les)," in *Dictionnaire de théologie catholique* 14/2 (1941): 1860–84, at 1862. According to William J. Courtenay, however, there is no conclusive evidence to show that lectures on the *Sentences* ever took more than one year in the bachelors' career, with the exception of the mendicant orders at Oxford, which may have had a two-year requirement in the thirteenth century; see his article, "Programs of Study and Genres of Scholastic Theological Production in the Fourteenth Century," in *Manuels, programmes de cours et techniques d'enseignement dans les universités médiévales* (cited in note 8 above), 325–50, esp. 333–36.

64 The manuscript in question is Oxford, Lincoln College, Lat. 95. The Roman *Sentences* commentary preserved in this manuscript has recently become available in a printed edition: Thomas Aquinas, *Lectura romana in primum Sententiarum Petri Lombardi*, ed. Leonard E. Boyle, O.P., and John F. Boyle, Studies and Texts 152 (Toronto: Pontifical Institute of Mediaeval Studies, 2006).

65 John F. Boyle, "Introduction," in ibid., 1–57, at 11.

66 Thomas Aquinas, *Summa theologiae*, prologus, in S. Thomae de Aquino *Opera omnia iussu impensaque Leonis XIII P. M. edita*, vol. 4 (Rome: Typographia Polyglotta, 1888), 5.

67 See Glorieux, "L'enseignenen au moyen âge," 123–36, and the important study by Olga Weijers, *Le maniement du savoir. Pratiques intellectuelles à l'époque des premières universités (XIIIᵉ–XIVᵉ siècles)*, Studia artistarum, Subsidia (Turnhout: Brepols, 1996), chaps. 4 and 5. Weijers concentrates on the practices that prevailed at the faculty of arts.

68 S. Thomae de Aquino *Tabula libri Ethicorum*, ed. René-Antoine Gauthier, O.P., in *Opera omnia iussu Leonis XIII P. M. edita*, vol. 48 (Rome: Santa Sabina, 1971).

69   The entry occurs ibid., B126. For Gauthier's commentary, see ibid., B49f.

70   My account of the rise of indexing techniques in the twelfth and thirteenth centuries is based upon Mary A. Rouse and Richard H. Rouse, *Authentic Witnesses: Approaches to Medieval Texts and Manuscripts* (Notre Dame, Ind.: University of Notre Dame Press, 1991), esp. chap. 6 ("*Statim invenire*: Schools, Preachers, and New Attitudes to the Page") and chap. 7 ("The Development of Research Tools in the Thirteenth Century").

71   For a brief description of this project, see ibid., 234. The Rouses' account is based on research by Daniel A. Callus, O.P., "The 'Tabula super Originalia Patrum' of Robert Kilwardby O.P.," in *Studia mediaevalia in honorem admodum Reverendi Patris Raymundi Josephi Martin* (Bruges: De Tempel, 1948), 243–70; idem, "New Manuscripts of Kilwardby's *Tabulae super originalia patrum*," *Dominican Studies* 2 (1949): 38–45; and idem, "The Contribution to the Study of the Fathers Made by the Thirteenth-Century Oxford Schools," *Journal of Ecclesiastical History* 5 (1954): 139–48.

72   The list appearing in Stegmüller, *Repertorium*, 1: 5 (no. 10, 1), should be complemented by the manuscripts identified by Callus (on which see the previous note).

73   MS. London, British Library, Royal 9.B.VI, fol. 2r: "Hic incipit diuisio primi libri sententiarum. primo in generali respectu 4 librorum postremo diuisio in speciali respectu primi solum."

74   Therefore, there is no "general plan of the *Sentences*," as Callus claimed ("The 'Tabulae super Originalia Patrum,'" 253).

75   See Richard Fishacre, *In tertium librum Sententiarum*, Teil 2: Dist. 23–40, ed. Klaus Rodler, Bayerische Akademie der Wissenschaften—Veröffentlichungen der Kommission für die Herausgabe ungedrucker Texte aus der mittelalterlichen Geisteswelt 23 (Munich: Verlag der Bayerischen Akademie der Wissenschaften, 2003); for images of *arbores ramificatae* in manuscripts of Fishacre's commentary, see R. James Long and Maura O'Carroll, S.N.D., *The Life and Works of Richard Fishacre OP: Prolegomena to the Edition of his Commentary on the "Sentences,"* Bayerische Akademie der Wissenschaften—Veröffentlichungen der Kommission für die Herausgabe ungedrucker Texte aus der mittelalterlichen Geisteswelt 21 (Munich: Verlag der Bayerischen Akademie der Wissenschaften, 1999), figures 7, 8, 10, 15, 16, 29, 30, 31.

76   See Robert Kilwardby, *Quaestiones in librum quartum Sententiarum*, ed. Richard Schenk, Bayerische Akademie der Wissenschaften—Veröffentlichungen der Kommission für die Herausgabe ungedrucker Texte aus der mittelalterlichen Geisteswelt 17 (Munich: Verlag der Bayerischen Akademie der Wissenschaften, 1993), 39* and 253–70.

77   See Robert Kilwardby, *Quaestiones in quatuor libros Sententiarum*, Appendix: *Tabula ordine alphabeti contexta (Cod. Worcester F 43)*, ed. Gerd Haverling, Bayerische Akademie der Wissenschaften—Veröffentlichungen der Kommission für die Herausgabe ungedrucker Texte aus der mittelalterlichen Geisteswelt 19 (Munich: Verlag der Bayerischen Akademie der Wissenschaften, 1995).

78 I edited this text some years ago in Robert Grosseteste, *Tabula*, ed. Philipp W. Rosemann, Corpus Christianorum, Continuatio Mediaevalis 130 (Turnhout: Brepols, 1995), 233–320. Also see my study, "Robert Grosseteste's *Tabula*," in *Robert Grosseteste: New Perspectives on His Thought and Scholarship*, ed. James McEvoy, Instrumenta Patristica 27 (Steenbrugge: in Abbatia S. Petri; Turnhout: Brepols, 1995), 321–55.

79 Rouse and Rouse, *Authentic Witnesses*, 204.

80 Ibid., 214.

81 See Z. Alszeghy, S.J., "Abbreviationes Bonaventurae. Handschriftliche Auszüge aus dem Sentenzenkommentar des hl. Bonaventura im Mittelalter," *Gregorianum* 28 (1947): 474–510.

82 See Stegmüller, *Repertorium*, 1: 138 (no. 301). My account is based on the study by Kent Emery, Jr., "The 'Sentences' Abbreviation of William de Rothwell, O.P. University of Pennsylvania, Lat. MS. 32," *RTAM* 51 (1984): 69–135. This essay has been reprinted in the same author's volume of collected articles, *Monastic, Scholastic and Mystical Theologies from the Later Middle Ages*, Collected Studies Series CS 561 (Aldershot, England, and Brookfield, Vt.: Variorum, 1996), essay II.

83 See Martin Grabmann, "Handschriftliche Mitteilungen über Abbreviationen des Sentenzenkommentars des seligen Papstes Innozenz V. (Petrus de Tarantasia O.P. † 1276)," *Divus Thomas* (Fribourg) 24 (1946): 109–12.

84 This expression is from Russell L. Friedman, "The *Sentences* Commentary, 1250–1320: General Trends, the Impact of the Religious Orders, and the Test Case of Predestination," in *Mediaeval Commentaries*, 41–128, at 47.

85 See Emery, "The 'Sentences' Abbreviation of William de Rothwell, O.P.," 133.

Notes to Chapter Three

1 See Jean-Luc Marion, *Being Given: Toward a Phenomenology of Givenness*, trans. Jeffrey L. Kosky, Cultural Memory in the Present (Stanford, CA: Stanford University Press, 2002).

2 Russell L. Friedman, "The *Sentences* Commentary, 1250–1320: General Trends, the Impact of the Religious Orders, and the Test Case of Predestination," in *Mediaeval Commentaries*, 41–128, at 90. Also see the remarks by William J. Courtenay, *Schools & Scholars in Fourteenth-Century England* (Princeton, NJ: Princeton University Press, 1987), 253. If there was any systematic coverage of the *Book of Sentences* in the fourteenth-century classroom—which is quite possible—this was not judged to be sufficiently important to be published and circulated.

3 On this phenomenon, see the classic study by Constantin Michalski, "Die vielfachen Redaktionen einiger Kommentare zu Petrus Lombardus," in *Miscellanea Francesco Ehrle: scritti di storia e paleografia pubblicati sotto gli auspici di S. S. Pio XI. in occasione dell'80 natalizio dell'e.mo card. Francesco Ehrle*, Studi e testi 37 (Rome: Biblioteca Apostolica Vaticana, 1924), 1: 219–64.

4   This chronology is based upon Charles Balić, O.F.M., "The Life and Works of John Duns Scotus," in *John Duns Scotus, 1265–1965*, ed. John K. Ryan and Bernadine M. Bonansea, Studies in Philosophy and the History of Philosophy 3 (Washington, DC: Catholic University of America Press, 1965), 1–27, esp. 11–13. In this article, Father Balić revised some of his theses advanced in his earlier book, *Les commentaires de Jean Duns Scot sur les quatre livres des Sentences*, Bibliothèque de la Revue d'histoire ecclésiastique 1 (Louvain: Bureaux de la Revue, 1927).

5   The manuscript in question is MS. Assisi, Biblioteca municipale, 137. On this remarkable manuscript, see Charles Balić, O.F.M., "Die kritische Textausgabe der Werke des Johannes Duns Scotus," *Archiv für Geschichte der Philosophie* 43 (1961): 303–17, at 308–10. A much more complete examination of the manuscript is to be found in the introduction to the critical edition: Duns Scoti *Opera omnia*, ed. Charles Balić, vol. 1: *Ordinatio, Prologus* (Vatican City: Vatican Polyglott Press, 1950), esp. 12★–28★ and 259★–70★.

6   The Vatican edition provides marginal numbers to help identify the principal steps in Scotus's argument.

7   Friedman, "The *Sentences* Commentary, 1250–1320," 92.

8   Charles Balić, O.F.M., "The Nature and Value of a Critical Edition of the Complete Works of John Duns Scotus," in *John Duns Scotus, 1265–1965*, 368–79, at 373.

9   *Ordinatio, Prologus*, pars 1, qu. unica, nos. 57 and 60. For commentary on this passage, see Allan B. Wolter, O.F.M., *The Philosophical Theology of John Duns Scotus*, ed. Marilyn McCord Adams (Ithaca, N.Y., and London: Cornell University Press, 1990), chap. 6: "Duns Scotus on the Natural Desire for the Supernatural" (125–47), and Olivier Boulnois, *Duns Scot, la rigueur de la charité*, Initiations au moyen âge (Paris: Cerf, 1998), chap. 1: "Philosophes et théologiens—la controverse" (27–72). Boulnois's book is written as a running commentary upon the entire prologue to the *Ordinatio*.

10 Boulnois writes: "Si la révélation a une origine surnaturelle, sa réception est purement naturelle" (*Duns Scot*, 80).

11 Ibid., 80–91.

12 Ioannis Duns Scoti *Opera omnia*, ed. Charles Balić, vol. 5: *Ordinatio, Liber primus, a distinctione undecima ad vigesimam quintam* (Vatican City: Vatican Polyglott Press, 1959), dist. 17, pars 1, qu. 1–2, no. 165: "Quantum ad tertium articulum, posset dici quod Magister non negat omnem habitum supernaturalem ..."

13 *Ordinatio, Prologus*, pars 1, qu. unica, no. 12.

14 Ibid., no. 18.

15 Ibid., no. 55.

16 William J. Courtenay, "The Dialectic of Divine Omnipotence," in his *Covenant and Causality in Medieval Thought: Studies in Philosophy, Theology and Economic Practice*, Collected Studies Series CS206 (London: Variorum Reprints, 1984), Study IV, 6.

17 The covenantal dimension of the distinction between *potentia absoluta* and *po-*

tentia ordinata is strongly emphasized in William Courtenay's study *Covenant and Causality in Medieval Thought*, cited in the previous note. For an overview of recent scholarship on the distinction, see Francis Oakley, *Omnipotence and Promise: The Legacy of the Scholastic Distinction of Powers*, The Étienne Gilson Series 23 (Toronto: Pontifical Institute of Mediaeval Studies, 2002).

18 On the logic of nominalism, see Heiko Oberman, *The Dawn of the Reformation: Essays in Late Medieval and Early Reformation Thought* (Grand Rapids, MI: Eerdmans, 1986), 27–9. The limitations of a merely logical and epistemological definition of nominalism were recognized as far back as 1925, by Cardinal Franz Ehrle, S.J., in his book, *Der Sentenzenkommentar Peters von Candia, des Pisaner Papstes Alexanders V. Ein Beitrag zur Scheidung der Schulen in der Scholastik des vierzehnten Jahrhunderts und zur Geschichte des Wegestreites*, Franziskanische Studien, Beiheft 9 (Münster: Aschendorff, 1925), 106–12. While Ehrle refuses to view Scotus as a nominalist, he calls him a *Bahnbrecher* (110), or "pathbreaker," of the developing nominalist current (which he views in extremely negative terms).

19 Boulnois, *Duns Scot*, 150.

20 The theses are quoted here according to the new edition by David Piché, who has restored them to their original order; see David Piché, *La condamnation parisienne de 1277*, Sic et non (Paris: Vrin, 1999).

21 For a representative statement of this line of interpretation, see Alain de Libera, *Penser au moyen âge*, Chemins de pensée (Paris: Seuil, 1991), esp. 179 and 194.

22 On the Oxford condemnations, see Daniel A. Callus, O.P., *The Condemnation of St. Thomas at Oxford*, The Aquinas Society of London, Aquinas Paper No. 5, 2nd ed. (London: Blackfriars Publications, 1955), and P. Osmund Lewry, O.P., "Grammar, Logic and Rhetoric, 1220–1320," in *The History of the University of Oxford*, vol. 1: *The Early Oxford Schools*, ed. J.I. Catto (Oxford: Clarendon Press, 1984), 401–33, esp. 419–26.

23 Richard A. Lee, Jr., *Science, the Singular, and the Question of Theology*, The New Middle Ages (New York: Palgrave, 2002), vii. Also see 59–60, 103–04, 117. For an assessment and critique of Lee's book, see my review in *Speculum* 79 (2004): 785–87.

24 See Kent Emery, Jr., and Andreas Speer, "After the Condemnation of 1277: New Evidence, New Perspectives, and Grounds for New Interpretations," in *Nach der Verurteilung von 1277. Philosophie und Theologie an der Universität von Paris im letzten Viertel des 13. Jahrhunderts. Studien und Texte*, ed. Jan A. Aertsen, Kent Emery, Jr., and Andreas Speer, Miscellanea Mediaevalia 28 (Berlin and New York: de Gruyter, 2001), 3–19, esp. 5f. (with relevant literature on p. 6, n. 9).

25 Ibid., 15.

26 That Ockham knew Scotus personally was the considered opinion of Philotheus Boehner, O.F.M., *Collected Articles on Ockham*, ed. Eligius Buytaert, O.F.M., Franciscan Institute Publications, Philosophy Series 12 (St. Bonaventure, NY: Franciscan Institute; Louvain: Nauwelaerts; Paderborn: Schöningh, 1958), 2.

27 See ibid., 6f. and 96–110. The editors of the *Ordinatio* prefer to speak of "incomplete" and "complete" versions of the work, rather than of several redactions, since Ockham provided for numerous blank spaces when he first composed the *Ordinatio*—a clear indication of the fact that he did not consider the first version or versions to be finished products. On this point, see Guillelmi de Ockham *Scriptum in librum primum Sententiarum (Ordinatio), prologus et distinctio prima*, ed. Gedeon Gál, O.F.M., and Stephen Brown, Guillelmi de Ockham Opera philosophica et theologica, Opera theologica 1 (St. Bonaventure, NY: Franciscan Institute, 1967), 19*–23*.

28 Guillelmi de Ockham *Scriptum in librum primum Sententiarum*, prol., qu. 1 (3, ll. 3–4).

29 In this claim, I am following Volker Leppin, *Wilhelm von Ockham: Gelehrter, Streiter, Bettelmönch*, Gestalten des Mittelalters und der Renaissance (Darmstadt: Wissenschaftliche Buchgesellschaft, 2003), 48.

30 For this theory, see *Summa theologiae* I, qu. 1, art. 2: "Utrum sacra doctrina sit scientia." On medieval theories of subalternation from Robert Grosseteste to John of Reading, see Steven J. Livesey, *Theology and Science in the Fourteenth Century: Three Questions on the Unity and Subalternation of the Sciences from John of Reading's Commentary on the Sentences*, Studien und Texte zur Geistesgeschichte des Mittelalters 25 (Leiden: Brill, 1989), chap. 2 (20–53).

31 See Courtenay, *Schools & Scholars in Fourteenth-Century England*, 206: "... the rigor of logic and rational demonstration could be restored, since they no longer had to be bent to the service of natural theology."

32 Guillelmi de Ockham *Scriptum in librum primum Sententiarum*, prol., qu. 2, art. 2 (87, 20–88, 2).

33 Ibid., prol., qu. 1, art. 5 (49, 10–13).

34 My summary of Ockham's difficult argument is based upon the commentary by Robert Guelluy, *Philosophie et théologie chez Guillaume d'Ockham*, Universitas catholica lovaniensis, Dissertationes ad gradum magistri in Facultate Theologica vel in Facultate Iuris Canonici consequendum conscriptae, Series II, 39 (Louvain: Nauwelaerts; Paris: Vrin, 1947), esp. 157–69 (for Ockham's examination of the scientific character of a theology based upon evident knowledge of God granted *de potentia absoluta*). Guelluy provides detailed commentary on the entire text of the prologue to the *Ordinatio*.

35 Guillelmi de Ockham *Scriptum in librum primum Sententiarum*, prol., qu. 7 (183, 4f.).

36 Ibid., 197, 22; repeated at 205, 7.

37 See *Nicomachean Ethics* VI.3, 1139b16–7.

38 Guillelmi de Ockham *Scriptum in librum primum Sententiarum*, prol., qu. 7 (200, 16–201, 3). The words, "because it is not evident, although it is certain (*quia non est evidens, quamvis sit certus*)," were added to the text later by Ockham.

39 Ibid., 206, 4f. For a more detailed description of the theological habit, see ibid., 196, 20–197, 22.

40 Ibid., book I, dist. 1, qu. 5 (455, 7–10).

41 On this development, see Hastings Rashdall, *The Universities of Europe in the Middle Ages*, new ed. by F.M. Powicke and A.B. Emden, vol. 3 (Oxford: Oxford University Press, 1936), 71f.

42 See Friedman, "The *Sentences* Commentary, 1250–1320," 100: "... the *Sentences* commentary was no longer a work that was nearly exclusively associated with a student's pursuit of the doctorate, it was a work that was a—perhaps the— preferred format for the theologian."

43 See Leppin, *Wilhelm von Ockham*, 46.

44 The quotation (1 Cor. 12:8) occurs at the beginning of qu. 7 (183, 18f.).

45 Guelluy, *Philosophie et théologie chez Guillaume d'Ockham*, 357: "Nul souffle sous ces textes arides et denses."

46 Guillelmi de Ockham *Scriptum in librum primum Sententiarum*, prol., qu. 7 (196, 20–197, 5).

47 See the remarks in Courtenay, *Schools & Scholars in Fourteenth-Century England*, esp. 255: "... it is certainly true that metaphysical questions and a number of other favored topics of thirteenth-century theology all but disappear from the folios of *Sentences* commentaries and disputed questions in the fourteenth century."

48 Friedman, "The *Sentences* Commentary, 1250–1320," 87ff.

49 None of the medieval authors referred to in this question is identified by name; references remain anonymous, using such phrases as "some people" (*quidam*) or "another opinion" (*alia opinio*).

50 See Courtenay, *Schools & Scholars*, 171–8 (on the formation of schools); and Chris Schabel, "Haec Ille: Citation, Quotation, and Plagiarism in 14th-Century Scholasticism," in *The Origins of European Scholarship*, ed. Ioannis Taifacos (Stuttgart: Franz Steiner, 2006), 163–75 (on the identification of contemporary sources).

51 Guillelmi de Ockham *Scriptum in librum primum Sententiarum (Ordinatio), distinctiones IV–XVIII*, ed. Girard I. Etzkorn, Guillelmi de Ockham Opera philosophica et theologica, Opera theologica 3 (St. Bonaventure, NY: Franciscan Institute, 1977), dist. 17, qu. 3 (476, 12f.).

52 See ibid., 477, 21–478, 1.

53 Ibid., 479, 2.

54 Ibid., 478, 2.

55 For the chronology of Gregory's career, see Venício Marcolino, "Einleitung," in Gregorii Ariminensis OESA *Lectura super primum et secundum Sententiarum*, ed. A. Damasus Trapp O.S.A. and Venício Marcolino, vol. 1: *Super primum (Dist. 1–6)*, Spätmittelalter und Reformation 6 (Berlin and New York: de Gruyter, 1981), xi–ciii, esp. xi–xvii. The same author has published an impressively thorough examination of Gregory's career at the University of Paris, in light of all the available evidence, in his article "Der Augustinertheologe an der Universität Paris," in *Gregor von Rimini: Werk und Wirkung bis zur Reformation*, ed. Heiko A. Oberman, Spätmittelalter und Reformation 20 (Berlin and New York: de Gruyter, 1981), 127–94.

56 Gregorii Ariminensis OESA *Lectura super primum et secundum Sententiarum*, vol. 1: *Super primum (Dist. 1–6)*, Book I, dist. 3, qu. 1, Additio 9 (p. 323, l. 3).

57 Ibid., qu. 3 (398, 16). Other references to Books III and IV are listed in Marcolino, "Der Augustinertheologe," 164 n. 36.

58 See Pascale Bermon, "La *Lectura* sur les deux premiers livres des *Sentences* de Grégoire de Rimini O.E.S.A. (1300–1358)," in *Mediaeval Commentaries*, 267–85, esp. 272 n. 22.

59 See Marcolino, "Der Augustinertheologe," 148f.

60 See ibid., 165–67.

61 See ibid., 168–74.

62 Gregorii Ariminensis OESA *Lectura super primum et secundum Sententiarum*, vol. 1: *Super primum (Dist. 1–6)*, prologus, qu. 1 (1, l. 5).

63 Ibid. (1, 3f.).

64 Ibid., qu. 2 (57, 23).

65 Ibid., qu. 3 (92, 22).

66 Ibid., qu. 4 (121, 16).

67 Ibid., qu. 5 (147, 2).

68 The expression is from Damasus Trapp, O.E.S.A., "Augustinian Theology of the 14th Century: Notes on Editions, Marginalia, Opinions and Book-Lore," *Augustiniana* 6 (1956): 146–274, at 149.

69 See Gregorii Ariminensis OESA *Lectura super primum et secundum Sententiarum*, ed. A. Damasus Trapp, O.S.A., Venício Marcolino, and Manuel Santos-Noya, vol. 2: *Super primum (Dist. 7–17)*, Spätmittelalter und Reformation 7 (Berlin and New York: de Gruyter, 1982), 215–481.

70 Trapp, "Augustinian Theology," 188.

71 Gregorii Ariminensis OESA *Lectura super primum et secundum Sententiarum*, vol. 1: *Super primum (Dist. 1–6)*, prologus, qu. 1 (1, respectively ll. 11f., 20f., and 26).

72 See Christoph Peter Burger, "Der Augustinerschüler gegen die modernen Pelagianer: Das 'auxilium speciale dei' in der Gnadenlehre Gregors von Rimini," in *Gregor von Rimini: Werk und Wirkung bis zur Reformation*, 195–240.

73 Gregorii Ariminensis OESA *Lectura super primum et secundum Sententiarum*, vol. 1: *Super primum (Dist. 1–6)*, prologus, qu. 1, art. 2 (13, 3) and art. 4 (40, 15).

74 Trapp, "Augustinian Theology," 200, writes: "Under such circumstances it is much more plausible to credit the marginal notes of Gregory to Gregory himself, aided perhaps by a Socius." Marcolino, "Einleitung," c and cii, agrees.

75 Gregorii Ariminensis OESA *Lectura super primum et secundum Sententiarum*, vol. 1: *Super primum (Dist. 1–6)*, prologus, qu. 1, art. 1 (2, 14, n. 6).

76 Ibid. (10, 25).

77 Gregorii Ariminensis OESA *Lectura super primum et secundum Sententiarum*, vol. 7: *Indices*, Spätmittelalter und Reformation 12 (Berlin and New York: de Gruyter, 1987), Tabula primi libri, 226, 20f.

78 Ibid., 272, 28f.

79 Ibid., 226, 3–18.

80 The editors of the *Lectura* arrived at the same conclusion; see ibid., vii: "… mit

hoher Wahrscheinlichkeit ist daher davon auszugehen, daß der Tabulator diese Register im Auftrag des Autors erstellt hat."

81 Guillelmi de Ockham *Scriptum in librum primum Sententiarum*, prol., qu. 9 (266, 18–20).

82 Ibid., 269, 1.

83 Ibid., 266, 20f.

84 Gregorii Ariminensis OESA *Lectura super primum et secundum Sententiarum*, vol. 1: *Super primum (Dist. 1–6)*, prologus, qu. 1 (3, 32–4, 5).

85 See ibid. (6, 20–7). Gregory refers to *Nicomachean Ethics*, book VI, chap. 3 (1139b19–24), and *Posterior Analytics*, book I, chap. 2 (71b9–15).

86 On this point, see the incisive remarks in Lee, *Science, the Singular, and the Question of Theology*, 79f.

87 Gregorii Ariminensis OESA *Lectura super primum et secundum Sententiarum*, vol. 1: *Super primum (Dist. 1–6)*, prologus, qu. 3 (102, 18–20).

88 I am following the interpretation by Volker Wendland, "Die Wissenschaftslehre Gregors von Rimini in der Diskussion," in *Gregor von Rimini: Werk und Wirkung bis zur Reformation*, 241–300, esp. 292–8.

89 See Gregorii Ariminensis OESA *Lectura super primum et secundum Sententiarum*, vol. 1: *Super primum (Dist. 1–6)*, prologus, qu. 1 (8, 31–9, 7).

90 Volker Wendland, "Die Wissenschaftslehre Gregors von Rimini in der Diskussion," provides a detailed survey of the literature on the topic.

91 See Gedeon Gál, O.F.M., "Adam of Wodeham's Question on the 'Complexe Significabile' as the Immediate Object of Scientific Knowledge," *Franciscan Studies* 37 (1977): 66–102. More recently, Jack Zupko has argued that Gregory failed to understand an important element in Adam's theory, namely, its holistic character; I do not find this conclusion entirely convincing. See Jack Zupko, "How it played in the *rue de Fouarre*: The Reception of Adam Wodeham's Theory of the *Complexe Significabile* [sic] in the Arts Faculty at Paris in the Mid-Fourteenth Century," *Franciscan Studies* 54 (1994–97): 211–25.

92 See Hubert Élie, *Le complexe significabile* (Paris: Vrin, 1936); reprinted under the title, *Le signifiable par complexe. La proposition et son objet: Grégoire de Rimini, Meinong, Russell* (Paris: Vrin, 2000).

93 Trapp, "Augustinian Theology," 148.

94 Gregorii Ariminensis OESA *Lectura super primum et secundum Sententiarum*, vol. 1: *Super primum (Dist. 1–6)*, prologus, qu. 1 (18, 2–4).

95 Ibid. (56, 9f.). Theology, then, is not "the exclusive province of the believer" for Gregory, "the sole property of the faithful," as Gordon Leff maintained; see his *Gregory of Rimini: Tradition and Innovation in Fourteenth-Century Thought* (Manchester: Manchester University Press, 1961), 218 and 234, respectively. Leff must have read only the first half of the conclusion just quoted.

96 Courtenay, *Schools & Scholars*, 359.

97 See Damasus Trapp, O.S.A., "Clm 27034: Unchristened Nominalism and Wycliffite Realism at Prague in 1381," *RTAM* 24 (1957): 320–60. For the date of 1384, 324.

98 Ibid., 345.

99   Ibid., 344.

100   On Stephen Patrington's biography, see the entry in *Dictionary of National Biography*, ed. Leslie Stephen and Sidney Lee (Oxford: Oxford University Press, 1949–50), 15: 492–3, and, more recently, the article by Barthélemy Xiberta, "Étienne de Patrington," in *Dictionnaire de spiritualité* IV/2 (Paris: Beauchesne, 1961): 1517.

101   The index of the notebook has been edited by Leonard A. Kennedy, C.S.B., "A Carmelite Fourteenth-Century Theological Notebook," *Carmelus* 33 (1986), 70–102.

102   The first question is available in an edition of Leonard A. Kennedy, C.S.B., "Late-Fourteenth-Century Philosophical Scepticism at Oxford," *Vivarium* 23 (1985): 124–51. Also see the same author's "Philosophical Scepticism in England in the Mid-Fourteenth Century," *Vivarium* 21 (1983): 35–57.

103   John Wyclif, *Tractatus de universalibus*, ed. Ivan J. Mueller (Oxford: Clarendon Press, 1985), chap. 2, 65, ll. 300–07.

104   See Paul J.J.M. Bakker and Chris Schabel, "*Sentences* Commentaries of the Later Fourteenth Century," in *Mediaeval Commentaries*, 425–64.

105   On Simon of Cremona, see Trapp, "Augustinian Theology," 250–63. Chris Schabel, "Haec Ille: Citation, Quotation, and Plagiarism in 14th-Century Scholasticism," 175, does not believe that readings *secundum alium* were any more prevalent in the second half of the fourteenth century than in the first.

106   Trapp, "Augustinian Theology," 250.

107   See Bakker and Schabel, "*Sentences* Commentaries of the Later Fourteenth Century," 443–61.

108   See Maarten J.F.M. Hoenen, "The Commentary on the *Sentences* of Marsilius of Inghen," in *Mediaeval Commentaries*, 465–506, esp. 465f.

109   On Marsilius's career, see Marsilius of Inghen, *Quaestiones super quattuor libros Sententiarum*, vol. 1: *Super primum, quaestiones 1–7*, ed. Manuel Santos Noya, Studies in the History of Christian Thought 87 (Leiden: Brill, 2000), xvii–xxvi. On the intellectual climate at Paris in Marsilius's time, see William J. Courtenay, "Parisian Theology, 1362–1377," in *Philosophie und Theologie des ausgehenden Mittelalters. Marsilius von Inghen und das Denken seiner Zeit*, ed. Maarten J.F.M. Hoenen and Paul J.J.M. Bakker (Leiden: Brill, 2000), 3–19.

110   This edition is available as a modern reprint: *Questiones Marsilii super quattuor libros Sententiarum* (Frankfurt/Main: Minerva, 1966).

111   On the challenges posed by the 1501 edition, see Marsilius von Inghen, *Quaestiones super quattuor libros Sententiarum*, vol. 1, xlvi–liii; also see M.J.F.M. Hoenen, "Einige Notizen über die Handschriften und Drucke des Sentenzenkommentars von Marsilius von Inghen," *RTAM* 56 (1989): 117–63, esp. 153–60. A reader consulting this article must deal with a large number of mistakes in its German text.

112   Marsilius of Inghen, *Quaestiones super quattuor libros Sententiarum*, vol. 1: *Super primum*, qu. 2, art. 5 (129, ll. 15f.).

113   Ibid., art. 3 (81, 17–20 and 24f.).

114 Ibid., 91, 7–32.

115 See Maarten J.F.M. Hoenen, "Marsilius von Inghen in der Geistesgeschichte des ausgehenden Mittelalters," in *Philosophie und Theologie des ausgehenden Mittelalters*, 21–45, esp. 27–42.

116 *Questiones Marsilii super quattuor libros Sententiarum*, lib. 1, dist. 45, art. 2, fol. 191v. (This is a reference to the reprint of the 1501 edition, given the fact that the critical edition has not yet advanced beyond qu. 21 of Book I.)

117 See Dorothea Walz, "Marsilius von Inghen als Schreiber und Büchersammler," in *Marsilius von Inghen, Werk und Wirkung. Akten des zweiten internationalen Marsilius-von-Inghen-Kongresses*, ed. Stanisław Wielgus (Lublin: Redakcja Wydawnictw KUL, 1993), 31–71.

118 Marsilius of Inghen, *Quaestiones super quattuor libros Sententiarum*, vol. 1: *Super primum*, qu. 3, art. 1 (138, 10–12). On the privileged place of Thomas Aquinas within Marsilius's theology, see the remarks in Manuel Santos Noya's excellent article, "Die 'auctoritates theologicae' im Sentenzenkommentar des Marsilius von Inghen," in *Philosophie und Theologie des ausgehenden Mittelalters*, 197–210, at 203f.

119 Marsilius of Inghen, *Quaestiones super quattuor libros Sententiarum*, vol. 1: *Super primum*, qu. 2, art. 2 (75, 15–76, 20). For a detailed historical commentary on this passage, see Manuel Santos Noya, "Schrift, Tradition und Theologie bei Marsilius von Inghen," in *Marsilius von Inghen, Werk und Wirkung*, 73–91.

120 Marsilius of Inghen, *Quaestiones super quattuor libros Sententiarum*, vol. 1: *Super primum*, qu. 2, art. 2 (76, 21f.). On Marsilius's use of canon law as theological authority, see Santos Noya, "Die 'auctoritates theologicae,'" 199–203.

121 See Marsilius of Inghen, *Quaestiones super quattuor libros Sententiarum*, vol. 2: *Super primum, quaestiones 8–21*, ed. Manual Santos Noya, Studies in the History of Christian Thought 88 (Leiden: Brill, 2000), qu. 20 (275, 8–26).

122 Ibid., art. 1 (279, 14–18).

123 Gerhard Ritter, *Studien zur Spätscholastik*, vol. 1: *Marsilius von Inghen und die ok-kamistische Schule in Deutschland*, Sitzungsberichte der Heidelberger Akademie der Wissenschaften, Philosophisch-historische Klasse, 1921/4 (Heidelberg: Winter, 1921; reprinted, 1985), 151.

124 This is a point made by Santos Noya, "Die 'auctoritates theologicae,'" 203. On the Council of Vienne, see Ewald Müller, *Das Konzil von Vienne, 1311–1312. Seine Quellen und seine Geschichte*, Vorreformationsgeschichtliche Forschungen 21 (Münster: Aschendorff, 1934). The Council of Vienne did not pronounce itself directly on the question of charity; but in defining the infusion of the theological virtues at baptism, it can be read as implying that charity is such a virtue.

125 Marsilius of Inghen, *Quaestiones super quattuor libros Sententiarum*, vol. 1: *Super primum*, qu. 2, art. 3 (110, 8f.).

126 Ibid., art. 5 (127, 13f.).

127 Ibid., 127, 17–19.

128 Ibid., 129, 7f.

129 *Questiones Marsilii super quattuor libros Sententiarum*, lib. 1, fol. 1r.

130 Walter J. Ong, S.J., *Ramus, Method, and the Decay of Dialogue: From the Art of Discourse to the Art of Reason* (Cambridge, Mass.: Harvard University Press, 1958; reprinted, Chicago and London: University of Chicago Press, 2004).

131 Marsilius of Inghen, *Quaestiones super quattuor libros Sententiarum*, vol. 1: *Super primum*, qu. 5 (205, 3–5).

132 Maarten Hoenen provides a table showing the correspondence between Marsilius's questions and the Lombard's distinctions; see Hoenen, "The Commentary on the *Sentences* of Marsilius of Inghen," 495.

133 Marsilius of Inghen, *Quaestiones super quattuor libros Sententiarum*, vol. 1: *Super primum*, qu. 1 (1, 6–9).

134 On Marsilius's *principia*, see the remarks in Hoenen, "Einige Notizen," 123f. For a fuller treatment of the *principia* at the University of Heidelberg, see Gerhard Ritter, *Die Heidelberger Universität im Mittelalter (1386–1508): ein Stück deutscher Geschichte*, 3rd ed. (Heidelberg: Winter, 1993), 208, 419, and 509–10.

135 Marsilius of Inghen, *Quaestiones super quattuor libros Sententiarum*, vol. 1: *Super primum*, qu. 1 (1, 11–13).

136 On the opening lecture for Book I, see M.J.F.M. Hoenen, "Neuplatonismus am Ende des 14. Jahrhunderts. Die Prinzipien zum Sentenzenkommentar des Marsilius von Inghen," in *Marsilius von Inghen, Werk und Wirkung*, 165–94.

137 Marsilius of Inghen, *Quaestiones super quattuor libros Sententiarum*, vol. 1: *Super primum*, qu. 2 (61, 5f.).

138 Ibid., art. 2 (71, 22–72, 3).

139 The manuscripts of Marsilius's *Quaestiones* usually contain a table of contents and marginal notes that draw attention to the main components of the text (questions, articles, *notabilia*, *dubia*, etc.), together with underlining of quotations and of structuring elements within the text (words such as "corollary," "it is to be noted," and so forth); in addition, the Strasbourg incunabulum also carries an alphabetical subject index. But, unlike the case of Gregory of Rimini's *Lectura*, it does not appear that the author himself was involved in the preparation of these research tools.

Notes to Chapter Four

1 Heiko Oberman, *The Two Reformations: The Journey from the Last Days to the New World*, ed. Donald Weinstein (New Haven, CT, and London: Yale University Press, 2003), 7.

2 Ibid., 27.

3 On Heidegger's philosophy of history, see my article, "Heidegger's Transcendental History," *Journal of the History of Philosophy* 40 (2002): 501–23.

4 I have discussed the dangers that accompany the transformation of *sacra pagina* into *scientia divina* in my article, "*Sacra pagina* or *scientia divina*? Peter Lombard, Thomas Aquinas, and the Nature of the Theological Project," *Philotheos: International Journal for Philosophy and Theology* 4 (2004): 284–300.

5 The term "the long fifteenth century" is from an essay that Heiko Oberman published under the same title in 2001; it is reprinted, in a revised version, as chapter 1 in *The Two Reformations*, cited in note 1 above.

6 A point emphasized by Stefan Swieżawski, *Histoire de la philosophie européene au XVe siècle*, adaptée par Mariusz Prokopowicz (Paris: Beauchesne, 1990), 290–93. In its original Polish edition, Swieżawski's history of European philosophy in the fifteenth century comprises eight volumes. The French abridgment, unfortunately, represents only a very general survey of some currents in fifteenth-century intellectual life; references to primary literature have been almost completely omitted. For an overview of Swieżawski's research, see Mieczysław Markowski, "*In memoriam* Stefan Swieżawski," *Bulletin de philosophie médiévale* 46 (2004): 319–22.

7 See Heiko Oberman, *The Dawn of the Reformation: Essays in Late Medieval and Early Reformation Thought* (Grand Rapids, MI: Eerdmans, 1986), 21: "The most obvious and pervasive factor in our period is the phenomenon of crisis."

8 Oberman, *The Two Reformations*, 18.

9 A first overview of the *Sentences* literature in the fifteenth century was presented some twenty years ago by John Van Dyk, "The Sentence Commentary: A Vehicle in the Intellectual Transition of the Fifteenth Century," in *Fifteenth-Century Studies*, vol. 8, ed. G.P. Mermier and E.E. DuBruck (Detroit: Fifteenth-Century Symposium, 1983), 227–38.

10 On the *vesperiae* and the *resumptio*, see Hastings Rashdall, *The Universities of Europe in the Middle Ages*, new ed. by F.M. Powicke and A.B. Emden, vol. 1 (Oxford: Oxford University Press, 1936), 486.

11 On the events surrounding the condemnation of John of Montson's theses, see the lively account in Palémon Glorieux, "Pierre d'Ailly et saint Thomas," in *Littérature et religion. Mélanges offerts à M. le chanoine Joseph Coppin à l'occasion de son 80e anniversaire*, Mélanges de science religieuse 23, tome supplémentaire (Lille: Facultés catholiques, 1966), 45–54. Further remarks, based upon Glorieux's article, can be found in Ruedi Imbach, "Le contexte intellectuel de l'œuvre de Capreolus," in *Jean Capreolus et son temps (1380–1444)*, ed. Guy Bedouelle, Romanus Cessario, and Kevin White, Mémoire dominicaine, numéro special 1 (Paris: Cerf, 1997), 13–22, esp. 17–21.

12 See Imbach, "Le contexte intellectuel," 19.

13 On the biography of John Capreolus, scholarship has not advanced much since the seminal article by Thomas-M. Pègues, O.P., "La biographie de Jean Capréolus," *Revue thomiste* 7 (1899): 317–34.

14 The modern edition of the work, based upon the *editio princeps* of 1483, was prepared by the Dominicans Ceslas Paban and Thomas Pègues: Johannis Capreoli *Defensiones theologiae divi Thomae Aquinatis*, 7 vols. (Tours: Cattier, 1900–08; reprinted, Frankfurt am Main: Minerva, 1967). The Paban-Pègues edition allows itself some liberties with the text, such as the internal renumbering of arguments and the conjectural emendation of passages that are defective in the 1483 edition. On the principles followed by the editors in their work, see

Thomas-M. Pègues, O.P., "Capreolus 'thomistarum princeps.' À propos de la nouvelle édition de ses œuvres," *Revue thomiste* 7 (1899): 63–81, esp. 74–81.

15 Not "Guido of Carmello," as Romanus Cessario and Kevin White translate *Guido de Carmelo* in John Capreolus, *On the Virtues*, trans. Romanus Cessario, O.P., and Kevin White (Washington, D.C.: Catholic University of America Press, 2001), xxix.

16 Johannis Capreoli *Defensiones theologiae divi Thomae Aquinatis*, prologus, qu. 1 (vol. 1, 1).

17 It is also true, however, that such large-scale theological composition was no longer the central preoccupation of most fifteenth-century schoolmen. As Daniel Hobbins has convincingly argued, the tract—shorter, focused on a specific topic, directed at a larger audience—was becoming the preferred literary genre of this period; see his article, "The Schoolman as Public Intellectual: Jean Gerson and the Late Medieval Tract," *American Historical Review* 108 (2003): 1308–37.

18 See Martin Grabmann, "Johannes Capreolus O.P., der 'Princeps Thomistarum' († 1444), und seine Stellung in der Geschichte der Thomistenschule," in his *Mittelalterliches Geistesleben*, vol. 3 (Munich: Hueber, 1956; reprinted, Hildesheim: Olms, 1984), 370–410, at 375f.

19 The Paban-Pègues edition, however, does contain references, which are due to the editors themselves. On this subject, see Pègues, "Capreolus 'princeps thomistarum,'" 80f.

20 For example, in qu. 1, art. 2 on the prologue (1: 9), where John uses a passage from Book III, dist. 24, qu. 1 of Scotus's *Sentences* commentary, he identifies the reference.

21 Thomas-M. Pègues, O.P, "Le rôle de Capréolus dans la défense de saint Thomas," *Revue thomiste* 7 (1899): 507–29; the characterization of Peter Auriol as John's *principal adversaire* occurs on p. 525.

22 Grabmann, "Johannes Capreolus O.P.," 388.

23 See, for instance, Romanus Cessario and Kevin White's introduction to their translation of John Capreolus, *On the Virtues*, xxx: "Within each book, he raises questions, each of which is related to one or several of Lombard's distinctions.... Then follow three 'articles' which constitute the main part of the question." Apparently, the mistake goes back to the usually meticulous Grabmann, "Johannes Capreolus O.P.," 376.

24 Johannis Capreoli *Defensiones theologiae divi Thomae Aquinatis*, prologus, qu. 1 (1: 1).

25 The structural differences between Book I, on the one hand, and Books II through IV, on the other, also confirm that John completed Book I significantly earlier than the others, and that Book I underwent no major revisions at Rodez. These questions have been subject to some controversy in the literature; see the remarks in Pègues, "La biographie de Jean Capréolus," 321–23.

26 Johannis Capreoli *Defensiones theologiae divi Thomae Aquinatis*, Bk. I, dist. 1, qu. 1 (1: 61).

27 Ibid., prologue, qu. 4, art. 2 (1: 61).

28 See Grabmann, "Johannes Capreolus O.P.," 388.

29 On this genre of Thomistic literature, see Martin Grabmann, "Hilfsmittel des Thomasstudiums aus alter Zeit (Abbreviationes, Concordantiae, Tabulae)," in his *Mittelalterliches Geistesleben*, vol. 2 (Munich: Hueber, 1936; reprinted, Hildesheim: Olms, 1984), 424–89, esp. 452–81. Grabmann regards the *Defensiones* of John Capreolus as the natural culmination of the development of the Thomistic concordances literature; see his remarks ibid., 475–78. The concordance *Articuli in quibus frater Thomas melius in Summa quam in Scriptis* has been edited by R.-A. Gauthier, O.P., in *RTAM* 19 (1952): 271–326.

30 This accusation is contained in a long sermon in defense of the actions of the theology faculty (*Apologia facultatis theologiae parisiensis*); on which see Glorieux, "Pierre d'Ailly et saint Thomas," esp. 48–53.

31 Johannis Capreoli *Defensiones theologiae divi Thomae Aquinatis*, Bk. I, dist. 17, qu. 1, art. 1 (2: 73).

32 These principles were first described by Grabmann, "Johannes Capreolus O.P.," 377–80.

33 Consider, for example, the following remark: "Sed dico quod hoc non est contradictio, nisi secundum apparentiam" (Johannis Capreoli *Defensiones theologiae divi Thomae Aquinatis*, Book I, dist. 8, qu. 1, art. 1; 1: 313).

34 See ibid., Book II, dist. 17, qu. 1, art. 3 (4: 123).

35 See ibid., Book IV, dist. 43, qu. 1, art. 3 (7: 29): "… [t]amen teneo cum sancto Thoma, in *Quodlibeto*, unde sumptae sunt conclusiones. Qualitercumque enim sensit in *Scriptis*, vel visus fuerit sensisse in *Tertia Parte*, determinatio *Quodlibeti* videtur mihi rationabilior: quia ibi solum tractavit istam materiam a proposito et in formam; in aliis vero locis incidenter solum, et cum suppositione, et respondendo magis ad hominem quam ad rem."

36 Ibid., Book II, dist. 13, qu. 1, art. 3 (4: 38).

37 See ibid., Book IV, dist. 22, qu. 2, art. 3 (6: 451–2): "… [i]llud dictum ultimum sanctus Thomas in praesenti distinctione et responsione dixit forte inadvertenter, non recolens de prioribus dictis suis in oppositum. Hoc enim facile contingit in tam longo opere, sicut est Scriptum 4 *Sentent.* …."

38 Ibid., Book II, dist. 1, qu. 3, art. 1 (3: 87).

39 Ibid., Book II, dist. 13, qu. 1, art. 3 (4: 38).

40 See ibid., Book II, dist. 17, qu. 1, art. 3 (4: 123) and Book IV, dist. 22, qu. 2, art. 3 (6: 452).

41 I have borrowed the expression, "spirit of 'back-to-the-sources'" from Van Dyk, "The Sentence Commentary," 230.

42 D. Dionysii Cartusiani *Commentaria in primum librum Sententiarum*, Doctoris Ecstatici D. Dionysii Cartusiani Opera Omnia 19 (Tournai: Typis cartusiae S. M. de Pratis, 1902), prooemium, 36. A parallel text is to be found in the prologue to the *Elementatio theologica*, Opera Omnia 33 (Tournai: Typis cartusiae S. M. de Pratis, 1907), 112. For commentary, see Kent Emery, Jr., "Denys the Carthusian and the Doxography of Scholastic Theology," in his *Monastic,*

Scholastic and Mystical Theologies from the Later Middle Ages, Variorum Collected Studies Series CS 561 (Aldershot, England, and Brookfield, VT: Variorum, 1996), essay IX, esp. 332f.

43 D. Dionysii Cartusiani *Commentaria in primum librum Sententiarum*, prooemium, 35.

44 Ibid., dist. 8, qu. 7 (408D). On Denys's biography, see Kent Emery, Jr., *Dionysii Cartusiensis Opera selecta, Prolegomena*, 2 vols., Corpus Christianorum, Continuatio Mediaevalis 121/121A (Turnhout: Brepols, 1991), 15–19.

45 On the development of the Carthusian order in the fourteenth and fifteenth centuries, with special consideration of the role of study, one may read Dirk Wassermann, *Dionysius der Kartäuser. Einführung in Werk und Gedankenwelt*, Analecta cartusiana 133 (Salzburg: Institut für Anglistik und Amerikanistik, 1996), 16–43.

46 Emery, "Denys the Carthusian and the Doxography of Scholastic Theology," 389. For a list of Denys's works, see Anselme Stoelen, art. "Denys le Chartreux," in *Dictionnaire de spiritualité*, vol. 3 (Paris: Beauchesne, 1957), 430–49, at 432–34.

47 See Emery, "Denys the Carthusian and the Invention of Preaching Materials," in his *Monastic, Scholastic and Mystical Theologies from the Later Middle Ages*, essay X.

48 D. Dionysii Cartusiani *Commentaria in primum librum Sententiarum*, prooemium, 37.

49 Ibid., 38. A parallel text occurs in the prologue to the *Elementatio theologica*, 111f. For commentary, see Emery, "Twofold Wisdom and Contemplation in Denys of Ryckel (Dionysius Cartusiensis, 1402–1471)," in his *Monastic, Scholastic and Mystical Theologies from the Later Middle Ages*, essay VI, 108–10, and the same author's "Theology as a Science: The Teaching of Denys of Ryckel (Dionysius Cartusiensis, 1402–1471)," ibid., essay VIII, 377f.

50 D. Dionysii Cartusiani *Commentaria in primum librum Sententiarum*, prooemium, 42f.

51 See Emery, *Dionysii Cartusiensis Opera selecta, Prolegomena*, 22.

52 Wassermann, *Dionysius der Kartäuser*, 50, plays down the extent of Denys's knowledge of his sources, claiming that it was largely derived from contemporary anthologies. He adduces no evidence for his thesis.

53 D. Dionysii Cartusiani *Commentaria in primum librum Sententiarum*, prooemium, 37.

54 Emery, *Dionysii Cartusiensis Opera selecta, Prolegomena*, 27.

55 See ibid., 26–9.

56 See ibid., 228, no. 49.

57 Stoelen, "Denys le Chartreux," 432.

58 Emery, *Dionysii Cartusiensis Opera selecta, Prolegomena*, 25. Also see the remarks in the same author's article, "Denys the Carthusian and the Invention of Preaching Materials," 380f.

59 D. Dionysii Cartusiani *Commentaria in primum librum Sententiarum*, expositio prologi, 52A.

60 Ibid., dist. 3, expositio, 215A/B.

61 Ibid., dist. 4, summa, 292A.

62 D. Dionysii Cartusiani *Commentaria in primum librum Sententiarum*, Doctoris Ecstatici D. Dionysii Cartusiani Opera Omnia 20 (Tournai: Typis cartusiae S. M. de Pratis, 1902), dist. 17, qu. 1, 16A/B.

63 Ibid., 9B/C. Question 1 of distinction 17 occupies pp. 9–18.

64 Ibid., 9D´.

65 Ibid., 13B´.

66 Ibid., 13C´/D´.

67 Ibid., 14C/D.

68 For textual references, see Stoelen, "Denys le Chartreux," 445.

69 *Elementatio theologica*, proposition 6, 118A/B.

70 D. Dionysii Cartusiani *Commentaria in primum librum Sententiarum*, dist. 17, qu. 1, 15A/B.

71 Ibid., 15C´.

72 Franz Joseph Burkard notes that, in the first half of the fifteenth century, students frequently opted to study both at Erfurt and at Cologne in order to acquaint themselves with the two "ways"; see his book, *Philosophische Lehrgehalte in Gabriel Biels Sentenzenkommentar unter besonderer Berücksichtigung seiner Erkenntnislehre*, Monographien zur philosophischen Forschung 122 (Meisenheim am Glan: Hain, 1974), 6. My account of Biel's life follows the dates provided by Burkard. Also see the important article by William J. Courtenay, "Gabriel Biel as Cathedral Preacher at Mainz and His Supposed Sojourn at Marienthal," *Research Studies of the Washington State University* 33 (1965): 145–50.

73 Friedrich Stegmüller has argued that Biel's *Sentences* commentary grew out of his teaching at houses of the Brethren; see his article, "Literargeschichtliches zu Gabriel Biel," in *Theologie in Geschichte und Gegenwart. Michael Schmaus zum sechzigsten Geburtstag*, ed. Johann Auer and Hermann Volk (Munich: Karl Zink, 1957), 1: 309–16, esp. 316. But Heiko Oberman raised doubts over this thesis in his classic work on Gabriel Biel, *The Harvest of Medieval Theology: Gabriel Biel and Late Medieval Nominalism* (Cambridge, MA: Harvard University Press, 1963), 25.

74 On the textual history of Biel's *Sentences* commentary, one may consult the introduction to its critical edition: Gabrielis Biel *Collectorium circa quattuor libros Sententiarum*, ed. Wilfrid Werbeck and Udo Hofmann, 5 vols. and Index (Tübingen: J.C.B. Mohr/Paul Siebeck, 1973–92), 1: xiv–xxxiii.

75 Gabrielis Biel *Collectorium circa quattuor libros Sententiarum*, praefatio, 1: 6, 1–5. Lawrence F. Murphy, S.J., translated portions of Biel's preface in his dissertation, comparing Biel's remarks with Luther's attitude toward Peter Lombard, theology, and philosophy; see *Martin Luther, Commentator on the "Sentences" of Peter Lombard: Theological Method and Selected Theological Problems* (Ph.D. thesis, Marquette University, 1970), esp. 117–30.

76 Gabrielis Biel *Collectorium circa quattuor libros Sententiarum*, praefatio, 1: 6, 5–14. The last sentence is a quotation from Peter Lombard's own prologue (*Sentences* 1: 4, 24–6).

77 Gabrielis Biel *Collectorium circa quattuor libros Sententiarum*, praefatio, 1: 6, 14–18.

78 The "metes" (*metae*) were stones used in the Roman circus to indicate the turning-points for chariot races. Gabriel Biel's Latin is eloquent, and his use of ancient imagery reminds us of the fact that he is writing in the age of humanism.

79 Gabrielis Biel *Collectorium circa quattuor libros Sententiarum*, praefatio, 1: 6, 19–7, 30.

80 Ibid., 7, 41–56.

81 The critical edition contains an excellent *Index auctoritatum* which provides a quick overview of the material that Biel digested in his *Collectorium* (see Gabrielis Biel *Collectorium circa quattuor libros Sententiarum*, Indices: 65–144).

82 See John L. Farthing, *Thomas Aquinas and Gabriel Biel: Interpretations of St. Thomas Aquinas in German Nominalism on the Eve of the Reformation*, Duke Monographs in Medieval and Renaissance Studies 9 (Durham and London: Duke University Press, 1988), 191.

83 This claim is corroborated by Wilhelm Ernst, *Gott und Mensch am Vorabend der Reformation. Eine Untersuchung zur Moralphilosophie und -theologie bei Gabriel Biel*, Erfurter theologische Studien 28 (Leipzig: St. Benno-Verlag, 1972), 92–3 (although Ernst counted 389 references to Aquinas). Pages 92–3 of Ernst's book offer a detailed table of all of Biel's sources in each of the four books of the *Collectorium*.

84 Farthing, *Thomas Aquinas and Gabriel Biel*, 192.

85 Gabrielis Biel *Collectorium circa quattuor libros Sententiarum*, Book I, dist. 35, art. 2, concl. 2 (1: 636, C24–7).

86 Ibid., Book III, dist. 1, qu. 2 (3: 36, A4–37, A15).

87 Ibid., Book I, dist. 35, art. 2, concl. 2 (1: 636, C27)—this passage has already been quoted earlier.

88 Ibid., prologue, qu. 1 (1: 8, A3–5).

89 See ibid., Book III, dist. 20, qu. unica (3: 330–36).

90 Ibid., art. 1 (331, B1–2).

91 Ibid., art. 2 (334, D1–2 and D11–12).

92 For the contents of the 1501 edition, see the introduction to the critical edition: Gabrielis Biel *Collectorium circa quattuor libros Sententiarum*, 1: xvi–xvii. The *inventarium generale* is printed in the index volume of the critical edition, 1–43.

93 Ibid., Indices: 5.

94 *D. Martin Luthers Werke. Kritische Gesammtausgabe* (Weimar: Böhlau, 1883–), TR 3: 3722 (dated 1538): "wenn ich darinnen las, da blutte mein hertz." On the history of this standard edition of Luther's works, one may read Ulrich Köpf, "Kurze Geschichte der Weimarer Lutherausgabe," in *D. Martin Luthers Werke. Sonderedition der kritischen Weimarer Ausgabe. Begleitheft zur Deutschen Bibel* (Weimar: Böhlau, 2001), 1–24.

95 A good introduction to Erfurt's humanist circles is Dieter Stievermann's article, "Marschalk (ca. 1470–1525), Spalatin (1484–1545), Mutian (ca. 1470–1526), Hessius (1488–1540) und die Erfurter Humanisten," in *Große Denker Erfurts und der Erfurter Universität*, ed. Dietmar van der Pforten (Göttingen: Wallstein,

2002), 118–42. The following volume contains the proceedings of a conference devoted to Erfurt's humanist movement: *Humanismus in Erfurt*, ed. Gerlinde Huber-Rebenich and Walter Ludwig, Acta Academiae Scientiarum 7/Humanismusstudien 1 (Rudolstadt: Hain-Verlag, 2002).

96 See Helmar Junghans, *Der junge Luther und die Humanisten* (Göttingen: Vandenhoeck & Ruprecht, 1985).

97 The literature on Luther's *Sentences* glosses is abundant. I have found the most comprehensive and incisive study to be Josef Wieneke, *Luther und Petrus Lombardus. Martin Luthers Notizen anläßlich seiner Vorlesung über die Sentenzen des Petrus Lombardus, Erfurt 1509/11*, Dissertationen, Theologische Reihe 71 (St. Ottilien: EOS Verlag, 1994). Wieneke develops his argument in dialogue with the entire scholarship dealing with Luther's *Sentences* glosses. On the modalities of Luther's lectures on the *Sentences*, see esp. p. 64.

98 Luther's glosses on the *Sentences* have been edited in *D. Martin Luthers Werke*, 9: 28–94. The edition is, however, not entirely free from transcription errors.

99 See Oberman, *The Dawn of the Reformation*, 77 n. 159: "The relatively long opening statement … is undoubtedly not from Luther, but from another hand, contemporary, probably slightly older."

100 For these graphological analyses, see Junghans, *Der junge Luther*, 98–103.

101 *D. Martin Luthers Werke*, 9: 29, 1–19; reading *irremeabilis* for *irreplicabilis* in line 10 (according to the new transcription in Junghans, *Der junge Luther*, 96–7). I have consulted the translation in Murphy, *Martin Luther*, 77f., but have modified it in many places.

102 See Augustine, *De doctrina christiana*, chap. 2, nos. 144–8 (based on Ex. 3:21–22, 11:2, and 12:35–36).

103 Murphy, *Martin Luther, Commentator on the "Sentences,"* 98 n. 34. Also see the translation in Junghans, *Der junge Luther*, 98.

104 I wish to thank my colleague Francis Swietek for suggesting the translation of *popularis familiaritas* as "secular familiarity."

105 See Wieneke, *Luther und Petrus Lombardus*, 52, who distinguishes three kinds of glosses, using length as his criterion of differentiation.

106 *D. Martin Luthers Werke*, 9: 31, 30 and 32, 32.

107 Ibid., 76, 18 and 30.

108 Ibid., 30, 35–7.

109 Ibid., 30, 1f.

110 Ibid., 31, 29.

111 Ibid., 55, 27.

112 For further analysis of Luther's references to Peter Lombard's sources, see Junghans, *Der junge Luther*, 119–21.

113 *D. Martin Luthers Werke*, 9: 31, 6f.

114 Wieneke, *Luther und Petrus Lombardus*, 65, claims that Luther must have been immersed in studying *On the Trinity* as he was reading the *Book of Sentences*; but Wieneke's remark should be extended to many other texts with which Luther exhibits close acquaintance in his glosses.

115 See *D. Martin Luthers Werke*, 9: 32, 26f.

116   See Wieneke, *Luther und Petrus Lombardus*, 51.

117   *D. Martin Luthers Werke*, 9: 29, 20–6. The quotation is from Hilary of Poitiers, *De Trinitate*, Book 7, chap. 38. Luther's expression *nostri subtiles magis quam illustres* is modeled on Peter Lombard's phrase in *Sentences* I, dist. 2, chap. 3 (p. 63), *garrulos ratiocinatores, elatiores quam capaciores*, which is itself a quotation from Augustine, *De Trinitate*, Book I, chap. 2.

118   *D. Martin Luthers Werke*, 9: 47, 6.

119   Ibid., 43, 5.

120   Ibid., 62, 17f.: *Respondet Magister et bene, quod ...*

121   Ibid., 74, 8–11.

122   See Wieneke, *Luther und Petrus Lombardus*.

123   Augustine, *De Trinitate*, Book VIII, chap. 7, 10.

124   Ibid., chaps. 7–8, 11–12.

125   Peter Lombard, *Sentences*, I, dist. 17, chap. 1, no. 2 (142). For the text of Luther's glosses, see *D. Martin Luthers Werke*, 9: 42, 6–16.

126   In the critical edition of Luther's works, the text commented upon in note *k* is given as *nisi deus plenus est* (*D. Martin Luthers Werke*, 9: 42, 16). This should correctly read, *nisi deo plenus est*.

127   *D. Martin Luthers Werke*, 9: 42, 35–43, 8. For *nisi sit forte determinatum essentiae in oppositum* in ll. 7f., read *nisi sit forte determinatio ecclesiae in oppositum*. This emendation was first proposed by Erich Vogelsang, *Der junge Luther*, Luther in Auswahl 5 (Berlin: de Gruyter, 1933), 7.

128   See Paul Vignaux, *Luther, commentateur des Sentences (livre I, distinction XVII)*, Études de philosophie médiévale 21 (Paris: Vrin, 1935). Ironically, Vignaux spends only a few pages on Luther's glosses on distinction 17 (pp. 39–43); the bulk of his work is devoted to the glosses leading up to distinction 17, as well as the nominalist background to Luther's thought.

129   See the incisive analysis by the Finnish Reformation scholar Risto Saarinen in his article, "*Ipsa dilectio Deus est*. Zur Wirkungsgeschichte von 1. Sent. dist. 17 des Petrus Lombardus bei Martin Luther," in *Thesaurus Lutheri. Auf der Suche nach neuen Paradigmen der Luther-Forschung*, ed. Tuomo Mannermaa, Anja Ghiselli, and Simo Peura, Veröffentlichungen der finnischen theologischen Literaturgesellschaft 153/Luther-Agricola-Gesellschaft, Schrift A24 (Helsinki: Suomalainen Teologinen Kirjallisuusseura, 1987), 185–204, esp. 191.

130   "Et videtur Magister non penitus absurdissime loqui: in eo quod habitum dicit esse spiritum sanctum." Literally, *absurdissime* means "most absurdly" or "extremely absurdly."

131   See Saarinen, "*Ipsa dilectio Deus est*," 202.

132   On Luther's rejection of the Aristotelian concept of habit, also see Junghans, *Der junge Luther*, 157f. Luther's critique of the Christian adaptation of the *habitus* theory appears prominently in the *Disputatio contra scholasticam theologiam* of 1517; see *D. Martin Luthers Werke* 1: 226, 8–11.

133   Namely, in the Council of Vienne (1311–12).

Note to the Conclusion

1 See Claude Panaccio, *Les mots, les concepts et les choses: la sémantique de Guillaume d'Occam et le nominalisme d'aujourd'hui*, Collection Analytiques 3 (Paris: Vrin; Montreal: Bellarmin, 1991). On some aspects of the debate over Panaccio's theses, see Kurt Flasch, *Philosophie hat Geschichte*, vol. 2: *Theorie der Philosophiehistorie* (Frankfurt am Main: Klostermann, 2005), 294–318. Panaccio has also published a book on Ockham in English: *Ockham on Concepts*, Ashgate Studies in Medieval Philosophy (Aldershot, England, and Burlington, VT: Ashgate, 2004).

Index

Bold page numbers indicate glossary entries.